I0092111

North Korean Defectors in Diaspora

Crossing Borders in a Global World: Applying Anthropology to Migration, Displacement, and Social Change

Series Editors

Raúl Sánchez Molina (ersanchez@fsof.uned.es)

Nancy Anne Konvalinka (nkonvalinka@fsof.uned.es)

Advisory Board

Maria Eugenia Bozzoli, Adi Bharadwaj, Monica Bonaccorso, Lucy M. Cohen, Yasmine Ergas, Andrés Fábregas Puig, Carles Feixa, Ubaldo Martínez Veiga, Marit Melhuus, Alicia Re Cruz, Amy Speier, Meenakshi Thapan, and María Amelia Viteri

Mission Statement

Current migrants, refugees, and travelers cross political, social, cultural, and identity borders and directly confront the challenges of globalization in the process of displacement, incorporation, and adaptation to new settlements. This series addresses these challenges and their intersections with national, ethnic, gender, and generational identities. Books in this series provide a range of interdisciplinary theoretical and methodological frameworks that scholars and practitioners can use both in the classroom and in applied work. This series is of value to scholars, advanced undergraduate and graduate students, and practitioners interested in the impact of displacements, migration, and social and cultural changes in contemporary societies.

Books in Series

Iranian Hospitality, Afghan Marginality: Spaces of Refuge and Belonging in the City of Shiraz, by Elisabeth Yarbakhsh

North Korean Defectors in Diaspora

Identities, Mobilities, and Resettlements

Edited by

HaeRan Shin

LEXINGTON BOOKS
Lanham • Boulder • New York • London

Published by Lexington Books
An imprint of The Rowman & Littlefield Publishing Group, Inc.
4501 Forbes Boulevard, Suite 200, Lanham, Maryland 20706
www.rowman.com

6 Tinworth Street, London SE11 5AL, United Kingdom

Copyright © 2022 The Rowman & Littlefield Publishing Group, Inc.

All rights reserved. No part of this book may be reproduced in any form or by any electronic or mechanical means, including information storage and retrieval systems, without written permission from the publisher, except by a reviewer who may quote passages in a review.

British Library Cataloguing in Publication Information Available

Library of Congress Cataloging-in-Publication Data Available
ISBN 978-1-7936-5149-5 (cloth)
ISBN 978-1-7936-5150-1 (electronic)
ISBN 978-1-7936-5151-8 (pbk.)

Contents

Acknowledgments

This work was supported by the Institute for Peace and Unification Studies, Seoul National University.

Introduction

HaeRan Shin, Kyung Hyo Chun, and Hyunuk Lee

When a Korean declares "I am from Korea" outside the Korean peninsula, the oft-asked question is "Which one?," signifying South Korea or North Korea. Koreans have spread across the globe to settle in myriad different countries, but of those the readers might have met, most if not all would be from South Korea. Members of the Korean diaspora, those who have left their homeland to live abroad, have in recent years come to include an invisible minority from North Korea. The majority of North Koreans escape across the border into China where an estimated thirty to fifty thousand have remained, but many have also continued on to South Korea. While a preponderance of North Koreans remained in South Korea, there are those that have moved on again for other countries. According to statistics in 2021 calculated with a reasonable margin of error, there are more than thirty thousand North Korean defectors in South Korea.[1] Of those North Koreans that left South Korea, approximately one thousand live in the United Kingdom, four hundred in Canada, one to three hundred in the United States, three hundred in Japan, and seventy in Australia.

Beyond the borders of North Korea, many including South Koreans view North Korean defectors as victims. News of starvation and human rights violations in North Korea succeeded by stories of perilous river crossings in the process of escaping and tales of human trafficking in China after escape reinforce the image of victim. Their willingness to face life-threatening circumstances in order to escape validated the impression the world has of the atrocities committed in North Korea. Their stories confirmed reports of labor camps, deprivation, and big brother control over every aspect people's daily lives. Yet despite the state's complete control, there were still skeptics, those who would willingly risk their lives to discover for themselves the reality beyond the North Korea's borders. Once in South Korea, some North Koreans seemed prepared to relinquish their North Korean identity and have been vocal in their condemnation of their homeland.

Though many North Koreans voluntarily discussed the traumas they suffered, the contributors of this edited volume found that this focus on the past to be problematic for the fact that it simplifies their past and ignores their present. By collecting and analyzing qualitative data on North Korean defectors not just in South Korea but in the United Kingdom, the United States, and Japan, we found that their stories have evolved. Those North Korean defectors that we encountered that constantly renegotiated settlement in and adapted their identities to the new society presented a dynamic and complex picture. They were not very different from other transnational migrants in that they wanted to maintain their connections to family and friends left behind and at the same time develop networks linking them to their destination's populace. It is for this reason that the book chapters of this edited volume have adopted methods similar to those used in migrant studies.

As one of the world's last closed societies, North Korea has attracted both scholarly interest and global curiosity, as evidenced by the number of academic publications and mass media commentaries. Most studies on North Korean defectors portray them as either witnesses to or victims of the dictatorship in North Korea, which disregards the agency they practice in escaping and rebuilding their lives. Of those in-depth migrant studies that chronicle North Korean defectors' resettlement, the research primarily focuses on cultural assimilation, preoccupied with proving a marked improvement in their post-escape lives. Alternatively, journalistic approaches have sensationalized the defectors' descriptions of deprivation, repression, and human rights violations in North Korea, as well as their dangerous journey to escape. Those defectors, being conditioned by such representations, attempted to construct and control their own images (Chun, 2020).

For those who are unfamiliar with the history of Korea, it is a country that has been divided for the last seventy years. In 1945, after the end of both World War II and Japan's colonization of Korea, the Soviet Union and the United States came to the decision to divide Korea into two occupation zones. This division eventually led to the North Korean invasion of the South in 1950 in a bid for reunification. A cease-fire was declared in 1953, but it became evident in 1954 when the Cold War's preeminent figures discussed the Korean question in Geneva that a peace accord was unlikely. Since South Korea and North Korea are still technically at war, political tension and on occasion outright hostility have continued to this day. The two countries have developed significantly different economic, political, and social systems and institutions, and after seventy years of division, people's daily culture, ideologies, and even language have diverged.

The two countries, however, do align on one thing: both forbid their citizens to contact the other's citizens. Legally, North Korea is not a country but an anti-governmental organization according to South Korea's constitutional

law. To call or exchange letters, emails, or any other form of communication is illegal. As a result, family members who have been separated by the
ongoing Korean War are still prohibited from contacting each other except
on those rare occasions when the two governments allowed brief interactions. These few government-sanctioned interactions aside, all other contact
between the citizens of these two countries is unauthorized and therefore
unlawful. Even those South Koreans and North Koreans living outside Korea
are expected to adhere to this law, and South Koreans are legally obliged to
report to their nearest embassy if any contact was made. This expectation
does not account for the reality that South and North Koreans work and live
in the same community outside the Korean peninsula, forming a part of each
other's daily lives.

This edited volume is a collection of case studies on a diaspora of North
Korean defectors living in various societies including the United Kingdom,
the United States, Japan, and South Korea. The South Korean scholars who
contributed to this book have interviewed North Korean defectors to attempt
to understand their movements, reasons for settlement and resettlement, and
through it all the reinvention of their identities. We identify key aspects of the
defectors' background to situate North Korean defectors more accurately in
the broader context of spatial strategies and help explain the motivation for
their multiple mobilities. We also study their process of renegotiation in their
post-settlement lives and the identity issues that prompt repeated mobilities.

SITUATING NORTH KOREAN DEFECTORS

Due to the uniqueness of North Korean escapees' circumstances, categoriz-
ing them is challenging. Let us explain why we decided to use the term
"defectors" rather than refugees when referring to those North Koreans who
escaped. In choosing a word that can be applied to all North Koreans living
outside their country, "defector" describes the one endeavor they all have
in common: their defection. We avoid the word refugee, unless it is used in
general or when other authors use it, because there is an ambiguity to that
term. For instance, North Koreans who lived in South Korea before applying for refugee status in the US and the UK are no longer considered to be
refugees according to the policies of those countries. Further confusion as
to their status as refugees arises from the fact that the Convention Relating
to the Status of Refugees refutes their claim while the United Nations High
Commissioner for Refugees supports it. Countries also differ on how they
view North Korean defectors. China does not recognize them as refugees
at all but as illegal immigrants and as such are returned to North Korea. In
Japan, those Koreans who left Japan as part of the repatriation project to later

return to Japan are called Zainichi returnees. In South Korea, they are called "defected ethnic North Koreans," "North Korean refugees," "defected North Korean residents" and more recently "North Korean migrants" (Kim, 2012).

By their definitions, the terms migrants and refugees evoke two quite different images, but in reality, an individual may exhibit characteristics that belong to more than one category depending on the situation and setting (De Coninck, 2020). Some contemporary academic discussions have moved past debates on the distinction between migrants and refugees to discuss the migratory experiences themselves that some feel neither category can adequately summarize. In fact, many believe that the existing categories do not provide an accurate or realistic picture of migration motivations and experiences (Collyer, 2010; Crawley and Skleparis, 2018). In creating categories, there is a risk of stigmatizing entire groups of people and limiting their rights through labels that could come to have negative associations (Crawley and Skleparis, 2018). Aware of this risk, the contributors of this book use the term of defectors to identify them by their agency and actions in escaping rather than requests for refuge.

In addition, there is also the fact that not all North Koreans continue on the same trajectory. Many North Koreans arrive in South Korea, which is defection rather than migration because it is strictly forbidden, and never move again. While others will relocate for a better jobs and their children's education, sharing motivations and characteristics with migrants. For these reasons, we decided that to identify them by the one experience they all share, escaping from North Korea, and chose to identify them by the neutral word defectors. Using the name in a broad way, we seek to understand the diversity of individuals intertwined with their historical circumstances and the different contexts of their lives in this book.

NORTH KOREAN DEFECTORS' DIASPORA—THEIR IDENTITIES, MOBILITIES, AND RESETTLEMENT

The late 1990s in North Korea is a period known as the Arduous March (1995–2000). The collapse of other communist countries and allies cut off political and financial support, which was exacerbated by the economic blockade by the United States that further isolated North Korea. During that same time, natural disasters destroyed crops, leading to a food crisis. The national distribution system that provided North Koreans with all their needs ground to a halt. Faced with starvation, an increasing number of people chose instead to risk execution if caught escaping and crossed into China usually by forging the river that divides the countries. From there, many continued to South Korea. Since North Korea had sent spies under the guise of defectors in the past, South Korean society tended to view all North Korean defectors as spies. The South Korean government established a system that supports escapees from North Korea while the National Security team investigates the veracity of their claims. Once their claims were deemed legitimate, the South Korean government would provide financial support through monthly stipends and social assistance such as housing, job training, medical care, and education.

This edited collection attempts to add depth to the studies on North Korean defectors' resettlement processes and uncover the motivations for their repeated mobilities. Since the ground has been well-trodden pertaining to assimilation in resettlement, we focused on questions that would uncover why they did not assimilate. How did they adapt to South Korean society? Why did some of them leave South Korea and relocate to other countries? Did they acclimate to other societies? Did they develop relationships with South Koreans or native speaking populations in other countries? How did their defection redefine their relationships with those family members with them and those left behind in North Korea? What constitutes their new identity and new networks? And lastly, how could we improve our interactions with North Korean defectors? By answering these questions, we hope to offer current and future scholars and interested readers a better understanding of North Korean defectors and the state of the two Koreas.

To arrive at a better understanding, we must look at how North Koreans are differentiated. For example, migration studies on South Koreans that explore their transnational mobilities and identities in transition do not consider North Koreans' similar migration struggles. Instead, most of the existing books and articles on North Korean defectors narrowly focus on only one or a few individuals' shocking tales of survival and escape from North Korea. Moreover, the current scholarship is predominantly focused on North Korean defectors' traumatic experiences in labor camps or stories of starvation and deprivation in North Korea. Others have focused on North Koreans' experiences in China and human rights violations they suffer while there before escaping yet again to other countries like the United States. There are some studies that reflect on North Koreans' post-settlement life but focus tends to be on their assimilation to South Korea.

Our book differs in that it offers information on a wider range of experiences in various destinations and includes a variety of issues from personal struggles to global dynamics. This edited collection has gathered and analyzed information on defectors' repeated mobilities, daily lives and encounters with South Koreans or other populations, for one purpose. This is to understand North Korean defectors' family relations, identity dynamics, and networks in the making. We contend that North Korean defectors' experiences and strategies ought to be scrutinized to understand how they influence the evolving processes of their lives and identities. Beside this introduction and the epilogue, we have compiled eight individual chapters on contemporary North Korean defectors exploring the issues of (1) mobilities, (2) settlements, and (3) identities from the perspectives of geography, anthropology, child education studies, and North Korean studies.

To the best of our knowledge, this is one of the first books to study North Korean defectors across the globe and has the potential to add incalculable value to this important scholarship on North Korean defectors.

KEEPING MOVING AND MAINTAINING NETWORKS

When we discuss North Korean defectors, this includes not only those who settled in South Korea after their defection but also those who left South Korea for other countries. North Korean defectors have emerged as a quite mobile group, migrating to United Kingdom, the United States, and Australia, the three most popular destinations after South Korea. You might wonder what could have compelled North Koreans to leave South Korea, the country they had dreamed about, where they shared a language and could live freely. The simple answer appears to be that they became disillusioned by the society there.

Explanations regarding why they left South Korea are of course more complicated than that. In-depth interviews conducted for the research in this book revealed that many North Korean defectors left South Korea because of discrimination. They explained that the discrimination of people of the same ethnicity was worse than the disdain of total strangers. It is likely, due to their cultural similarity, that they could decipher the cultural codes and facial expressions to recognize even when they were being subtly disrespected. In addition to the discrimination, it is clear that many North Koreans felt as if South Korea was akin to a foreign country where they could speak the language.

If discrimination was their reason for leaving, then their children's welfare and education was often what motivated them to relocate. Experiencing discrimination firsthand, many North Korean parents explained that did not want their children to experience the same intolerance and consequent disadvantages that they had. They also wanted to give their children the benefit of an education in an English-speaking country and the advantages of having that language skill. Like many other transnational migrant groups, North Korean defectors are heavily invested in their children's well-being and future. In that sense, their repeated mobilities can be understood as attempts to provide a better life for themselves but more importantly their families.

Other reasons North Koreans had for leaving South Korea sometimes include financial or legal troubles. In those cases, the pull factors of the next destination were not so important as the push factors forcing North Koreans to leave South Korea. Another reason North Koreans left was that they thought if they could find work in a more affluent country, then they could send more money to their families in North Korea.

Their willingness to depart for other countries that they felt might offer more could also be motivated by a wish to maximize the opportunities that the risks they took to defect had given them. In the end, some North Koreans returned to South Korea, explaining that their life in a third country did not go well. The first generation of North Korean defectors did not speak English and were unfamiliar with capitalist systems, so it can be said that they were unprepared to survive in those countries. Yet if they heard that they could easily qualify for refugee status and welfare in another country, they considered migration to those other countries just the same.

They might have left South Korea feeling diminished, but the support and sense of fellowship they derived from North Korean diaspora networks in other countries helped regain some confidence. North Korean defectors who migrated previously established transnational and informational ethnic networks that play a critical role in the mobilities of newly arriving North Koreans. These networks disseminated information that would benefit and support North Koreans in a system that spanned the globe.

POST-SETTLEMENT LIVES AND RESETTLEMENT IN SOUTH KOREA AND OTHER COUNTRIES

While the focus of this edited volume is on the diverse experiences of North Korean defectors in different countries, it cannot be overlooked that the majority of those North Korean defectors had settled in South Korea first. It is for this reason that North Koreans' experiences and interactions in South Korea are not only valuable sources of information on their post-settlement lives but also on what compelled some to relocate to another country. In fact, the examination of the adaptation process and the discourse on integration in South Korea is essential in understanding and addressing the transnational landscape of North Korean defectors. Scrutiny of North Korean defectors' post-settlement lives in South Korea and abroad even has future implications in prefiguring possible scenarios if Korea should be unified (or alternatively two Koreas with an open border without restrictions on movement). The influence of the policies, structural conditions, and popular discourses that shape North Korean defectors' settlement in South Korea continues even after they relocate and will have ramifications in the event of future reunification.

However, before discussion of a possible reunification there is first the defection. After defecting or relocating to another country, North Korean defectors would apply for political refugee status. Since North Korea is considered by many countries to be a dictatorship, North Koreans would be accepted as refugees, but the application processes and welfare for refugees varied by country. The United Kingdom was more popular than many other countries due to its exceptional welfare for refugees. Another reason the UK was a preferred destination was that the authorities there did not share fingerprint identification information with the South Korean government until 2014. North Korean defectors who once lived in South Korea could claim to have come directly came from North Korea knowing that this would not be verified and contradicted. Once the UK and Canada started to collaborate with South Korea and disclose fingerprint identification information, the number of North Korean refugees in those countries dropped dramatically.

Even though North Koreans left South Korea dissatisfied, many choose to settle in or near the Koreatowns established by South Korean migrants in cities such as London, Los Angeles, and Osaka. This was to have access to the businesses that South Koreans had developed, working in their restaurants, grocery shops, and businesses or in their house cleaning and babysitting. Their initial preference for South Korean employers was because they were not yet fluent in English. In some cases, if their South Korea employers were agreeable, North Koreans would be paid in cash to avoid any official record of their employment. This was often arranged between them so that North Koreans could continue to claim unemployment aid.

It was also to South Korean employers' advantage to hire North Korean defectors who they viewed as cheap laborers. For example, in London and Los Angeles, previous to the arrival of North Korean defectors, South Koreans had employed *Joseonjok* migrants, ethnic Koreans who were born and raised in China. In the 2000s when Korean Chinese migrants started returning to China, this left a need for labor that North Korean defectors filled. Many North Koreans had worked in South Korea before leaving, but the dynamics of the job market in the destination country was slightly different. When they worked for South Koreans in South Korea, due to the hierarchical culture of the society and job market, North Koreans faced discrimination in the workplace. In South Korea, North Koreans felt powerless to change the system, but in other countries their way of thinking changed. North Koreans were less accepting of the discrimination, citing the fact that both they and South Koreans are foreigners and therefore on a more equal footing. Knowing that the labor regulations in the destination countries protected them, North Koreans tended to be less submissive than they had been in South Korea (Shin, 2018).

Despite gaining a measure of security from the laws that protected them in the destination country, they still felt that they had to carefully monitor what they said and did as they had in North Korea. This would sometimes cause family members to filter what they shared even with other family members, which in some cases led to suppressed emotions and unhealthy behaviors. Once they settled in South Korea or in a third country, parents were preoccupied by the family's survival in the new setting. This preoccupation put stress on their own and their children's mental health, leaving them vulnerable to outside dangers and pressure.

Many found relief in close relations with other North Korean families and the North Korean ethnic community that was established by defectors to offer each other support. In London, their community was quite active in founding community organizations as well as political organizations. There they started a North Korean Ethnic Association, cultural groups including a dance group, and a Korean language school for the second generation. The success of the language school for children and other North Korean organizations were in part due to an amicable partnership with South Korean migrants. They were invited to participate in South Korean organizational activities and reciprocated by inviting South Koreans migrants to their events.

In Los Angeles, however, North Koreans defectors' efforts were less successful. An ethnic association did exist at one time, but it did not last long. Now all that is left is one small group of politically minded North Korean defectors (Shin, 2021). In Japan, there was no visible political organization, but that is not difficult to understand considering the small number of North Koreans. They tended to focus on creating a stable life there instead of pursuing political change in North Korea.

North Koreans living in Japan, however, could offer insight to any changes that may have occurred in North Korea through their uninterrupted connection to the country. The large-scale migration of Koreans from Japan over twenty-five years, which was a factor in changing North Korean society, continues today through short-term visits. Though it is rare, those Koreans who had decided to stay in Japan rather than be repatriated shuttle back and forth between South Korea and North Korea. Even though lines of communication between North Korea and South Korea have opened, they are sporadic at best, and we may yet find the way to connect the Koreas is through Japan.

NORTH KOREAN DEFECTORS' IDENTITIES RENEGOTIATED

It is debated just how much North Koreans have come to adopt South Koreans' culture and adapt their identities to include South Korean philosophy, common sense, and attitudes towards jobs, family, and the state. Even with surveys and in-depth interviews, it is difficult to determine how much some North Koreans have been unable to adapt due to cultural differences, lack of relationships with South Koreans, or other factors. Many North Korean defectors reported that they found life difficult in South Korea usually due to the economic system and job markets that were unlike anything they had ever experienced. They also found it difficult to connect with South Koreans, which left them without the assistance they needed to navigate a society that was foreign to them. Some North Koreans stated that they were unwilling to adapt to a society that discriminated against them or resisted because they were repelled by the pressure to assimilate.

The pressure to assimilate can be attributed to the South Korean society's firm belief in a homogenous Korean ethnicity. Due to this belief, there was the expectation that North Korean defectors would want to become like South Koreans, given that they share the same ethnicity and language. The reality turned out quite different from what the South Koreans expected. Since the two countries' languages had developed differently, with new South Korean words tending to be westernized, North Korean defectors often could not understand contemporary South Korean vocabulary. In addition to differences in vocabulary, North Korean defectors' particular accents and tones had become a cultural marker that differentiated them from South Koreans. Against a backdrop of expected commonality between the people of two the Koreas, North Korean defectors' difference from South Koreans is all the more pronounced (Shin, 2019). Unlike foreign migrants in South Korea who are purely foreign, North Korean defectors occupy an ambivalent place as foreign but not foreign due to the chasm between expected similarity and realized difference.

Like many other transnational migrants, however, North Korean defectors have kept their identities even as they continued to renegotiate who they are. One way they have stayed connected to their roots was to send remittances to their families in North Korea, although prohibited, no matter where they were in the world. The majority of North Korean defectors send remittances through brokers, usually Korean Chinese or other North Koreans. One reason South Korea is not a popular destination for North Korean defectors is that it is especially difficult to send remittances from there. In contrast, Japan has a direct and legal link to North Korea through Chongryon, Korean descendants of laborers sent to Japan during that country's colonization of Korea, and also North Korean defectors in Japan. It is not only the act of sending money that maintains their connection to family, however, but also the accompanying phone call to confirm receipt of funds. During this call, the conversation with their family members in North Korea reinforces their national identity as well as cultural identities.

So as a number of migrant studies have demonstrated, though North Koreans might reject their government, they do not necessarily reject their identity. Their identity is not only based on the hardship they experienced in their home country and in the process of escaping but on the national, regional, and family identities that they have developed. When those identities encounter new people such as brokers, NGO activists, governmental officials, and community members, they begin to adapt and incorporate new characteristics while negotiating to keep aspects of their old identity.

DISCUSSING THE CONTRIBUTIONS
AND IMPLICATIONS OF THE BOOK

There have been academic studies and journalist works on North Korean defectors that emphasized past traumatic experiences to juxtapose them to their current life in the new destination. Of the various South Korean surveys on North Korean defectors, the assumption is that North Korean defectors' final destination could be none other than South Korea. Hence in both popular discourse and public sectors in South Korea, the belief is that North Koreans' ultimate goal is to become good citizens of South Korea. The purpose of this book is to offer a different perspective not based on assumptions. As chapters of this volume address defectors' life in different parts of the world, this book expands on the hitherto narrow view taken by previous studies on North Koreans. A transnational perspective on North Korean defectors provides a fuller understanding of their lives that also facilitates comparative analysis of North Korean defectors living in different countries.

This book offers insight to this highly singular group of people, North Korean defectors, whose uniqueness stems not just from their status as refugees but also the insularity of their home country. Identifying North Korean defectors solely as witnesses to or victims of atrocities in their homeland and beleaguered refugees abroad but not as migrants does them a disservice. Once we begin to identify those characteristics that are unique to them as a people and not as victims or refugees they are not so unlike other migrants. Commonalities emerge such as the migrants' desire for a better life for themselves and their children. As we pull all these elements that characterize North Koreans together, a picture emerges that transcends the images of victim and defector.

Since their evolving identities were in part shaped by the destination society, we include references to their experiences in South Korea, the United Kingdom, Europe, the United States, and Japan. We evaluate the transnational identities of those defectors who, following contemporary migrants' trends, engaged in repeated migrations supported by information networks.

Regarding the mobilities of North Korean defectors, this volume discusses the practical issues of social integration in a Korean peninsula where at least the border has been demilitarized or at most the countries have been reunified.

REFORMING RESEARCH METHODS AND POLICIES

To close, we suggest a need to reform the research methods and policies that concern North Korean defectors. To present a comprehensive discussion on North Korean defectors, the contributing authors provide different perspectives on North Koreans living in various host country settings. The inclusion of statistics on North Korean defectors collected in the UK and other countries, however, presents new challenges. Unlike the official statistics compiled by South Korean authorities, other countries' official statistics tend not to be as comprehensive or as precise. First, the official statistics on the number of North Koreans tend to only include those who applied for and were granted refugee status. This does not include those who are waiting for a result, who failed to obtain refugee status but stayed without documents, as well as those who chose not to apply at all. Second, as ethnic Koreans, *Joseonjok* migrants are sometimes included in these statistics, which skews the total number of North Koreans. As a result of these sometimes too specific and other times too general statistics, those ethnic associations that assist incoming refugees are often better positioned to calculate the number of North Koreans more accurately than the official statistics. For this reason, previous studies employing qualitative research methods note that the sample size often depends on the context.

Statistics provide valuable hard data that quantitative research methods can then analyze usually in conjunction with other research results to attain a generalized view of a wider population (Schreier, 2017). Our focus, however, is on ethnographic qualitative methods that include in-depth interviews, participant observation, focus groups, and archival studies to explain rather than quantify North Korea defectors' experiences. Unlike quantitative research methods, qualitative research methods generate a limited generalization based on statistically representative samples that instead offer a rich and in-depth analysis of a specific context that is transferable to another similar one (Schreier, 2017). Both research methods have their strengths and limitations. Qualitative research methods, for instance, can be challenging especially when potential interviewees are hesitant or outright refuse to give their permission for an interview, as is the case with North Korean defectors. In order to supplement the sample size of interviewees, chapters of the edited volume also included participant observations in North Korean church activities and informal exchanges with those North Koreans. In addition to these recognized methods for collecting information, we have included South Korean migrants' observations of North Koreans. After all, North Korean defectors do not exist in a vacuum and this edited volume is not based solely on their perspectives but also includes their relations with South Koreans and other ethnic groups.

South Korean research interests in North Korean defectors can be broadly divided into two groups based on the ultimate purpose of the research. The first group is interested in the information North Korean defectors can provide so they may learn about North Korean society, which is inaccessible to most researchers. North Korean defectors are like a window into North Korea through which interviewers can remotely observe the people living there and possibly predict how they would view South Korean rule. The second group interviews North Korean defectors to gain knowledge of the state of their adaptation and level of social integration. Both groups focus on the cultural differences of North Korean defectors and South Koreans. They use cultural differences to demonstrate how North and South Korean societies have diverged, or as the source of North Korean defectors' difficulties integrating into South Korean society.

While issues directly related to North Korean defectors are often attributed to cultural differences, public discussion on the factors and conditions that constitute and shape cultural difference has not been actively pursued. Although there are annual surveys by research institutions such as Korean Hana Foundation and the Institute for Peace and Unification Studies at Seoul National University, progress in understanding cultural difference from the North Korean perspective is lacking. The difficulty in eliciting information lies in the fact that respondents are questioned about cultural difference in a manner that assumes that they have the same understanding of the term as the people conducting the survey.

The information collected by surveys based on quantitative research methods for statistical analysis has provided much of the information on North Korean defectors' previous life in North Korea, the society and characteristics. However, this method does not provide insight into the motivations and dynamics of North Korean defectors' mobilities as they settle and then resettle in various societies. For this reason, we draw from these various standpoints as we discuss the complicated nature of those North Korean defectors as well as implications for future possibilities and policy.

Fortunately, encounters between South Koreans and North Koreans outside the Korean peninsula that have acted as a pilot study for a reunified Korea or at least two countries reconciled have provided useful information. It is likely that the reality will likely fall somewhere between how North and South Koreans interact outside the Korean peninsula and in South Korea.

How people perceive cultural difference and how they mobilize it to create social conflict are much more important than the cultural difference itself. To understand how the issue of cultural difference has affected North Korean defectors, we need to make an active inquiry into three important points. First, we must ask how North Korean defectors perceive cultural difference. Second, it is necessary to discover how North Korean defectors view the relationship between cultural difference and social prejudice. Third, there must be an inquiry into the strategic choices North Korean defectors make in an attempt to overcome the negative effect of perceived cultural difference. It is difficult to find the information needed to address these points with surveys limited by multiple choice answers and an interviewer that directs the dialogue while the interviewee is denied space for self-expression. To remedy this, it is critical to have qualitative research based on in-depth interviews with North Korean defectors and rich descriptions of their lived experience of cultural difference and social prejudice. We recommend redesigning the survey-oriented approach, which has been helpful so far but constraining, to offer a deeper understanding through qualitative research approach in academic debates and public policy.

THE STRUCTURE OF THE BOOK

Together, the contributors to this book map North Korean defectors' circular or repeated mobilities to countries that include South Korea, Japan, the United Kingdom and the United States. They ask the questions that will elicit answers to North Koreans' motivations for their mobilities, experiences in resettlement and how those experiences influence their identity formation. This book on North Korean defectors is divided into three distinct sections covering topics that on occasion overlap: (1) mobilities, (2) settlements, and (3) the North Korean defectors' identities in different contexts. It should be noted that though the chapters discuss North Koreans' lives in the UK and other countries, this edited volume is not concerned so much with the different regions where North Koreans have settled as their experiences there. The focus remains on North Koreans' mobilities, settlements, and identities, the comprehensive implications of which will be summarized in the concluding chapter.

Section 1. "Keep Moving—North Korean Defectors," is broken down into three chapters each a different empirical study. In chapter 1 of this volume, "From Linked to Linking Agency: Transnational Ties of North Korean Defectors Living in Japan," Hyunuk Lee and Seok Hyang Kim deliberate on North Koreans' circular mobilities between Korea and Japan. North Korean defectors living in Japan are powerful examples not considered in this monochromatic framework, and help analyze the range of North Korean understandings of a colorful existence. Our goal is to describe not only the regional diversity of North Korean defectors in Japan, the United Kingdom, and South Korea, but also the dynamic range of these people, including their social relationships, memories, and historical backgrounds. This chapter investigates the history and the complicated relationship those returnees had with North Korea and Japan and analyzes the transnational networks that their multiple moves forged. They chronicle the passage of those Koreans who under Japanese Occupation in the early twentieth century were expatriated to Japan to provide cheap labor, then in the 1960s were repatriated to North Korea. Then in the 2000s, when the remittances from relatives in Japan stopped usually because they had died or money had run out, a trickle of so called "returnees" started leaving North Korea to re-migrate to Japan. The focus of this chapter is on the mobilities of the few hundred returnees that escaped North Korea to return to Japan and the transnational ties connecting ethnic Koreans living in Japan and defectors in South Korea to family in North Korea.

In chapter 2, "Adaptation of North Korean Defector Families Who Resettled in South Korea after Having Left the South," Heuijeong Kim concentrates on North Koreans' circular mobilities involving multiple moves to several different countries to arrive back in South Korea. Kim traces North Korean families who escaped to South Korea then chose to emigrate to the United Kingdom only to return to South Korea. She pays particular attention to how the repetitive mobile experiences initiated an adaptation process that ultimately altered and shaped North Korean defectors' identities. The chapter demonstrates that North Korean defectors in the process of repeated transnational movements have developed a hybridized identity that is part North Korean and part other. It also examines the effects of repeated migrations on adolescents and young adults, who already experiencing accelerated identity formation due to rapid physical changes and mental development are deeply affected. This combined with the intergenerational transmission of North Korean identity from their parents further confuses youths and impacts their psychological adaptation negatively. The chapter concludes by suggesting policy and education for adaptation and social integration for youths.

Chapter 3 is titled "'I Opened my Eyes'—Female North Korean Defectors' Journey from Precarity to Empowerment" by HaeRan Shin. Here she illustrates how the famine in North Korea in the 1990s accustomed women to hardship and became a source of their strength in surviving the rigors of escape and the challenges of resettlements. She argues that through their mobilities, their defection to South Korea and their subsequent settlement in London, many women became empowered. These women's adaptability and ethnic networks enabled them to not only survive uncertain situations but thrive. The shift from caregiver to breadwinner that started in North Korea was consolidated in the UK as they once again turned adversity to their advantage when the UK government decreased financial support. In the Korean community, by engaging in educational and cultural activities instead of political associations, those women have been able to move forward. As a result, they have found a power in themselves to make a difference in their lives. This chapter challenges existing literature and schools of thought that exclude agency in their studies on the mobilities of North Korean female defectors.

Section 2. "Life Outside the Korean Peninsula—North Korean Defectors' Settlements," discusses their settlement processes and their lives in countries other than South Korea over three chapters. In South Korea, North Korean defectors were scattered throughout the country, making it difficult to document those defectors' coping mechanisms and empowerment strategies as they responded to precarious situations. Korean enclaves in cities in other countries, however, offer neutral ground that closely simulates a control group that not only facilitate observation of North Koreans' strategies but also interactions with South Koreans. Furthermore, tracing the networks connecting North Korean defectors to each other as well as to their families still in North Korea is less complicated in enclaves than when they are in South Korea.

Chapter 4, "Do They Get Along? Interactions between North Korean Defectors and South Korean Migrants in London," is the first chapter of this section. Author HaeRan Shin selects a Korean enclave in London to observe the interactions of North Korean defectors and South Korean migrants in situations that revolve around employment, children's education, and recreational activities. The empirical findings demonstrate, first, that the geopolitical hierarchy and tensions among the origin societies of *Joseonjok*, South Korean, and North Korean migrants contributed to the reterritorialization of the ethnic enclave of transnational migrants. Second, the transnational enclave is being constantly reterritorialized by conflicting and adapting interactions between established South Korean migrants and newcomers. Third, the power relations of origin societies have intruded on individual migrants' lives by means, in part, of different religious and ethnic organizations. This chapter demonstrates the effects of transnational practices and geopolitical relationships on migrant communities and how they create a territorialized and relational space within ethnic enclaves.

In chapter 5, "Communication of North Korean Defector Families through Transnational Migration," Heuijeong Kim surveys the same Korean enclave in London observed in the first chapter of this section. She considers to what degree the continuous fear of discovery before and during defection inhibited and restrained their communication with their family in North Korea even after their resettlement lest they be punished. Transnational family communication was largely limited to contact through remittances facilitated by a network of brokers, usually Chinese or North Koreans, that connected defectors however indirectly to their family in North Korea. This chapter explores communication within and between families, which despite being a source of significant information has been overlooked, and how it relates to transnational care, the roles family play, and adaptation patterns.

Chapter 6 is titled "De-bordering North Korea: Remittances and Global Networks." In this chapter, HaeRan Shin describes the obstacles North Korean defectors living in London and Los Angeles faced in sending remittances to their families and the methods they used to overcome them. She argues that the North Korean defectors' financial and social remittances challenged the North Korean border control, which encouraged defectors to establish governments-in-exile to oppose the North Korean sovereignty. This research demonstrates that, first, through their practices of financial and social remittances, North Korean defectors have successfully breached North Korea's border and proved that the state's control is not absolute. Second, North Korean defectors developed global and regional networks to challenge the North Korean sovereignty. These networks played important roles in the daily lives of North Korean diaspora as well as the geopolitics of North Korea.

Section 3. "North Korean Identities Reconstituted as They Muddle Through," is the last section in this book. Two chapters are dedicated to understanding the period after settlement when North Korean defectors could finally process their experiences and living situation, which inevitably impacted their identity as North Koreans. In the past, scholars and journalists often assumed that defectors would rush to divest themselves of all reminders of the harsh conditions and horrible experiences in North Korea, their identities included. As a result, previous studies emphasized the assimilation perspective. These chapters refute the notion that North Koreans would simply adopt entirely new identities by demonstrating their complex and contextualized identity re-formation. Muddling through new experiences, North Korean defectors have defended their identities, adapting to the practices of South Koreans and other populations in ways that might modify but not rewrite their identity.

In chapter 7, "Representation and Self-Presentation of North Korean Defectors in South Korea: Image, Discourse, and Voices," Kyung Hyo Chun outlines why outsiders might imagine North Korean defectors would prefer to distance themselves from memories of North Korea. This chapter then juxtaposes the images others have of North Koreans as victims with the images they have of themselves as determined and capable. In this pilot study, the four North Korean defectors interviewed expressed frustration with the biased editorials circulated by the South Korean media and a desire to rectify the discrepancy between media representation and self-presentation. North Korean defectors have been actively working to gain control of the construction and management of their own images, rejecting and revising the identities that have been hitherto nationalized, gendered, and ethnicized. Their self-presentation, which itself is a product of strategic choices conditioned by social discourse and media representation, exposes the discrepancy between the conscious and the unconscious, public and personal, and front stage and back stage.

Chapter 8, "North Korean Nation-Building outside North Korea," examines those North Korean transnational refugees' discourses and practices that constitute a new version of the nation outside the materially bordered geography of their homeland. The findings of HaeRan Shin's study in this chapter are twofold. First, she establishes how the global network of North Korean refugees contributed to extraterritorial nation-building through the flow of ideas, discourses, and activities. These efforts supported a vision of a future version of the North Korean nation proper as network members collaborated to initiate political activities and measures that would establish an exile government. Second, she deliberates on how nation-building efforts in relations were vital in distinguishing the North Korean identity from South Korean and Korean Chinese migrants. Shin discusses those North Korean defectors who had initially attempted to assimilate in South Korea but feeling rejected by South Koreans moved to the UK and established a new North Koreanness. Over time, as they connected with other North Koreans in their efforts to maintain their identities this laid the groundwork for an alternative version of North Korea, or nation-building through relations.

"Conclusion: Looking to the Future" first summarizes the findings of the case studies and then asks how North Korean defectors would respond to a unified Korea or two Koreas at peace in the near future. Considering the various scenarios for North Koreans in the event of reunification or at least reforms in North Korea, this concluding chapter extends the volume's discussions on the main themes: mobilities, resettlements, and identities. HaeRan Shin and Kyung Hyo Chun collaborate in the concluding chapter to examine future possibilities from the perspective of North Korean defectors who have experienced life in North Korea, South Korea, and a third country. To arrive at a place of understanding, Shin and Chun argue for the pursuit of qualitative research over quantitative research. They believe that contextualized, nuanced, and process-oriented qualitative approaches will expose the divisions in understanding been North and South Koreans and redirect Koreans to a path based on knowledge and not assumptions.

NOTE

1. Ministry of Unification, https://www.unikorea.go.kr/eng_unikorea/whatwedo/support/. Accessed on October 27, 2021.

REFERENCES

Chun, Kyung Hyo. "Representation and Self-Presentation of North Korean Defectors in South Korea: Image, Discourses, and Voices." *Asian Journal of Peacebuilding* 8, no.1 (2020): 93–112.

Collyer, M. "Stranded Migrants and the Fragmented Journey." *Journal of Refugee Studies* 23, no. 3 (2010): 273–293.

Crawley, Heaven, and Dimitris Skleparis. "Refugees, migrants, neither, both: categorical fetishism and the politics of bounding in Europe's 'migration crisis.'" *Journal of Ethnic and Migration Studies* 44, no. 1 (2018): 48–64.

De Coninck, David. "Migrant categorizations and European public opinion: Diverging attitudes towards immigrants and refugees." *Journal of Ethnic and Migration studies* 46, no. 9 (2020): 1667–1686.

Kim, Sung Kyung. "'Defector,' 'Refugee,' or 'Migrant'? North Korean Settlers in South Korea's Changing Social Discourse." *North Korean Review* (2012): 94–110.

Shin, HaeRan. "The Geopolitical Ethnic Networks for De-bordering: North Korean Defectors in Los Angeles and London." *Asian Journal of Peacebuilding*. 9, no. 2 (2021): 1–24 doi: 10.18588/202111.00a189

Shin, HaeRan. "Extra-territorial nation-building in flows and relations: North Korea in the global networks and an ethnic enclave." *Political Geography*, 74 (2019): 102047 (online).

Shin, HaeRan. "The territoriality of ethnic enclaves: dynamics of transnational practices and geopolitical relations within and beyond a Korean transnational enclave in New Malden, London." *The Annals of the American Association of Geographers*, 108, no. 3 (2018): 756–772.

SECTION 1

Keeping Moving—North Korean Defectors

Chapter 1

From Linked to Linking Agency

Transnational Ties of North Korean Defectors Living in Japan

Hyunuk Lee and Seok-hyang Kim

In an era of global migration, North Korean defectors, once a rarity, are scattered all over the world today. This chapter focuses on those North Korean defectors who first migrated from Korea under colonial rule to Japan, then from Japan to North Korea, and finally, from North Korea back to Japan.[1] Their migration is part of a flow of movement formed over a long period of time that could also be conceptualized in terms of diaspora and diaspora return. Defectors, including those discussed in this chapter as they fled North Korea craving better lives, are the core of the North Korean diaspora. As transnational migrants with high mobilities, they constantly exploit their mobilities to survive, and there is an opportunity here to reinterpret North Korean defectors as pioneering migrants.

Today, there are more than 30,000 North Korean defectors living in South Korea and more than 300 living in Japan (Bell, 2018). Those living in Japan have a very long history and crucial transnational networks that though not constantly active will when needed function to this today. Our focus here is on those North Korean defectors that have connections to Japan as a home they left behind to move to North Korea, believing Korea to be their "motherland."

This chapter explores the history and background of these North Korean defectors, as well as their transnational networks linking North Korea, South Korea, and Japan, focusing on connectivity through remittances and the exchange of goods. The chapter uses the term "ex-Zainichi" (在日) to describe those North Korean defectors who once lived in Japan as Zainichi Josenjin (在日朝鮮人) rather than "Korean-Japanese defectors." Using the term "ex-Zainichi North Korean defectors" expresses the origin as well as the mobilities in history of the group that is the focus of this study, i.e., North Korean defectors now living in Japan. This is especially true of North Korean defectors who are second-generation Zainichi and remember Japan as their original and home before their move to North Korea. Also, the term Korean-Japanese mainly refers to South Koreans who migrated to Japan after the division of Korea rather than the people transported there during the Japanese colonial rule.

RETURN OR REPATRIATION?

The return of Zainichi Koreans to Korean society from Japan is considered by many as the return of the Zainichi diaspora. However, this chapter focuses narrowly on the return of Zainichi Koreans to North Korea, which had a more aggressive repatriation policy than South Korea did. December 14, 2019, marked the 60th anniversary of the official start of the repatriation project, but this group is struggling to inform the world about their historically forgotten mass migration to North Korea and related human rights violations. More victims of the political divisions separating the Korean peninsula into South Korea and North Korea, these migrants are perhaps among those whose existence is slowly being forgotten in our society.

In 1960 alone, more than 49,000 Zainichi Koreans traveled to North Korea, and over the entire duration of the repatriation project—from December 1959 to July 1984–93,340 people made the journey (Morris-Suzuki, 2011). Very few have since had a chance to visit, or to go back to, Japan or South Korea, and those who did had to defect from North Korea.

The vast majority of Zainichi Koreans were originally from the southern half of the Korean peninsula, but nevertheless they were excited to find a new dream in North Korea. From the point of view of the Zainichi, this was a "return migration" even though 96 percent of the Zainichi living in Japan at that time came from the southern part of the Korean peninsula (Inoue, 1956). Despite how they might have felt, the subsequent migration of Koreans living in Japan to North Korea cannot be considered a "return migration" in the strictest sense.

Since Choch'ongnyŏn (General Association of Korean Residents in Japan) is affiliated with North Korea, the term "return migration" was intentionally used to describe this migration flow. Like Choch'ongnyŏn, Japan also referred to it as a "return migration movement" (Kawashima, 2011). However, the South Korean government and Mindan (Korean Residents Union in Japan) insisted that migration to North Korea was "repatriation to North Korea."

However, Masan Ilbo published a series of articles, titled "Repatriation to North Korea," in March and April 1959, almost a year before the repatriation project began. These articles indicated that South Korea and North Korea strongly disagreed on the issue of repatriation to North Korea even at the time. The newspaper cited Choch'ongnyŏn's estimation of 117,000 Zainichi Koreans who wanted to return to their homeland. It also cited Choch'ongnyŏn's refusal to follow the "free will to move" verification procedures the International Committee of the Red Cross (ICRC) requested. Other articles discussed accusations made by Mindan and the South Korean government that Japan and North Korea were engaging in a political conspiracy to essentially "sell" Zainichi Koreans to North Korea (Masan Ilbo, 1 April 1959). Mindan and the South Korean government expressed doubts about Choch'ongnyŏn's explanation for vehemently opposing the ICRC demand to officially confirm Zainichi Koreans' intention to migrate to North Korea. Another article contended that the reason Choch'ongnyŏn opposed scrutiny of their claims was that the number of applicants who wanted to go to North Korea was no more than two to three thousand (Masan Ilbo, 11 March 1959).

The term "North Korea repatriation project" emphasizes that expatriates are being returned to their country of origin if not their region. What needs to be remembered is that when the migrants left the Korean peninsula, their homeland was a unified if occupied nation called "Joseon." The Zainichi left for North Korea, firmly believing that though the country was divided now, the motherland (Joseon or Korea) would soon be reunited (Morris-Suzuki, 2009a).

The political propaganda of North Korea leveraged Zainichi Koreans' firm belief in a "motherland" to convince them that the division of Joseon into two regimes would not affect them. Thus, the concept of the "motherland" emphasized by the North Korean government could have persuaded countless returnees to migrant to North Korea. North Korean government's propaganda and the promise of the free education and free habitation was also a strong push factor in the migration of Zainichi. Above all the propaganda of North Korea, building a new state, became a powerful incentive for large-scale migration, as people who have experienced the loss of their country achieve independence and dream of building a new state. However, since the 2000s, many so-called "returnees (Zainichi's returning to North Korea)" have attempted to escape from North Korea to Japan or South Korea for a better life.

LITERATURE REVIEW

There has been a noticeable increase in global interest in North Koreans. One reason is that these are people who are accustomed to very limited freedoms and almost nonexistent exchanges with the outside world under North Korea's dictatorships. Another reason is that due to the COVID-19 pandemic there is a greater concern for the welfare of people living in isolated environments with little health care.

As countries around the world place restrictions and controls on their population's movements at home and abroad, people are confronted with global socio-economic changes and crises caused by restricted mobility. No one is immune to the current spread of the pandemic. North Koreans too will have to develop new survival strategies for even greater social isolation than in the past, as well as those attempting to flee. In these precarious times, it is important to continue research on North Korea and its defectors.

Since the early 2000s, research on North Korean defectors has been continuous. The focus, however, has been on North Korean defectors in South Korea, the main place of settlement for North Korean defectors (Choo, 2006; Yoon, 2001; Jeon, 2000; Jeon et al. 2012; Hough, 2021). The discussions have centered on their networks and strategies in defecting as well as identity issues (Kim et al. 2009; Lim, 2008; Kim, 2014; Song, 2017; Kook, 2018).

Other research on the activities of North Korean defectors, such as nation-building in Asia and Europe, provided important insights for this study (Oh, 2012; Shin, 2018, 2019; Watson, 2015; Bell, 2021) on issues that include belonging and integration. However, despite many studies on North Korean defectors, we still do not know that much about the particular circumstances of their backgrounds. Although it has been established that many of the defectors are from the North Korea-China border region, it is assumed that the reason for this is that geographical proximity meant they their escape would be easier. Is proximity to the border the only reason these people escaped? If there were a specific group of people whose circumstances were more dire and need to flee North Korea more desperate, what group would that be? Do all North Koreans who escape intend to live permanently in South Korea? Are there other minorities like the Chinese diaspora in North Korea that Tertitskiy (2015) discusses who experience harsher treatment than other minorities? With these questions in mind, we believe that more attention needs to be paid to the diversity of these defectors' motivations and their networks.

Just as ethnic networks have a significant influence on defectors (Shin, 2018), how do their meaningful or even casual relationships influence the formation of their own networks? When and how did North Koreans in the outside world form a network with those still in North Korea? To get a little closer to answering this question, we focus our study of North Korean defectors on those who—contradictorily—relocated to North Korea.

There has always been interest in large-scale migration to socialist countries, which historically is an anomaly. In what follows, we will first provide an overview of studies on the North Korean repatriation project as well as the main findings of research on North Korean defectors in Japan.

There have been previous studies that analyzed the North Korea repatriation project, notably the purpose and significance of the project (Shin, 1979; Jang, 2003; Morris-Suzuki, 2007; Nam, 2012; Kikuchi, 2009). Several studies have found that repatriation was used by the Japanese as a means to evict the Koreans in Japan (Morris-Suzuki, 2007). However, other studies identify North Korea the driving force behind the North Korea repatriation project. Some believe that North Korea used the "return project" as a way to secure manpower (including technicians and businessmen) and to demonstrate the superiority of the socialist system in North Korea (Shin, 1979; Jang, 2003; Nam, 2012).

There are several research studies that have analyzed the development process of the North Korea repatriation project (Morris-Suzuki, 2011; Kim, 2003; Park, 2011). Based on International Committee of the Red Cross archives, Morris-Suzuki (2011) has shown that secret negotiations involving the Japanese government, the Japanese Red Cross, their North Korean counterparts, in a large-scale repatriation began in 1955.

Considering the enormous roles played by Japan, the Japanese Red Cross, Choch'ongnyŏn and North Korea in this repatriation project, we can infer that there must have been considerable cooperation in making the project successful. There must have been sufficient reasons for promoting the mass migration of a refugee-like population (Zainichi Koreans) to a country not recognized as a state (North Korea). As an impartial organization, the fact of the Red Cross's involvement in repatriating a large number of people gave credence to the humanitarian mission that was supposedly behind this project. However, as the International Committee of the Red Cross noted, it was up to the Japan to administer its border and determine the fate of the Zainichi in Japanese territory. Therefore, it seems that the return project could not have existed without the Japanese government's cooperation with the North Korean government, the Red Cross, and the Choch'ongnyŏn.

Japan had agreed to the idea of "return migration" due to the financial burden of supporting the largely unemployed Zainichi. The Japanese Red Cross, which conducted a survey of the Zainichi Korean population before the repatriation project, emphasized that their unemployment rate was high and most were unskilled laborers. It was at this time that Japanese Congress began discussing solutions for the Zainichi burden on the country's finances.

In 1945, it is estimated that between 2 million and 2.4 million Koreans lived in Japan (Morita, 1996). By 1956, according to the statistical data, about 90,000 Koreans living in Japan (about 90 percent of foreigners) were entitled to subsistence assistance, and at over 200 million yen per year, the assistance amount was a large expenditure. According to a report from Japan Red Cross, written by Inoue (1956), the chairman of the Japanese Red Cross' foreign affairs, the Japanese government must accept the fact that expulsion of the troublesome Koreans from Japan had advantages. Apart from the issue of whether it was beneficial to decrease Japan's population, it was also thought that expulsion would preemptively prevent any potential conflict that might arise between the Japanese and Koreans (Morris-Suzuki, 2005a).

The Japanese Red Cross report, however, also stressed that the Zainichi should return to their homeland (North Korea) of their own free will, and the Japanese government should respect their decision to stay. Recognizing the importance of the Zainichi's freedom of residence on humanitarian grounds, it was recommended that the International Committee of the Red Cross obtain their consent.

In this context, the political and economic situation in Japan seems to have played an important role in the relocation of Zainichi. Though the repatriation project was devised supposedly for humanitarian reasons, in reality, it seems the Japanese government's policy on the Zainichi was the underlying motivation. Related to this point, Shin (1979) has stressed that the Japanese Red Cross had to have persuaded the ICRC to repatriate Koreans in Japan to North Korea.

Although the International Committee of the Red Cross requested confirmation of free will in the migration process to North Korea, this request provoked strong resistance from the Choch'ongnyŏn and the North Korean Red Cross. Resistance from North Korea further hindered cooperation with Japan and the ICRC. The confirmation process to prove "free will to move" back then could absolve the current the Japanese Red Cross, the Japanese government and ironically the North Korean government of accusations of misconduct in the repatriation project.

That said, the provision for freedom of movement was nonetheless not respected, and this should be seen as a real problem. The fact that children under the age of 16 were obliged to submit to parents' decisions points to a situation in which many young people could have been, in effect, forced to migrate to North Korea. Despite their lack of free will, according to our interviewees, many young students were nonetheless enchanted by North Korean propaganda and ideological education. As a result, more than half the students in Choch'ongnyŏn-run schools boarded ships to North Korea to "contribute to the progress of the motherland" and for "free education" (Kim, 1999).

Additionally, as Kawashima (2011) has noted, unlike the previous two phases (1959–1967 and 1971), in the third phase (1971–1984) the Red Cross procedure for confirming "free will to move" was not carried out. He has, thus, suggested that it is appropriate to understand the post-1971 North Korea repatriation project as an entirely different and separate project.

The reasons for the large influx of Zainichi from Japan into North Korea can be summarized as follows. First, the Japanese government and Japanese Red Cross encouraged the migration to reduce the Zainichi minority in Japan. Second, North Korean propaganda aroused a desire to return to their homeland with promises of free education and jobs. Third, Koreans in Japan voluntarily left for North Korea due to the hardships and discrimination they faced in that country.

Regarding previous studies on Zainichi who escaped from North Korea to return to Japan, there is little research into their lives in North Korea, though several research studies have been initiated as the number of former Zainichi to defect from North Korea has increased recently (Yi, 2006; Jong, 2009; Bell, 2014, 2016, 2018; Kim, 2017; Kim, 2018). In previous studies, researchers conducted interviews with North Korean defectors in Japan (Jong, 2009; Bell, 2014, 2018) and South Korea (Kim, 2018). They noted that Zainichi in North Korea were discriminated against but were also often the subjects of envy and jealousy if they received gifts and money from Japan.

Despite previous studies' significant contributions to the subject of North Korean defectors' return to Japan, they have only partially examined the transnational connections that have been formed as a result. They focus only on fragmentary aspects of transnational connections, which limits our ability to understand the long-term connections between North Korea, Japan, and South Korea. The importance of these connections should not be underestimated; they provide valuable clues as to why the number of North Korean defectors currently defecting to Japan is increasing.

Though these connections through remittances and goods from Japan for the past sixty years offer insights, it is necessary to concede that there continues to be a lack of information regarding the changes in North Korean society. While immigrants play an important role in transnational relations, the actions of non-immigrants such as those family members in Japan also have a major impact on the success or failure (Jørgen Carling, 2008) of transnational networks. In fact, the role of non-immigrants in transnational networks is amplified in those cases where freedom is severely restricted because their family's rights in North Korea are so limited.

RESEARCH METHODOLOGY

To examine the characteristics of the transnational networks and lives of ex-Zainichi North Korean defectors in Japan, this study analyzed literature reviews and conducted in-depth interviews.

First, we reviewed a wide range of existing Korean as well as international studies on North Koreans and Koreans living in Japan that related to the repatriation project. These studies shed light on the political and historical reasons for the North Korea repatriation project. They also clarified the process by which Koreans living in Japan at the time migrated to North Korea.

Second, we conducted two- to three-hour individual interview with sixteen in Japan and South Korea, focusing on those who had followed similar migration routes from Japan to North Korea in the past. Interviewees tended to fall into three groups. The first group was composed of those Koreans who migrated from Japan as children (the first generation). The second group included the children born to those repatriated North Koreans (the second generation). The third group was made up of Zainichi Koreans living in Japan who were witnesses to the repatriation efforts. The interviews were conducted in the suburbs of Osaka, Japan, and locations in Korea over the span of a year in 2019. We were able to discover that the repatriated Koreans were spread throughout North Korea, but of our interviewees almost 45 percent of them were located in Hamgyeonbuk-do.

Third, we examined how Zainichi Koreans who moved to North Korea lived while maintaining transnational networks to Japan and South Korea. In this section, we demonstrate that the transnational networks that connect Japan, North Korea, and South Korea have remained constant since 1959. The issue here is not the strength of the connection but that it flows one way, either from Japan or South Korea to North Korea. This flow includes people and goods. From 1959 to 1984, Zainichi Koreans in Japan traveled to North Korea by ship, but almost none returned. When visits were permitted, family members in Japan could travel to North Korea but Zainichi Koreans could not leave to visit family in Japan. The same stands true of money and goods flowing from Japan to North Korea but nothing in return. Initially, people and goods were conveyed by ships, but since the last route was retired this current flowing from Japan to North Korea has been maintained with international flights. In addition, we conducted interviews of ex-Zainichi North Korean defectors in Japan to discover their transnational networks.

Through this research process, we find that the border crossing of ex-Zainichi North Korean defectors is associated with the return of the diaspora; and that a trend of continuous mobilities emerges through their networks between Japan, South Korea, and North Korea.

THE REPATRIATION TO NORTH KOREA

In the early years, a Soviet ship ferried Zainichi Koreans to North Korea; in later years, a North Korean vessel called the *Mangyongbong*[2] took on this task. Overall, however, the route from the port city Niigata in Japan to North Korea's port city, Chongjin remained relatively unchanged until the so-called "return project" was completed. After the repatriation project ended, *Mangyongbong* and later *Mangyongbong-92*[3] operated between the ports of Wonsan in North Korea and Niigata in Japan and served as an important life-line connecting migrants between North Korea and Japan.[4]

In 1959, the first repatriation ship departed from Niigata with 975 Zainichi on board bound for Chongjin. The migration of the Zainichi to North Korea continued for twenty-five years until 1984, when the 186th ship departed Niigata for Chongjin. However, the project did not run continuously for twenty-five years, but was divided into three phases, including a three-year hiatus: Phase One: December 1959 to October 1967, Suspension: 1968–1970, Phase Two: May to October 1971, Phase Three: December 1971–July 1984 (Kawasaki, 2011).

The controversy around why so many people (93,195) decided to move from Japan to North Korea[5] continues to this day. The largest number of Zainichi moved to North Korea in the first full two years of the project, 1960 and 1961. There could be several reasons for the high numbers of migrants that flocked to North Korea during those years. Based on the interviews that we conducted, in the beginning, many people returned to their (supposed) homeland because they believed North Korea's propaganda. However, the Zainichi still in Japan gradually understood through letters from family who had moved to North Korea requesting basic necessities that the shortages there made life unimaginably difficult (Ryang, 2014).

I use the soap and detergent you sent me. After we ate the macaroni you sent me from Japan, my husband said it had been too long since he had eaten macaroni, so the worms in his stomach were surprised. I hope you can send me the goods with the returnees. You can send goods up to 10 kilos per person, so please send us 20 kilos under the names of the two returners. (26 January 1963)[6]

As this excerpt describes a shortage of basic household goods and staples that was so dire that they needed as many goods and remittances as possible sent from Japan. Migrants who moved to North Korea early on would attempt to have people who moved to North Korea after them bring them goods.

Why, then, did some of the Zainichi go to North Korea, knowing or at least suspecting the severe conditions in North Korea? Often, Zainichi moved to North Korea because it was the only way to reunite with other family members (children, parents, siblings) who had gone to North Korea in the early days. Even today, free relations between North Korea and Japan are forbidden; and it is almost impossible to visit with family members in North Korea without paying the "visit to the motherland" fee. The "visit to the motherland" refers to a one- or two-week state-sanctioned visit to meet family in North Korea, for which a Zainichi must pay a large sum of money.[7] Most people could not afford to visit their families in North Korea, and if they wanted to see their families, they had to migrated too. For this reason, 200 to 300 people migrated continuously to North Korea each year until the project ended.

There had to have been cases in which people who faced adversity in Japan inevitably migrated despite the difficult situation, including supply shortages, in North Korea. Moreover, it must be mentioned that there was a group of people who subscribed to socialist ideas and the ideal socialist state that North Korea promoted. It was not difficult to discover examples through our interviews of one family member's determination to relocated to North Korea, which led to the entire family moving to North Korea.

ZAINICHI LIVES IN NORTH KOREA

Studies on diaspora returnees have discussed how the negative experiences in going back to their homelands have resulted in reorganization and negotiation of identity (Seol & Skrentny, 2009; Iglicka, 1998; Tsuda, 2000, 2003). However, the Zainichi Koreans who migrated to North Korea—the migration is often referred to as the return of the diaspora—faced a reality that went beyond the negative experiences of returning diaspora.

There is very little authentic data on the lives of the Zainichi after they migrated to North Korea.[8] Compared to the research studies that have evaluated the North Korea repatriation project, there are only a few studies on the lives of repatriated Zainichi Koreans in North Korea and just as few on the resettlement of defectors in Japan. This may be understandable in the context of the restrictions on information and travel in North Korea. It is less understandable in Japan where Zainichi Koreans' existence was arguably forgotten by Japanese society. However, with the recent increase in Zainichi North Koreans defectors, their lives post-repatriation in North Korea has gradually been revealed.

According to the South Korean government's White Paper on Human Rights in North Korea published in 1996, Zainichi Koreans (returners) are generally referred to as "Gwipo" or "Jaepo" (which means returners from Japan) in North Korea. This is seemingly because the North Koreans have treated Zainichi Koreans as a heterogeneous group from Japan.[9] In addition, the White Paper has testimony that if Zainichi Koreans (returnees) do not receive financial support from their families in Japan, they are treated with contempt by the local residents.[10] Due to harsh treatment and constant surveillance, some Zainichi Koreans (returnees) have suffered psychologically and committed suicide, and some are said to have been executed while escaping to China or Russia.[11]

Depending on their position in the North Korean societal hierarchy, nearly all citizens endure some degree of discrimination. Their standing could affect their entry into the Labour Party; college admissions; job hiring; promotion; executive appointment; changing residence; government provision; and even marriage. The lowest rung is comprised of North Korea who are classified as severely non-compliant with the North Korean regime and subject to constant surveillance and discrimination by the North Korean authorities (*Korean-English Glossary of North Korean Human Rights*, 2016).

Kim Il-sung's statements[12] (Niigatakenn Zainichi Chosenzin Kikokugkyouryokukai, 1980) promise the Zainichi a welcoming atmosphere and privileged treatment upon their arrival in North Korea. Expecting a warm welcome, the Zainichi's longing for their motherland must have increased and likely accelerated the migration to North Korea. However, the welcome Zainichi received upon arriving in North Korea was one of suspicion and they were viewed as bearers of capitalist ideas from Japan that could destroy the socialist order.[13] According to Kim (2018), ex-Zainichi North Korean defectors were suspected of being corrupted by capitalist society. Those Zainichi Koreans with Japanese spouses (Aoki, 2010),[14] sometimes neither of whom could speak Korean well, became the objects of increased vigilance by the North Korean government.[15]

The interviews conducted for this study attempted to draw out information on the lives of Zainichi Koreans (returnees) in North Korea. According to one interviewee, Zainichi Koreans (returnees) who received remittances or goods from Japan were less likely to be suspected or discriminated against in North Korea and could lead easier lives. After moving to North Korea, they wrote letters to their families in Japan to request items to sell in North Korea.[16] Most of them asked for nylon cloth, clothes, and wristwatches. Looking back, they recall that their North Koreans neighbors were very envious when goods arrived from Japan once or twice a year. The disdain mixed with envy was due to the fact that some Zainichi could eat rice and wear quality clothing thanks to remittances from relatives in Japan. They explained that without the remittances and goods from Japan they would be so poor that they would struggle to survive in North Korea. Generally speaking, Zainichi Koreans did not have any relatives in North Korea, which made it difficult to get help in North Korean society and why they relied so much on their relatives in Japan.

In an example of this envy and disdain, one interviewee told of an incident when other children throwing stones and tauntingly called "Jaepo":

> I was born in North Korea but I knew that my house was somehow different. We could eat rice in my house, not corn. Sometimes when my uncle, who lives in Japan, sent luggage to us (my grandfather and father in the North), people would come and look around curiously. There were also girls in my neighborhood who wanted to marry me because my house was rich. However, my great-grandfather's business was not doing well, so we could no longer get money from Japan, and my house became too expensive. Inevitably, my parents made me and my brothers live in another house and go to work. At that time, the children who had treated me well in the past started acting strangely toward me, throwing stones and calling me "Jaepo." That's when I realized that there was definitely discrimination against us. I belonged to the "Jaepo."

It is due to this type of incident that Zainichi intentionally maintained a certain distance from local North Koreans and secretly shared certain information only with Zainichi Koreans (returnees) in similar circumstances (Kim, 2018) by using Japanese. It is said that Japanese was commonly spoken, especially in the house since those doing the listening were government agents pretending to be neighbors. For this reason, it is not surprising that the second generation of ex-Zainichi born in North Korea are fluent in Japanese as it was one of their survival strategies in North Korea.

Mutual distrust meant social relationships as well as marriage options were limited (Kim, 2018).[17] According to one interviewee, a second-generation Zainichi woman born in North Korea, when she tried to marry a North Korean man, the man's family strongly disapproved. The reason for their opposition to the marriage was that if a North Korean man married a returnee, it would harm his chances for promotion in the Communist Party. In the end, she had no choice but to renounce the idea of marriage to this man of her own accord. In North Korea, to marry a returnee is to marry a person far down in the hierarchy of North Korean society. For this reason, opportunities for returnees to form various social relationships with North Koreans were extremely rare.

ENTERING AND SETTLING IN JAPAN

As mentioned in the introduction, approximated 300 ex-Zainichi North Korean defectors have resettled in Japan to date. Here, we explore how ex-Zainichi North Korean defectors decided to return to Japan.

North Korean defectors are understood to be refugees and accepted as worldwide. The South Korean government, though, recognizes them as citizens, not refugees, and has implemented policies to integrate them into

Korean society. Japan, however, does not indiscriminately grant the residency to North Korean defectors that it offers to ex-Zainichi Koreans previously registered as Josen-seki.[18] In the case of ex-Zainichi North Korean defectors, they do not need to apply for refugee status. They are eligible to enter Japan upon proving that they are Josen-seki. This is the main reason for ex-Zainichi North Korean defectors' migration to Japan. Their unimpeded entry into Japan reflects the complex historical background and relationships of migrants across generations.

In this section, we examine the lives of ex-Zainichi North Korean defectors residing in Yao, a suburb of Osaka, where Japan's oldest "Korea Town" is located. Ex-Zainichi North Korean defectors living in Japan often conceal that they have defected due to Japanese society's prejudice toward defectors.

The Japanese government allows returnees to enter and settle in Japan for humanitarian reasons, but the social assistance provided amounts, in practical terms, to nothing more than life support. In addition, they face various difficulties in finding jobs and housing, and readjusting to Japanese society.

Japanese society learned about the lives of ex-Zainichi North Korean defectors in a documentary called "North Korean Defectors in Osaka Yao"[19] aired approximately ten years ago. This documentary followed the more than thirty ex-Zainichi North Korean defectors living quietly in Yao city, a suburb of the Osaka metropolitan area,[20] as if they were in hiding.

Ex-Zainichi North Korean defectors in Japan tend to live in the Tokyo and Osaka in areas known for their Zainichi population since colonial times. It can be speculated that ex-Zainichi North Korean defectors live in places that historically had a high percentage of Zainichi to settle anew more easily.[21]

According to an interview with a North Korean defector, she was brought to Osaka's Korea Town, Tsuruhashi—the largest Korea Town—by the broker when she arrived in Japan after defection. She lived there for three months. However, due to the high cost of rent in Tsuruhashi, which is near Osaka's business district, she then moved to Yao, which is only fifteen minutes by train from Tsuruhashi and the city center. In the interview, we found out that there were other factors, besides rent, for her move.

> I came to Yao because there is an NGO office here that helped me escape from North Korea. I heard from another defector that there is a night school in Yao that teaches Japanese and it is free. Also, I need to start working and there was a bus from Yao station to the farm where I can work, so I thought it would be better to move here.

For her, a place with a lower cost of living and the nongovernmental organization (NGO)[22] that had helped her escape from North Korea nearby was a better prospect than the centrally located Korea Town. It was beneficial for her to get help, from the NGO, with the basic administrative processes of living in Japan. Moreover, we believe that being in a place where she could communicate with ex-Zainichi North Korean defectors in a similar situation, was more important than anything else, as she learned about Yao's night school from those who had defected earlier. Also, the place where other ex-Zainichi North Korean defectors live could help her—as someone who had returned to Japan after fifty years—feel better.

As this case shows, it is possible, through the interviews, to find out the general set of reasons for the gathering of North Korean defectors in Yao. However, we want to stress that the historical characteristics of the place is deeply related to the concentration of ex-Zainichi Korean in Yao.

It is important to understand the regional characteristics of Yao, to grasp the background reasons for the gathering of North Korean defectors in the city. The first is related to the characteristics of the job market in Tsuruhashi.[23] It is possible for ex-Zainichi North Korean defectors to find a job here because they understand both Japanese and Korean. Besides the job market, the fact that the Yao area has been home to a socially inferior group, compared to the surrounding suburbs is strongly related to the settlement of Zainichi Korean. Yao is a place where Zainichi Koreans have settled since long ago.[24]

The reason as to why many Zainichi have lived in Yao since long ago is related to the fact that this was an area where people of low social classes lived together in Japanese society (Cho, 2009). It needs to be mentioned that Yao is known as the "Dongwa problem" in Japan.[25] We would like to stress that the relationship between the Zainichi and Yao is significant. Yao used to be a "Dongwa district" near Osaka, and it was also a place where Zainichi Koreans, one of the groups that was discriminated against in Japanese society in the past, lived in high density.[26] The Dongwa district was the residential area where people who performed despised jobs in Japanese society (mainly butchers) gathered.[27]

The facts that the Dongwa district was the place of discrimination in Yao and that Zainichi had lived in this segregated place, indicate that Zainichi also lived in a very hard situation in Japanese society. Yao still has the highest density of Zainichi; and the fact that North Korean defectors cohabit in its society, implies that the defectors are living in a segregated space from Japanese society.[28] According to a survey conducted by Yao city, people in Osaka still have prejudices against the Dongwa district, and they believe that people from this area are socially discriminated against.[29]

Although ex-Zainichi North Korean defectors live in the same space (Yao) with the Zainichi Koreans who have the most similar background to them, there is a certain social distance between them. There are many Korean-Japanese (newcomers) living in Yao city, and there are several NGOs and social groups that support Zainichi Koreans and newcomers, but the ex-Zainichi North Korean defectors do not interact with them at all. The reason is that even though they are ex-Zainichi themselves, they think that being a defector places them in a very different situation.

I do not know what the Japanese think of me. It seems that the people around me know that I am not Japanese. Of course, it is not clear if they know if I am a North Korean defector. Maybe people heard a rumor that there are a lot of North Korean defectors in Yao, or they don't care. There's not much discrimination in Japan, but it's clear they'll know I'm different. I don't know what the Japanese think of me. I know I'm not Japanese or Zainichi. I'm not sure they know I'm a North Korean defector. I can't forget that I'm a North Korean defector. It's always labelled.

Living in Yao, which is currently densely populated by Korean-Japanese, it is possible that they are perceived as Koreans in Japan rather than as defectors from North Korea. However, they seem to feel that the fact they are from North Korea is more apparent than the fact that they used to be Zainichi. If, in North Korea, it was difficult for them to assimilate into North Korean society because they were Zainichi who migrated from Japan, now back in Japan, it seems that they remain outsiders or strangers, albeit now in Korean-Japanese (or Zainichi) society, and create their own community.

As second-generation ex-Zainichi North Korean defectors in Japan, who were born in Japan, are aging, their loneliness is expressed by staying alone, especially given that they could not bring their children with them after defecting from North Korea.

I escaped from North Korea alone, so it's hard for me. My family in North Korea may be fine because they are with their own, but I think it's hardest for me to be alone here. I cannot sleep without a drink when I feel lonely. I can't help but think about it. How good it is to be around someone, the worst thing is to be lonely. There are situations where I can't help but live, even if it's hard, while saying that today is already over. But I have a dream, so I have to live anyway. We must live with hope.

The reason they fled North Korea alone was that they were thinking primarily of their grandchildren, not their own children (born in North Korea). Their children (second-generation ex-Zainichi, born in North Korea) learned a little Japanese, so they could live in Japan, but their grandchildren know very little Japanese. So, one defector decided not to bring her children and grandchildren; so long as she could send money from Japan, her children and grandchildren could somehow eat and live in North Korea. As a result, if ex-Zainichi North Korean defectors live alone in Yao, they help each other to survive. Two or three times a week they talk to each other on the phone, and once a week they meet for dinner at each other's houses and share information.

As mentioned earlier, when they migrated to North Korea, they used Japanese within their community, so generally, they do not have much difficulty speaking daily Japanese. Generally, the second generation born in North Korea learned Japanese orally from their parents (first-generation returnees to North Korea), so they do not know difficult expressions, but even they are able to converse in everyday life. However, in order to get a job (unlike work at the NGO's farm in the earlier example) or to get higher education, Japanese education is necessary in the early days of settling in Japan.[30] New Japanese expressions and new cultural norms are a barrier for ex-Zainichi North Korean defectors to understanding and adapting to Japanese society, so Yao's night Japanese school helps in this regard.

Yao city's night Japanese school, conducted at Yao Junior High School, offers an opportunity to learn Japanese for free.[31] North Korean defectors would gradually become accustomed to life in Japan, if they started working after learning Japanese and understanding the workings of society (Bell, 2018).[32]

Speaking Japanese is very important in order to return and adapt to Japanese society. The following interview corresponds to a case where a woman who emigrated to North Korea at the age of ten, then fled North Korea at the age of sixty and currently lives in Japan.

> I speak as much Japanese as I can without feeling uncomfortable living in Japan. However, I cannot read the difficult Kanji, like written announcement from Yao city. So, before COVID-19, I tried to learn more Japanese kanji (Chinese characters) while attending night school in Yao. So I attended night school at Yao Junior High School in Japan, related with the registration, another defector told me that I could apply to Yao City Hall. They say all North Korean defectors go to night school. It's fine to go for 3 years, and even though it's free.

Their Japanese level also plays a big role in them being able to get a visa that allows them to live a stable life in Japan. One ex-Zainichi North Korean defector moved to Japan and then brought his wife and son over to join him in Japan later. However, since his wife is originally from North Korea, she could not speak Japanese at all, and their son was in the same situation. Because of their poor Japanese skills, life became difficult for the wife and son, who must renew their visas every year, to obtain a work permit in Japan, however poor Japanese skills make it hard to pass the visa renewal process. As in this case, especially if a Zainichi (returnee) marries a North Korean and defects to Japan with the partner, or brings a child born in North Korea to Japan, it is difficult for them to stay in a stable situation and to find work to survive in Japan.[33]

TRANSNATIONAL NETWORK THROUGH GENERATIONS

Here, we would like to address how the lives of Zainichi in North Korea and ex-Zainichi North Korean defectors who have settled in Japan form part of a transnational network. Typically, international migration involves remittances to the migrant's home country. However, in the case of migration to North Korea, remittances are continuously sent from Japan to North Korea. Transnational migrants may also receive remittances or support from the place of origin during the initial phase of migration, but the real purpose of migration is to transfer money to the place of origin. In this regard, migrants who have migrated to North Korea do not send money to their place of origin, but receive money until the time of defection.

Legally, remittances can be sent to North Korea from Japan through the post office, and the maximum amount that can be sent at one time is 100,000 yen, though this is limited to those who have personal ties to North Korea. The amount of 100,000 yen is equivalent to about 1,000 U.S. dollars and is the driving force to sustain the lives of families in North Korea.[34]

As discussed in the previous section, Zainichi, having returned to North Korea, maintained relations with their relatives living in Japan. They received considerable remittances from them. However, after returning to Japan, ex-Zainichi North Korean defectors try to send remittances again to families left behind in North Korea. The greatest concern and greatest source of suffering, common to North Korean defectors who have entered Japan, are the lives of their families remaining in North Korea and their safety. They try to use the small income that they earn by working in an unfamiliar environment, or the money that they save from their social welfare, for their North Korean families. Remittances, since 1959, are still continuing over the Zainichi generations.

In this section, we will look at the transnational linkage that still exists through the Zainichi generations. Towards that end, we will discuss the supplying of goods (based on requests for such goods from Japan through the medium of letters), as mentioned in the previous section, and which still provides the link between Japan and North Korea. Through analysis of this processes, we will show the continuous linkage of the Zainichi with the migrants (returnees) in North Korea. Also, we will suggest that the linkage continues, through the ex-Zainichi North Korean defectors in Japan, across Zainichi generations.

From 2003 to 2006, various media in Japan drew attention to the remittances and packages of Zainichi, connecting Niigata in Japan and Wonsan in North Korea. The attention was prompted by the North Korean kidnapping of Japanese in Niigata, which was officially announced in 2003.[35] In fact, the *Mangyongbong*—as discussed earlier—had been running between the two ports since the 1980s, enabling the exchange of many goods and people. Until the mid-2000s, North Korea's *Mangyongbong-92* and *Samjiyeon* regularly ran the Niigata-Wonsan route three to four times a month (Korea Maritime Institute, 2007). We can also reasonably assume that during the repatriation project period, new returnees brought many goods to North Korea, which were shipped on *Mangyongbong* and *Mangyongbong-92*.[36]

However, it has suddenly become an issue in Japanese society, especially since the early 2000s. In Japan, suspicions of kidnapping of Japanese citizens by North Korea increased in the 1990s, and when North Korea admitted such kidnapping in 2003, a great deal of opposition arose in Japanese society against the entry of *Mangyongbong-92* into the port of Niigata. As a result, the connection between North Korea and Zainichi Koreans, linking Wonsan and Niigata, received much attention.[37]

At this point, we would like to highlight the ongoing connection between Japan and North Korea, even after the repatriation project ended. The transnational connection linked families in Japan and the Zainichi in North Korea through "visit to the motherland" via *Mangyongbong-92*.

In 2003 alone, it appears that people, including 573 students,[38] traveled to North Korea. In the case of Joseon School, students are able to enter North Korea for the purpose of "visiting the motherland." North Korea's Department of "Overseas Koreans" allows their visit as visiting overseas Koreans. The students continued to make short visits until recently. After *Mangyongbong-92* stopped operating in 2006,[39] "visits to the motherland" were made by plane.[40] Nowadays, students fly to Pyongyang in North Korea.[41]

The amount of goods entering North Korea from Japan in August 2003, seven months after the last arrival of *Mangyongbong-92* in Niigata, the items on board a ship sailing from Japan to Wonsan mainly consisted of household items, such as medicines, spices, instant coffee, food, air conditioners, refrigerators, and other electronic equipment. When the ships approached Niigata, families from all over Japan began sending goods to Niigata.[42]

In 2004, *Mangyongbong-92* arrived at the port of Niigata sixteen times. About 5,000 students, including Japanese Koreans and students on school trips, and about 2,000 tons of goods connected Japan and North Korea that year (Asahi Shimbun, 1 February 2005). If 5,000 people moved or traveled from Japan to North Korea in a year, in 2005, it can be seen that about 312 people connected families and businesses between Japan and North Korea per month.[43]

In summary, the North Korea repatriation project that connected Niigata and Chongjin ended in 1985, but *Mangyongbong-92* continued to connect the lives of Zainichi in North Korea and Japan until 2006. Although *Mangyongbong-92* ceased operations in 2006, they were reconnected by the skyway connecting Osaka and Pyongyang (via Beijing).[44]

The connection between North Korea and Japan by air is significant, since North Korean defectors are now scattered all over the world. In other words, the air connection links Japan and North Korea even as South Korea and North Korea are not directly connected. Thus, when some ex-Zainichi North Korean defectors settle in South Korea, the connection is maintained with the help of ex-Zainichi North Korean defectors who have settled in Japan. To communicate with their families in North Korea, North Korean defectors connect with them through Japan.[45] Of course, ex-Zainichi North Korean defectors themselves are unable to travel to North Korea, but they can send items (maximum 20 kg per person) and letters, including money, through those Choch'ongnyŏn acquaintances "visiting the motherland."

This network of North Korean defectors plays a very important role for transnational migrants. The physical connection between North Korea and Japan, through human traffic and mail, reverses the previous prejudice associated with the severance of the relationship with North Korea. The connection has existed since Koreans moved from Japan to North Korea in 1959, and the operation of the transnational network has helped migrants survive in North Korea, while still connecting peoples in Japan, North Korea, and South Korea.

HIGH MOBILITIES AND STRATEGIES OF BEING FLEXIBLE

Transnational migrants are becoming firmly rooted in their new countries, but simultaneously maintaining multiple linkages to their homeland (Schiller et al., 1992). The various linkages of transnational migrants will proliferate as mobility increases, and networks with these linkages are activated according to need. Looking at the ex-Zainichi North Korean defectors as transnational migrants gives us a broader perspective, to understand how they solve the difficulties in their lives and distribute the risk of being a transnational migrant. Ex-Zainichi North Korean defectors as transnational migrants practice high mobility, which affects their lives in many ways and also leads them to accumulate strategies. We focus here on the ex-Zainichi North Korean defectors to discern the practice of mobilities and networking.

Their high mobility strategies have persisted over the generations, so ex-Zainichi North Korean defectors have been able to expand their network to survive. The migration path or settlement of North Korean defectors in the destination country takes place within a network of many social relations. Therefore, to understand the mobilities of ex-Zainichi North Korean defectors, it is necessary to briefly trace the path through the Zainichi generations.

During the Japanese colonial period, many Koreans migrated to Japan to overcome the constraints of their lives, even though migration across the country's borders entails a lot of energy and costs. Some of the Koreans had moved to Japan involuntarily because they had to do forced labor; while others were trying to escape the high level of poverty in Korean society. But the disadvantage due to their status as Koreans (Zainichi) caused by the end of Japanese colonial rule, motivated them again to move abroad. Meanwhile, due to the loss of (Japanese) nationality and the change to a new two-state system in their motherland of Korea (North Korea and South Korea), it would have been a difficult decision to simply uproot life in Japan and move back home. At the same time, migration to North Korea, which spread propaganda guaranteeing a life without discrimination and free education, must have been a strong pull factor for them. Therefore, North Korea must have been one of the options for individuals or families under these circumstances. If moving geographically to a new place offers a way to solve the various problems one faces and if the new place is part of the homeland which one previously left, one may not need to hesitate anymore.

After the migration of the Zainichi to North Korea, their mobility decreased in reality due to restrictions on the freedom of migration in North Korea. However, they activated their networks to move back to Japan or to other parts of the world when they had an opportunity to cross the border again. The mobility was triggered by the problem of famine in North Korea, but would have been difficult to undertake without a transnational network, including places and people which is the linkage of mobilities. According to the interviews we conducted, ex-Zainichi North Korean defectors contacted their relatives and old friends in Japan and got resources to cross the border.

To be precise, the main reason for the migration of ex-Zainichi from North Korea is that remittances from the place of origin have been cut off, that is, they have realized that continuing to live in North Korea is impossible. And the reason for the stopping of the remittances is that the remaining families of the Zainichi in Japan are either dying of old age or facing hardship in supporting their families in North Korea over a long period of time.

As mentioned earlier, Zainichi, after they had returned to North Korea, maintained relations with their relatives living in Japan, and had received considerable remittances from them. After they then returned to Japan, for the sake of helping their families left behind in North Korea and also to overcome the instability in their own lives, ex-Zainichi North Korean defectors have tried to find old family relations or acquaintances in South Korea and Japan, to establish another network.

It is possible that ex-Zainichi North Korean defectors, like other transnational migrants, respond flexibly to life problems through their mobility and social relations across different places and borders. According to the interviews, ex-Zainichi North Korean defectors often choose to live in Japan after acquiring South Korean citizenship. The reason why they stay in Japan is to minimize the uncertainties in their lives. By exploiting the fact that support for North Korean defectors is different in Korea and Japan, they try to get the best result using mobilities. Especially, if they are over 65 years of age and have no relatives in Japan, they can get protection as residents following a verification process by Japanese local governments. If they pass the verification process, they will receive about 115,000 yen (about $1,000) per month for living expenses. In such cases, the migrants are recognized as Koreans in Japan and North Korean defectors in South Korea at the same time. Meanwhile, while living as North Korean defectors in South Korea, when the situation becomes difficult because of the prejudice around them, they often only reveal the advantageous identity, which they acquired as a result of mobility, of Zainichi Korean. Of course, the opposite can also happen. In the case of ex-Zainichi North Korean defectors who did not manage to settle in Japan but moved to South Korea and started a business, their transnational network acquired through mobilities proliferates to gain resources.

In the case of family, members may live scattered across South Korea and Japan or in another country, to decrease the risks and instability. They do it with the intention to link up to fill the gaps in their lives. For example, an ex-Zainichi North Korean defector has two daughters, one in Gwangju in Korea and one in Osaka in Japan. The woman, who belongs to the second generation of Zainichi, has been living in Osaka with her daughter there since she migrated to Japan, but recently visited Gwangju for a while. She says that she is satisfied with having travelled to the two places in her life.

It is also worth paying attention to the fact that many Japanese items have been transported on *Mangyongbong* since the late 1950s and continue to link Japan to North Korean society. It is known that many goods flow through China in North Korea in the present day, but in reality, with the migration of 100,000 Zainichi Koreans living in Japan to North Korea in the late 1950s, many daily necessities have flowed to various parts of North Korean society.

As can be seen from the many testimonies, it is significant that people in North Korea were continuously exposed to Japanese goods (from spices to machinery) and that North Korean society was continuously exposed to capitalist goods and values and cultivated relationships. Such a continuous network most likely influenced the internal changes of North Korean society.

The network with Japan and South Korea would have had a continuous influence on North Korean society and potential migrants as it was and still.

CONCLUSION

Sixty years have passed since Zainichi moved to North Korea. The remittances from Japan for migrants to North Korea, which began 60 years ago, continue to connect the two countries, now also with some of the past recipients of the remittances having becoming senders. In other words, the ex-Zainichi defectors from North Korea are continuing the relations between people in the two societies, in the form of remittances from Japan to the rest of their families in North Korea.

The mobility of the first generation of Koreans to Japan distributed the risks in the lives of migrants and non-migrants and made them help each other transnationally. The first and second generation of Zainichi who lived in Japan were able to move to North Korea and maintain their lives in cooperation with their families in Japan, which is a mutual benefit of mobility. Also, as the families in Japan grew older, and it is no longer possible to remit money to the first/second and third generations of Zainichi living in North Korea, the second generation continues the transnational network again by moving to Japan.

We often get caught up in the term of "North Korean defector." The migrant's life, relationship building, and pioneering a new life should not be limited to the motives of migration in the sense of "defected." The term North Korean defection is a term that focuses on behavior at the time of leaving North Korea, rather than on migration and mobility. However, the moment they leave North Korea society, these migrants realize first hand, more than ever, the benefits of migration. The improvement in quality of life that can be enjoyed through movement can be felt more strongly than the regret and cost of leaving their hometown, and the belief that they can provide more opportunities and fullness of life to those they care about can create a constant inertia to move them.

As transnational migrants, ex-Zainichi North Korean defectors, reported in this chapter, are perhaps a little-known secret agent in the transformation of North Korean society. They have long been associated with Japan and North Korea are stationed throughout the country and supply Japanese goods to North Korean society. Even now, the North Korean society changes through various linkages. And this change based on the foundation because it was branched by the migration of Zainichi to North Korea, which we have been dealing with. If we include the families of the Zainichi Koreans in Japan and the Zainichi Koreans, who were naturalized at South Korea, a transnational relationship would have been formed with North Korea across many borders. Now many connections that had a relationship with this space are scattered all over the world, building a new transnational life.

Immigrants to Japan, migrants from Japan to North Korea, and migrants who defected to Japan, South Korea, China, and other neighbor countries show the formation of networks formed over a long period of time, which is central to transnational migration. And it shows us the workings of opportunities due to that network. Confidence that one has crossed boundaries on one's own leads to stronger confidence through experience. Crossing the country's borders made North Korean defectors feel like traitors, especially. However, the trigger that set off the act of crossing the border is the expression of the will "to live." By linking of the lives themselves, including crossing the borders sometimes, they are constantly moving in and out to challenge concrete and certain possibilities.

Crossing borders is not a betrayal, but is sometimes transformed into a diverse and comfortable sense of belonging. And in this, some of transnational migrants seem to be looking for ways to get rid of the identity of North Korean defectors that they felt like a stigma and live as free migrants. Such an act of searching tends to choose the method of movement again, and mobility increases again. Some of the migrants in this study lived in Japan and converted the resources given by the border (Japan or Korea) as needed after more than 10 years had passed since they settled in Japan.

Those who cross the border seem to know how to judge the right time to move, which also affect knowing the value of "time of waiting." Waiting can mean waiting for someone they miss to cross the border, or it can be a time to prepare for the next move. Could it be that North Korean defectors in Japan have the potential to move, acquire information about the wider world, and become more dynamic transnational migrants than they think?

As far as we find in the interview, many North Korean defectors of Japanese descent revealed that they live in a time of waiting for their next move and a strong will to live. Just as they have experienced the power of remittances and the charm of connection in the past while relying on the support of remittances from Japan, the changing situation of the termination of remittances is causing them to actively defect (move) themselves and attempt to reconnect with another connection of opportunity.

NOTES

1. This chapter is a revised version of the previously published article by Hyunuk Lee and Seok-hyang Kim. 2022. "Transnational Ties of North Korean Defectors Living in Japan." Journal of Peace and Unification, 11(2).

2. *Mangyonbong* was built in 1971 and sailed between North Korea and Japan. *Mangyonbong* means "peak of a thousand views" in Korean (https://koryogroup. com/travel-guide/mangyongbong-92-north-korea-travel-guide). *Mangyonbong* had a capacity of less than 200 passengers and belonged to the small class of cargo passenger ships (Nomura, 2002).

3. The added "92" simply indicates the year in which this ship was launched, differentiating it from the original *Mangyongbong*.

4. The main ports in North Korea, in the 1940s, were Cheongjin, Wonsan, Heungnam, Rajin, Yongampo, Jinnampo, and Haeju, among others. However, since the partition, the functions and roles of these cities have changed. In 2007, Nampo (860,000), Wonsan (300,000), Hamheung (790,000), Cheongjin (660,000), and Rajin (Raseon city: 300,000) became port cities. These ports are North Korea's representative trading ports, connecting the country to Japan (Osaka, Kobe, Yokohama, Niigata, Nagasaki, etc.) and with the Southeast Asian region. The route for regular passenger traffic runs from Wonsan, North Korea, to Niigata, Japan, and *Mangyongbong* is still in service.

5. Morris-Suzuki (2011) has noted that the question as to why the repatriation became a mass outflow of Zainichi cannot be answered simply. She identifies it as a very complex situation.

6. The contents of this letter are an excerpt from a collection of letters by Dr. Cho Ho-Pyung, a scientist who was repatriated to North Korea, written to his family in Japan. Circumstances surrounding Cho Ho-Pyong and his wife Koike Hideko "disappeared" and "detentioned" status were first described by Amnesty International in 1994 (Amnesty International, 1995). The family of Cho Ho-Pyung, who lived in Japan, published the letters that the Jo Ho-Pyong family had sent to Japan as an epistle named *Cho Ho-Pyong and Koike Hideko letter collection*, attesting to their miserable life in North Korea. The North Korean side said they put Cho Ho-Pyong in prison because he was a spy from Japan, and then executed him for trying to escape from prison. However, Cho Ho-pyeong's brother in Japan strongly disagreed and criticized the reckless behavior of North Korea and protested his brother's innocence.

7. Kim (2010), a Zainichi living in Japan, published about her own experience of visiting her family in North Korea several times. She describes that from 1980 onwards, ordinary people, not just Choch'ongnyŏn officials, could go to North Korea as part of a "visit to the motherland." However, to visit North Korea, Zainichi, who dealt in commerce and industry, donated a large amount of money to North Korea whenever they met repatriated family members, so that they might have secure livelihoods (Nam, 2012). As North Korea has been trying to solve the problem of lack of money and backward industrial technology since the 1980s, Korean-Japanese businessmen and entrepreneurs have been targeted. For Zainichi, donating factories was also one of the ways to take care of relatives who have migrated to North Korea (Lee, 2015).

8. There are also insufficient records to analyse how they have lived for decades since their arrival at Chongjin port in North Korea (Bell, 2018). This is because the North Korean authorities, who received the Zainichi from Japan, have not published accurate data on how they have lived after arriving at Chongjin. The data that is

available includes many publications—issued by the headquarters of the movement Niigata Return to Home—which describe how the migrants who have returned to North Korea have a good life in the motherland. However, these publications were a North Korean propaganda tool. The testimonies of North Korean defectors contradict their contents. According to these testimonies, due to the censorship of their letters by the North Korean government, people were forced to falsely convey that they were content with their lives in North Korea

9. In South Korea, information about the actual living conditions in North Korea and of Zainichi Koreans (returnees) is available until 1996 North Korean Human Rights White Paper, which includes a section on human rights violations against Zainichi Koreans in North Korea.

10. However, the substantive content of the section of the report on "Human Rights Violation Situation," dealing with repatriated Koreans in North Korea, has been greatly reduced since 1999. Specifically, the human rights issues faced by Zainichi Koreans (returnees) in North Korea have been analysed together with those faced by North Koreans, making it difficult to capture the specific aspects of life, including social discrimination, experienced by the former.

11. When people in Japan visited North Korea to meet their parents and relatives who had returned to that country, some of them were already missing, and no information about them could be found (Yi, 2006).

12. In a reported speech on the 10th anniversary of the founding of the Democratic People's Republic of Korea on September 8, 1958, Kim il sung stated,"Koreans living in Japan, suffering from lawlessness, ethnic discrimination and hardships, have recently been hoping to return to Democratic People's Republic of Korea. The Koreans in Japan are looking forward to returning to their homeland. As citizens of the People's Democratic People's Republic of Korea, which is developing day by day, the people living in Japan have the natural right to enjoy a happy life with their people in the homeland instead of Japan. The government guarantees all conditions for Koreans living in Japan to return to their homeland and lead a new life."

13. For Zainichi Koreans, the return to North Korea was successful in terms of migration to the homeland, but was a failure in terms of leading to a better life, which is the substantive purpose of migration. Of course, there are some people who have been able to live a better life in Pyongyang, through large donations to North Korea (Bell, 2018). However, most migrants to North Korea have faced the depressing reality of never being able to enjoy the freedom of seeing their families in Japan again.

14. It is known that about 6,000 Japanese citizens were repatriated to North Korea (Morris-Suzuki, 2005b).

15. Some second-generation Zainichi moved to North Korea without much knowledge of Korean. This was especially the case if one of their parents was Japanese or if they had lived in an area where there were not many Zainichi. After moving to North Korea, they have tried to learn the language quickly, even though sometimes they cannot quite change their Zainichi accent.

16. Related to this case, another testified about his experience once of meeting his visiting mother from Japan. The mother visited her son, M, in Wonsan in 1982 and gave him 100,000 yen to helping him in his life of poverty in North Korea. Among

those who have moved from Japan to North Korea, those who have family in Japan receive goods and money, and if the opportunity has arisen, their family in Japan has visited them in Wonsan on a "visit to the motherland" trip.

17. There was a saying: "Like magpies meeting magpies, and crows meeting crows," which meant that generally, Zainichi in North Korea could not marry North Koreans.

18. The term "Josen-seki (朝鮮籍)" refers to Zainichi Koreans who have lived in Japan since liberation in 1945, without taking South Korean citizenship or becoming naturalised. The "Josen-seki" Koreans are treated as being stateless in Japan (Ryang, 2014) and continue to be listed as "Josen" under Japanese immigration law, following the revocation of their Japanese citizenship upon the entry into force of the Treaty of San Francisco in April 1952. (Josen does not exist anymore, but is a historical name that continues to be used as a regional category; it does not imply nationality in Japan.) The normalisation of diplomatic relations between Korea and Japan in 1965, however, allowed them to obtain the right of permanent residence in Japan, if they opted for South Korean nationality. About 350,000 obtained the right of permanent residence in Japan, but some 250,000 refused to apply for this status and remain as Josen-seki (Kim, 2011). Josen-seki are often misleadingly referred to as "North Koreans in Japan" in English; being Josen-seki does not always mean that the person supports the North Korean regime (Morris-Suzuki, 2011).

Statistics on foreign residents show that the total number of Koreans and Josen-seki living in Japan, in 2020, was 480,000; this is the number of people whose "Nationality/Region" is listed as "Korean" and "Josen-seki" on the "Residence Card" issued to foreigners permanently residing in Japan. A "Special Permanent Resident Certificate" is issued to special permanent residents such as Koreans. According to the breakdown, there were 446,364 Korean nationals and 28,096 Joseon-seki, with a certain number Joseon-seki changing to become Koreans every year.

19. https://www.fujitv.co.jp/b_hp/fnsaward/20th/11-137.html

20. Yao is a city located in the eastern part of Osaka Prefecture, bordering the cities of Osaka and Higashi Osaka, and Nara Prefecture.

21. As mentioned in the previous chapter, it would have been easy for North Koreans defectors to live in a region where Zainichi culture had taken root. Such cases have also been pointed out in previous studies. As noted in one study of North Korean defectors abroad, they tend to choose a place near "Korea Town" in order to settle quickly into their new migration destinations (Shin, 2019).

22. One such NGO is the Society to Help Returnees to North Korea (北朝鮮帰国者の生命と人権を守る会), based in Yao, which plays an important role in supporting the lives of ex-Zainichi North Korean defectors. The NGO aims to help North Korean defectors in finding jobs and also by introducing them to Japanese culture. NGOs also help North Koreans access social welfare when they cannot find work in Japan and do not have family to take care of them.

23. In Tsuruhashi (Korea Town), many businesses are run by Zainichi, and Japanese and Korean skills are required to work in the service industry in this area.

24. The Zainichi were living in Yao before 1945 and still live in high density, compared to the other suburb of Osaka (Chung, 2020). There were more than 1,500

Zainichi in Yao in 1950. According to the "Yao Personnel Survey Form by Nationality" (2019) in Yao city, the total of "Koreans" and "Zainichi Korean" is 3,010.

25. The Dowa problem is unfounded and extremely unreasonable, as it involves discrimination against a person based only on their place of birth (Burakumin) and place of origin. This is the issue of Buraku discrimination.

26. Zainichi lived in underprivileged environments, often amounting to ethnic ghettoes, derisively referred to by the Japanese as "Josenburaku" or "Korean slum" (Ryang, 2014). Yao, for example, is one of buraku (Cho, 2009).

27. For this reason, the place is still the most important issue related to human rights in Japanese society. Both Mindan and Choch'ongnyŏn have had offices in Yao, and there are many human rights-related NGOs there. Efforts to address the "Dongwa problem" of Yao have continued until recently, and we can ascertain the situation by the measures taken by Yao city to get rid of its negative image as a Dongwa district.

28. In the 1970s, there was a campaign to condemn discrimination in employment, Park Jong-suk, which was the beginning of a protest movement against discrimination against Zainichi. In this regard, Yao is a significant place for Zainichi; it is where the Liaison Council was formed, to condemn the discrimination in employment. The Liaison Council in the Fight Against Ethnic Discrimination is a human rights organisation founded, in 1974, in Yao city by campaign officers, to condemn the discrimination against Zainichi in employment.

29. In 2010, the city of Yao conducted a survey on citizens' perceptions of the Dongwa district. Of the respondents, 39 percent answered: "I have been discriminated against in employment because of origin in Donghwa District." When it came to marriage, 52 percent of respondents said: "There is a tendency of rejection." Also, when people living in the Yao area were asked if there was a reluctance to choose the Donghwa Yao area for a house and school, 52 percent of respondents said "yes" (Public Awareness Survey Report on Human Rights, 2010).

30. With the increase in the use of new English expressions, they hardly understand new words, especially in Japanese.

31. In order to solve the problem of social disadvantage, Yao began to actively support educational activities voluntarily at an early stage. An example is the Yao night school. The night school was originally established to address the low education level in the Dongwa district (Yao), but it now helps ex-Zainichi North Korean refugees to learn Japanese and adjust to Japanese society.

32. Second-generation Zainichi (i.e., those born in Japan and who migrated to North Korea), who had a connection to Japan, find it natural and appropriate to return to Japan, where they grew up. However, their family members—such as those of the generation born in North Korea—find it very difficult to adapt in Japanese society, which for them is a different language and culture.

33. An NGO provides farm-related work in Osaka to them, based on the idea that if they can farm together and produce food in the future, this will supplement their livelihoods. However, this farm work may not be easy to continue. As the head of the NGO, Yamada, explains, in North Korea, farming was done by the lowest levels of society, and therefore, there was considerable resistance to it.

34. Until 2016, transfers to North Korea of up to 10 million yen were possible; more than 10 million yen required reporting to the Japanese Ministry of Finance. However, after North Korea conducted a nuclear test on 6 January 2016 and then fired a ballistic missile with an artificial satellite on 7 February 2016, Japan considered and decided to take measures to more effectively and comprehensively address problems such as hijacking, nuclear weapons, and missiles. The 19 February 2016 Cabinet Decision "Measures to Ban Payments to North Korea Based on Foreign Exchange and Foreign Trade Law," in principle, prohibited payments to people who have an address in North Korea, among other things. This was implemented from 26 February 2016. The exceptions to the measure are: payments not exceeding 100,000 yen to a natural person who has an address or residence in North Korea for the following: (1) the purchase of food, clothing, medicine, and other essential materials; and (2) the use of medical services. In addition, exception is made for payments deemed particularly necessary for humanitarian reasons.

35. When Prime Minister Koizumi visited North Korea in September 2002, North Korean leader Kim Jong Il said that five Japanese were alive and admitted the abduction (Miyatsuka, 2005).

36. Since 1963, the number of returnees has been decreasing every year. It was found in Japan at that time that the returnee ship was actually used for the purpose of transporting goods to North Korea (Kawashima, 2011).

37. This was fortunate, as we could obtain some data through the media.

38. Yamamoto (2019), accompanied by a third-year student, conducted a survey at Aichi Junior and Senior High School. The school is operated by Choch'ongnyŏn, so it is commonly called the "Joseon High School." Until recently, third-year students at Joseon High School took an annual school trip to North Korea. To them, North Korea is the "motherland"; and, generally speaking, the two-week trip is one of the most important school events. The visit usually takes place from late May to early June, often at the same time as visits by Kyushu Junior and Senior High School. Koryo Airline—operated by the General Administration of Civil Aviation of Korea—is in charge of these "visit to the motherland," Japan to North Korea.

39. As the movement against North Korean ship operations in Japan intensified, Japan began to undertake stringent inspections of ships coming from North Korea, beginning in 2003. As a result, ships from North Korea could no longer enter Niigata port, and the schedule shifted in unexpected ways. In 2006, three years later, the *Mangyongbong-92* completely stopped operating.

40. On 8 June 2003, for example, due to the sudden cancelation of the arrival of *Mangyongbong-92* in Niigata, Zainichi made desperate efforts to send necessary goods and money to their families in North Korea. Also, due to the cancelation, the scheduled two-week school trip of 110 high school students and 10 teachers from Aichi had to be postponed. About 250 students from Joseon University and elderly rural travellers also could not leave. On 9 June, when *Mangyongbong-92* could not enter Japan, 57 out of 140 Koreans in Japan boarded a plane and travelled to Pyongyang via Brazibostock, Russia. Some of the scheduled cargo was instead loaded on *Kusabong No. 2* and *Namsan* and departed from Kyoto for Wonsan. Also, due to the suspension of the *Mangyongbong-92* on 8 June, a cargo ship arrived at Naoetsu

port, Joetsu city, and Niigata city. Cargo ship *Howang-gunsan*, a 2,705-ton ship, left Chongjin on 14 June and arrived in Joetsu city, Japan. No cargo was brought from Chongjin. Forty-four used cars and daily necessities were loaded from Joetsu city in Niigata and returned to Chongjin.

41. In this case, there is a separate travel agency in charge of Choch'ongnyŏn. The trip consists of an overnight stay in Beijing and a visit to Pyongyang and the main tourist sites in North Korea (Yamamoto, 2019).

42. Goods sent by Zainichi living in Osaka, Hiroshima, etc. are sent to a warehouse in Niigata port.

43. Until the mid 2000s, there were about 3,000 to 5,000 visitors annually from Japan to North Korea, and most of them were "visiting motherland" students of Joseon School (Ryang, 2000; Nomura, 2002; Miyatsuka, 2005).

44. Looking at flights between North Korea and Japan, these have been operating irregularly on the Pyongyang-Nagoya and Pyongyang-Niigata routes since 1992. However, with the exception of some sections, the international flight performance of North Korea is almost stagnant at about 400 flights per year (Korean Marine Institute, 2007).

45. In Japan, before the COVID-19 pandemic, a certain amount and letters could be delivered through the mail.

REFERENCES

Amnesty International. 1995. *Democratic People's Republic of Korea (North Korea) Human Rights Violations behind Closed Doors*. Amnesty International.

Aoki, Atsuko. 2010. "Japanese wives of resident Koreans and their 'repatriation' to North Korea," *Acta Koreana*, 13(1): 91–112.

Asahi Shinbun, 1 February 2005.

Bell, Markus. 2014. "Ties that bind us: transnational networks of North Koreans on the move," *Resilience: International Policies, Practices and Discourses*, DOI: 10.1080/21693293.2014.914770.

Bell, Markus. 2016. "Making and Breaking Family: North Korea's Zainichi Returnees and 'the Gift,'" *Asian Anthropology*, 15(3): 260–276.

Bell, Markus. 2018. "Patriotic Revolutionaries and Imperial Sympathizers: Identity and Selfhood of Korean-Japanese Migrants from Japan to North Korea," *Cross-Currents: East Asian History and Culture Review*, 7(2): 237–265.

Bell, Markus. 2021. "Performing Death and Memory: Ancestral Rites of North Koreans in Exile," *Korean Studies*, 45: 141–164.

Carling, Jørgen. 2008. "The human dynamics of migrant transnationalism," *Ethnic and Racial Studies*, 31(8): 1452–1477.

Choo, Hae Yeon. 2006. "Gendered modernity and ethnicized citizenship—North Korean settlers in contemporary South Korea," *Gender & Society*, 20(5): 576–604.

Chung, Youngjin. 2020. "Minorities with a Focus on Koreans Living in Japan and Their Communities," *Hakusan review of Anthropology*, 23: 169–192.

Cho, Hyun Mi. 2009. "Segregation of the Lowest Social Class and Transformation of Communal Consciousness: As a Case Study of Douwa District in Yao City, Osaka." *Journal of The Korean Association of Regional Geographers*, 15(6): 803–819.

Editorial Board of The Forum on the Unification of Korea. 2010. "North Korea today: Remittance of separated families and easing in North Korea, banks," *The Forum on the Unification of Korea*, 7: 203–206.

Hough, Jennifer. 2021. "The racialization of North Koreans in South Korea: diasporic co-ethnics in the South Korean ethnolinguistic nation," *Ethnic and racial studies*, Early Access. DOI10.1080/01419870.2021.1921237

Iglicka, Krystyna. 1998. "Are They Fellow Countrymen or Not? The Migration of Ethnic Poles from Kazakhstan to Poland," *International Migration Review*, 32(4): 995–1014.

Inoue, Mastaro. 1956. *The Truth of the Return to the North Korea*. Tokyo, Japan: Red Cross Society.

Jang, Myong Soo. 2003. *Plot: North Korean Homecoming Project of the Japanese Red Cross Society*. Tokyo: Gogatsushobo.

Japan-North Korea Red Cross Agreement on the Return of Koreans in Japan (Agreement on the Return of Koreans in Japan between the Japanese Red Cross Society and the Red Cross Society of the Democratic People's Republic of Korea), 13 August 1959, https://worldjpn.grips.ac.jp/.

Jeon, Woo-Taek. 2000. "Issues and problems of adaptation of North Korean defectors to South Korean society: An in-depth interview study with 32 defectors," *Yonsei Medical Journal*, 41(3): 362–371.

Jeon, Woo-Taek. Yu, Shi-Eun, and Eom, Jin-Sup. 2012. "The Factors Affecting the Development of National Identity as South Korean in North Korean Refugees Living in South Korea," *Psychiatry Investigation*, 9(3): 209–216.

Jong, Eun Lee. 2009. "Re-illumination of North Korean System through Life of Korean Residents in Japan Returning to North Korea: Focusing on Testimony of North Korean Defectors in Japan," *The Journal of Asiatic Studies*, 52(3), 189–227.

Jung, Bong-min, ed. 2007. A Study on Integration of the Logistics System—Examination of Current Status and Derivation of Policy Direction for Integration of North-South Korea Logistics Systems, Korea Maritime Institute.

Kawashima, Takane. 2011. "A Study of Political and Humanitarian Aspects of Postwar Emigration and Immigration Control for the Japanese Abroad and Foreigner Residents in Japan," *Institute of Social Sciences Bulletin Meiji University*, 49(2): 31–45.

Kikuchi, Yoshiaki. 2009. *North Korean Homecoming Project*. Tokyo: Chuokoron.

Kim, Bumsoo. 2011. "Changes in the Socio-economic Position of 'Zainichi' Koreans: A Historical Overview," *Social Science Japan Journal*, 14(2):233–245.

Kim, Seok Hyang. 2018. *The story of the hometown of the northern land. First story, looking back at the village inminban that I left behind*. Seoul: Konrad Adenauer Stiftung.

Kim, Sung Kyung. 2014. "'I am well-cooked food': survival strategies of North Korean female border-crossers and possibilities for empowerment," *Inter-Asia Cultural Studies*, 15(4): 553–571.

Kim, Suk Ja. 2010. "The Korean Wave in North Korea—A Visit to North Korea by a Korean Resident in Japan," *Platform*, 1: 80–83.

Kim, Yeokyung. 2017. "What Is Homeland: Based on the Oral Histories of the Returnee-Refugees," *Korean Journal of Oral History*, 8(1): 95–135.

Kim, Yeong-dal and Takayanagi, Toshio. 1995. *Kita Chōsen Kikoku Jigyō Kankei Shiryōshū*, Tokyo, Shinkansha.

Kim, Young-soon. 1999. "Returning to North Korea of Koreans residing in Japan based on an agreement on return to North Korea," *Journal of Japanese Culture*, 7, 377–391.

Kook, Kyunghee. 2018. "'I Want to Be Trafficked so I Can Migrate!': Cross-Border Movement of North Koreans into China through Brokerage and Smuggling Networks," *Annals of the American Academy of Political of Political and Social Science*, 676(1): 114–134.

Lee, Ju Cheol. 1999. "A Study on the Adjustment by the North Korea Regime of Korean Residents in Japan," *The Korean Journal of Unification Affairs*, 11(1): 107–129.

Lim, Tai-Wei. 2008. "North Korea's Shady Transnational Business Activities and Their Future Prospects," *North Korean Review*, 4(2): 31–48.

Masan Ilbo, 11 March 1959.

Masan Ilbo, 1 April 1959.

Miura, Koutaro. 1999. "A young scientist and a Japanese wife who disappeared into the darkness of North Korea: Cho Ho-Pyong and Koike Hideko's letter collection," Cho Ho-Pyong and Koike Hideko's letter collection editorial committee.

Miyatsuka, Toshio. 2005. "Hitoto butuno nagarekara mita nihonnto kitachousenn," *Regional Policy*, 8(2): 199–204.

Morita, Yoshio. 1996. *Suuzigakataru zainichi kannkoku chousennzin no rekishi*, Akashi shotenn, Tokyo.

Morris-Suzuki, Tessa. 2005a. "Japan's Hidden Role in the 'Return' of Zainichi Koreans to North Korea," *The Asia-Pacific Journal: Japan Focus*, online journal, http://hdl.handle.net/1885/29083

Morris-Suzuki, Tessa. 2005b. "A Dream Betrayed: Cold War Politics and the Repatriation of Koreans from Japan to North Korea," *Asian Studies Review*, 29: 357–381.

Morris-Suzuki, Tessa. 2007. *Exodus to North Korea: Shadows from Japan's Cold War*, Lanham, MD: Rowman & Littlefield Publishers.

Morris-Suzuki, Tessa. 2009a. "Freedom and Homecoming Narratives of Migration in the Repatriation of Zainichi Koreans to North Korea" In *Diaspora without Homeland: Being Korean in Japan*, eds. Ryang, Sonia and Lie, John. Oxford: Oxford University Press, 39–61.

Morris-Suzuki, Tessa. 2009b. "Refugees, Abductees, Returnees: Human Rights in Japan-North Korea Relations," *The Asia Pacific Journal*, 7(3):1–23.

Morris-Suzuki, Tessa. 2011. "Exodus to North Korea Revisited: Japan, North Korea, and the ICRC in the "Repatriation" of Ethnic Koreans from Japan," *The Asia-Pacific Journal*, 9(22): 1–30.

Nam, Keun Woo. 2012. "Rethinking the North Korean Repatriation Program: The Change from an Aid Economy to a Hostage Economy," *Korean Social Sciences Review*, 2(2): 219–251.

National Human Rights Commission of Korea. 2016. *Korean-English Glossary of North Korean Human Right Terms*, The Human Rights Policy Division National Human Rights Commission of Korea.

Niigatakenn Zainichi Chosenzin Kikokugkyouryokukai. 1980. *Kikokuzigyouno 20nenn: Niigatakenn Zainichi Chosenzin Kikokugyouryokukaino Kiroku*. Niigatakenn Zainichi Chosenzin Kikokugkyouryokukai.

Nomura, Hataru. 2002. *Kitachousenn soukinn giwaku kaimei nicchou himitu shikinn ruuto*, bunnshunn bunko.

Oh, Ingyu. 2012. "From Nationalistic Diaspora to Transnational Diaspora: The Evolution of Identity Crisis among the Korean-Japanese," *Journal of ethnic and migration studies*, 38(4): 651–669.

Park, Jung-Jin. 2012. *Birth of the Cold War Structure between Japan and Korea: 1945–1965*. Tokyo: Heibonsha.

Park, Jung Jin. 2011. "North Korean Approach toward Japan and the Repatriation of Koreans in Japan," *North Korean studies review*, 15(1): 219–246.

Ryang, Sonia. 1997. *North Koreans in Japan: Language, Ideology, and Identity*. Boulder, CO: Westview Press.

Ryang, Sonia. 2000. *Koreans in Japan: Critical Voices from the Margin*. New York: Routledge.

Ryang, Sonia. 2014. "Space and Time: The Experience Of The 'Zainichi,' The Ethnic Korean Population of Japan," *Urban Anthropology and Studies of Cultural Systems and World Economic Development*, 43(4): 519–550.

Schiller, Nina Glick, Basch, Linda, and Blanc-Szanton Cristina. 1992. "Transnationalism: a new analytic framework for understanding migration," *Annals of the New York Academy of Sciences*, 645:1–24.

Seol, Dong-Hoon, Skrentny, John D. 2009. "Ethnic return migration and hierarchical nationhood Korean Chinese foreign workers in South Korea," *Ethnicities*, 9(2): 147–174.

Shin, HaeRan. 2018. "The Territoriality of Ethnic Enclaves: Dynamics of Transnational Practices and Geopolitical Relations within and beyond a Korean Transnational Enclave in New Malden, London," *Annals of the American Association of Geographers*, 108(3): 756–772.

Shin, HaeRan. 2019. "Extra-territorial nation-building in flows and relations: North Korea in the global networks and an ethnic enclave," *Political Geography*, 74, 102048 (online).

Shin, Jung Hyun. 1979. Japanese-North Korean relations 1953–1977: Linkage politics in a changing international system. City University of New York, Ph.D.

Song, Jiyoung. 2017. "Co-evolution of networks and discourses: a case from North Korean defector-activist," *Australian Journal of International Affairs*, 71(3): 284–299.

Tertitskiy, Fyodor. 2015. "Exclusion as a Privilege: The Chinese Diaspora in North Korea," *Journal of Korean Studies*, 20(1): 177–199.

Tsuda, Takeyuki. 2003. "Acting Brazilian in Japan: Ethnic resistance among return migrants," *Ethnology*, 39(1): 55–71.

Tsuda, Takeyuki. 2003. *Strangers in the Ethnic Homeland: Japanese Brazilian Return Migration in Transnational Perspective*. New York: Columbia University Press.

Watson, Iain. 2015. "The Korean diaspora and belonging in the UK: identity tensions between North and South Koreans," *Social Identity*, 21(6): 545–561.

Yamamoto, Kaori. 2019. "Our Trip to Homeland: Ethnography of My Participant Observation in School Trip to Pyongyang," *Bulletin of The Faculty of Education and Welfare Aichi Prefectural University*, 67: 41–50.

Yao city. 2010. *Public Awareness Survey Report on Human Rights*, Yao city.

Yi, In Ja. 2006. "Ekkyō joseitachi no ijusaki deno teichaku to jendā: Moto zainichi dappokusha no kurashi o jirei ni," *Japanese studies around the world*, 2005: 247–259.

Yun, Minwoo, Kim, Eunyoung, and Park, Mirang. 2009. "Cross border North Korean women trafficking and victimization between North Korea and China: An ethnographic case study," *International Journal of Law Crime and Justice*, 37(4): 154–169.

Yoon, In Jin. 2001. "North Korean Diaspora: North Korean Defectors Abroad and in South Korea," *Development and Society*, 30:1–26.

Chapter 2

Adaptation of North Korean Defector Families Who Resettled in South Korea after Having Left the South

Heuijeong Kim

In the early 2000s, North Korean defectors who had settled in South Korea began to leave for other countries that had an open-door refugee policy such as the United States, the United Kingdom and the EU (Park et al., 2011). The reasons for leaving South Korea were various, but four motives for this departure stand out, the lure of support policies for the defectors in the most developed welfare states in the world; curiosity about life in the West, better education for their children in an English-speaking environment and the recommendation of other North Korean defectors who had already migrated to the West (Kang, 2018; Park et al., 2011; Song, 2019). More than a decade has passed since large numbers of North Korean defectors left, but now there is a reversal in their course as some refugee families return to South Korea. This chapter examines the adaptation process of North Korean defector families as they resettle in South Korea after having lived for some years in the West.

North Korean defectors' psychological adaptation to a destination country depends largely on their family (Lee et al., 2007; Chin and Kim, 2018). To view transnational migration and adaptation as a "phenomenon" of the North Korean family may help uncover depths to the migration experience that are less evident in studies on individual North Korean defectors. It is necessary to examine the North Korean defector families through transnational resettlements to understand how the dissolution and reorganization of the family unit reflects their adaptation to the host society. Repeated transnational migration is usually closely linked to the family's inability to adapt to the destination country. If adaptation is too difficult, the entire process of dismantling and re-establishing the family elsewhere has in some cases led to two or three other countries before a return to South Korea (Song, 2019).

To date, studies on the migration and adaptation of North Korean defectors have mainly focused on the phenomena of migration. Lee Ji-yeon (2020), in her study of North Korean women in the era of postcolonial feminism, discusses the "vulnerability" that crossing boundaries that divide political systems and states creates. The lack of "situationality" or the awareness of what is normal in the destination society leaves these women vulnerable as they negotiate for refugee status and citizenship. There are, however, some studies that specifically address the migration of North Korean refugee families, for example "A serial migration study of North Korean refugee families" (Son and Kim, 2017) and "A study on the characteristics and types of North Korean refugee families' migrations" (Jin and Kim, 2018). Kim et al.'s 2019 exploratory study is particularly significant as it is the first to consider North Korean refugees' experiences on re-entry to South Korea on a case-by-case basis. The study conducted a survey to assess the reason for leaving and then returning to South Korea and to understand the context of North Korean residents' migrations (Kim et al., 2019). The survey also attempted to ascertain whether North Korean defectors felt the level of social prejudice they had faced in South Korea had in any way lessened with their second settlement. The study proposed a provision of customized services for the North Korean residents arriving back, and the provision of sufficient information and orientation for North Korean residents leaving for a third country (Kim et al., 2019).

Still, it is rare to find research that contemplates families of North Korean defectors that settle in South Korea for a second time. In previous studies, focus was on the experiences of individual of North Korean defectors and the country of residence tended to be Canada with very few samples from other destination countries. Hence, these studies have inherent limitations in examining North Korean defector families' settlement in and adaptation to Western countries. To rectify this omission to some degree, this study conducted in-depth interviews with two groups of North Korean defectors who had migrated to other countries after a limited period in South Korea. The main group and primary focus of this study consisted of five defectors. They were asked to discuss their transnational migration and overseas settlement experiences that started in South Korea and continued to either Europe or Canada only to arrive in South Korea again. The secondary group consisted of two defectors who had also lived in South Korea for a brief time then moved overseas, but they remained abroad. Their impartial observations of North Korean defectors who had left Western countries offered a more objective perspective on those factors that forced the defectors to resettle in South

Korea. Though the second group's observations were of the lived experiences of North Korean defectors not necessarily in the first group, the various perspectives of the two different groups offered a depth of understanding for the phenomenon of North Korean defectors returning to South Korea and their adaptation to the South Korean society in the process of resettlement.

ANALYSIS OF PRIOR RESEARCH: NORTH KOREAN DEFECTOR FAMILIES' OVERSEAS MIGRATION AND ADAPTATION TO A DESTINATION COUNTRY

As a multitude of North Korean defectors began to migrate to Western countries, their reasons for exiting South Korea drew interest. Kang Chae-yeon (2018) attributed North Korean defectors' repeated migration to an identity crisis caused by South Koreans' prejudice and discrimination against North Korean defectors, an inequality in opportunities, and treatment as second-class citizens. Many North Korean defectors pointed to the discrimination that they experienced in the South Korean society as their reason for their departure, as well as concerns about their children's education, personal safety issues, and political worries (Kim, 2018). Most North Korean defectors who had been granted asylum and citizenship in South Korea concealed this fact or created a new identity so they could apply for refugee status in another country. Their purpose in concealing that South Korea had offered them refuge and citizenship was that this disqualified them for refugee status in countries that accepted North Koreans defectors such as the UK and Canada. In 2009, Western countries started screening for camouflaged asylum seekers and became stricter about enforcing those policies that denied refugees who had found asylum already. However, in the event they could prove they had been persecuted for the political reasons stipulated in the Refugee Status Convention, North Korean defectors could qualify for refugee status even with South Korea citizenship (Park et al., 2011).

Before leaving South Korea, some North Korean defectors raised funds by all possible means such as, getting loans from banks within their personal credit limits, getting credit card loans and/or taking out illegal loans. This process was mostly aided and incited by brokers and later had socio-economic implications (Ryu, 2014)

The increased number of North Korean defectors' applications to other countries has been met with a rise in rejections. According to the *UNHCR Global Trends: Forced Displacement in 2018*, the UK rejected the largest number of North Koran refugee claims. With 355 cases rejected between 2000 and 2010 and an additional 209 cases denied between 2011 and 2017, the UK turned down a total of 564 North Korean refugee claims. Canada, which came after the UK, rejected a total of 253 refugee claimants with only twenty cases from 2000 to 2010 but a significant increase to 253 cases from 2011 to 2017. Canada, one of the countries that North Korean defectors migrated to the most, had revised the Refugee Protection Regulations in December 2012 (Lee, 2018), which accounted for fewer applicants being accepted. In cooperation with the South Korean government, Canada began a massive deportation campaign targeting North Korean defectors who held South Korean citizenship and therefore had applied for refugee status in Canada under false pretenses (Lee, 2018). This activity coincided with the United Kingdom's sharply declining acceptance rate of the North Korean refugees. Faced with deportation or outright rejection of their refugee status claims, North Korean defectors choose either to relocate to yet another country or to go back to South Korea. Some, however, chose to return to South Korea even after having been accepted as refugees in another country due to issues with the language barrier and difficulties adapting.

Given that the focus of this study is on North Korean defector families' need to adapt through repeated transnational migration, Mandelbaum's theory on adaptation seems to best describe what is required for adaptation. Mandelbaum defines adaptation as "a person's changing his/her behavior patterns in response to changed conditions in order to maintain the values and environment that one considers important in the course of one's life" (Mandelbaum, 1973). An individual's adaptation to a new or changed environment can be evaluated as "adapted well, or not at all adapted." It is this dichotomy of adaptation and maladaptation, of progression and regression, that make it difficult to discover unbroken continuity in an individual's adaptive behavior. In other words, "A life does not proceed in a projectable, unilinear curve like a cannon shot. Rather, it involved ongoing development in various spheres of behavior; it includes continuous adjustment and periodic adaptation" (Mandelbaum, 1973). The experience of repeated migrations from North Korea to China, South Korea, the UK, and then back to South Korea may characterize North Korean defector families and serve as a key factor in their adaptation to a new environment. It is regarded, therefore, that Mandelbaum's theory suffices as a framework for exploring the adaptation process revealed in the repeated transnational migration process of the participants.

THEORETICAL FRAMEWORK: RELATIONAL-CULTURAL THEORY

This study borrows from "relational-cultural theory" (RCT) to explain North Korean defector families' resettlement and adaptation to South Korean society. According to this theory, the source of the subject's or in this case the defector's pain is relational disconnection. The disconnection results from repeated experiences of being unacknowledged, outright rejected, abused and shamed by others and can cause psychological blocks to adaption (Judith and Linda, 2002; Judith and Jordan, 2008). The relational-cultural theory, introduced by Judith V. Jordan and Jean Baker Miller, stresses that without meaningful connections and mutually respectful relationships people's growth will falter. This challenges the existing human development model that emphasizes separation and individualization, autonomy over dependence, as not accurately reflecting the human experience (Judith and Jordan, 2008).

The concept of the separate self has suggested setting firm boundaries that in theory would strengthen the individual, and in becoming stronger, the individual would gain a sense of security and well-being. Conversely, the relational-cultural theory accentuates the importance of those relationships a person builds throughout life to achieve a sense of security and wellness (Judith and Jordan, 2008). At the core of this theory are the concepts of mutual empowerment, mutual empathy, authenticity, growth-fostering relationships, relationship image, self-critical alienation, controlled image, relational resilience, and relational competence (Judith and Linda, 2002; Judith and Jordan, 2008).

Initially, RCT was employed as a consultative tool intended to gather information and formulate policy. In doing so, it evaluated the participants' relationships and experiences usually within a cultural context. One study, however, explored North Korean defectors' various dynamic processes of disconnections and reconnections in a medical context as they battled tuberculosis (Yoo 2020). This theory has been adopted to assess minority groups for its ability to assess an individual's relationship with others in a microcosm of life far better than the theory of growth within a sociocultural context that focuses on the macrocosm of global events (Judith and Jordan, 2008). For this reason, some studies conducted on North Korean defectors have contemplated the possibility of engaging a counselor specialized in relational-cultural therapy techniques during interactions with North Korean defectors in the field (Kwon and Choi, 2011).

This study examines North Korean families' relational disconnection caused by various factors focusing on their experiences during resettlement in and adaptation to South Korea. To understand the migration of individuals and families, it is necessary to consider how the historical relevance and cultural pathways between the country and the migration destination affect their migration behavior (Park, 2009). Migration creates a partial or total disconnection from interpersonal relationships in social and structural contexts formed in the country of origin prior to migration. The relational-cultural theory in that it explains the disconnection and connection that North Korean defector families experience in the process of geographical, social, and cultural adaptations during transnational migration provides a framework for this study.

RESEARCH METHODS

In order to examine the disconnection North Korean families experience in their adaptation to another destination country that prompts them to return to South Korea, this study selected as research participants, two groups of North Korean defectors: one group being five North Korean defectors (A, B, C, D, and E) whose families left South Korea for another country but later returned, and the other North Korean defectors (F and G) who left for other countries and remained. Most of the adult participants, aged in their forties and fifties, migrated overseas with their families. Participants A, F, and G qualified for refugee status, while B, C, D, and E did not.

In-depth interviews with two North Korean defectors residing in New Malden, London, England, were conducted via a videoconferencing application over the month of October in 2020. Research participants in the study were sampled through the Association for North Korean defectors in New Malden, and all the study participants were interviewed solely by the researcher. Due to the time difference between the UK and South Korea, the interviews with participants F and G were schedule at 10 p.m. in GMT (7 a.m. in KST) for two hours and two times each. Interviews with participants A, B, C, D, and E, the North Korean defectors resettled in South Korea, were conducted from December 2020 and throughout January 2021 either at their home or a location of their choosing.

Prior to the interview, potential research participants were apprised of the purpose of the study and given a general idea of the interview questions so they could make an informed decision. Only those who indicated voluntary intention for participation were selected for this research. The author, at all stages of the study, abided by the research ethics related to voluntary participation, explained consent, the right to withdraw from participation without penalty, confidentiality, and storage and maintenance of data. The author created an atmosphere in which the participants could speak and ask questions freely. Once the interviews were completed, the participants' names were removed and replaced with an identifying number assigned by and only known to the author to safeguard their private information.

From 2016 to 2019, the author conducted a yearly visit to New Malden to study the lives of North Korean defectors from an observational perspective. During those visits, the author stayed at the home of one of the participants, which created a rapport. At this time, the author also conducted interviews with the other participant residing in New Malden to gain insight to North Korean defectors' experiences while living in the UK. In addition to participant observation, any newsworthy incidents about North Koreans in the UK that came to the author's notice contributed to data collected in a natural experiment. Rather than rely on what could be secondhand reporting, however, the author would contact the North Koreans in question through Zoom or "kakaotalk," a messenger application, to verify the details and avoid perpetrating hearsay. To fully understand why North Korean families resettled in South Korea, however, an account of North Korean defectors' experiences in Western countries is necessary, which will follow in the section.

This study employs the case method to gain a sense of North Korean defector families' adaptation to a destination country. Analyze of interview data collected on each of the five North Korean defectors' families of participants A to E using the relational-cultural theory helped detect difficulties the participants had in common. In addition, participants F and G provided general information that supported a basic analysis of the cases and the identification of common issues. That there is little research on North Korean defector families that have left then returned to South Korea only serves to underscore the importance of the close examination of each case in this study.

RESULTS

1. Case analyses

Participant A defected from North Korea at the age of fourteen, residing in China for six years before crossing into South Korea until the age of twenty. After being discharged from Hanawon, a settlement support center for North Korean refugees in South Korea, she married a fellow North Korean refugee and gave birth to two sons. Six years after entering South Korea, at the age of twenty-six, she and her family immigrated to Europe. At that time, they were financially well-off in South Korea, and she had grown bored of the tedium of everyday life and wanted the challenge of a new environment. She explained that she felt the same need to move when she was in North Korea and China, stating that "whenever she would find refuge and adjust to something, she couldn't stop thinking that she could not take root." She attributes her restlessness to her past lived experiences, which made her feel the need to wander and search for a better life.

The language spoken in the country where participant A settled was Dutch and her children quickly learned the language at school and day care centers. She also became proficient enough in the language that she could "offer a business translation for someone." After a relatively short waiting period, her family were granted refugee status. Since her husband had employment as a welding technician, the family lived comfortably. Once settled, she gave birth to their third son there. In the fourth year of residence, however, their eldest son was struck by a car on his way to school and died of his injuries. Her family initiated a criminal proceeding against the driver of the vehicle, but in the end, they lost the case. She believed that there were two main causes for the loss of their legal case. One was that the accused was influential in the area, and the other was their case had been mismanaged by the second-generation Korean lawyer they had hired. Still in shock after the death of their child and the lost lawsuit, she and her husband were persuaded by a someone else in South Korea to invest in a financial venture. Unfortunately, it was a fraudulent scheme and they lost their money. This financial loss was compounded by another accident that this time involved participant A as she was struck by a car while riding her bike. With her husband determined to leave, she and her family relinquished their refugee status and returned to South Korea.

After losing her first child during the economic crisis and famine in North Korea known as the Arduous March, participant B escaped across the border into China. She and her sister arrived there expecting that a broker would help them find jobs so they could earn money, but instead they were sold to a Chinese family by human traffickers. She became the unofficial wife of the son in the family and eventually gave birth to a son. In order to escape to South Korea, she had to leave her child with her mother in China and send for them after she had reached safety. Her mother suffered the ordeal of being repatriated to North Korea several times while caring for and protecting her grandson in China. Traumatized by the experiences escapes from North Korean prisons in searching for her grandson, her mother received psychological treatment after arriving in South Korea. Participant B met and became involved with a North Korean defector and gave birth to her second son in South Korea. Around the time the child turned three, her relationship with this man broke down. She was left to raise her two sons alone, but her failing health made it difficult. She realized that the stress of attempting to participate in South Korea's infamous education fever for her children was too much for her, and in 2015 she decided to immigrate to the UK. Her younger brother and his family had left for England in 2007, and having this contact there comforted her so she worried less about the move. The expectation of good social security for her family from a welfare state further reassured her and assuaged any lingering hesitation. She also considered the benefits for her children of learning to speak English freely. Her first son, who was eighteen at the time, thought he was too old for resettlement in a new country and said that he would not go, but she insisted. She and her two sons had had high expectations for British society, but following their arrival, they had a hard time both "mentally and financially."

When participant C was twenty-four, she decided to go to China for no longer than one month to earn money. She crossed the border and lived in China for five years and there gave birth to her first child. While attempting to cross from China into South Korea, she was repatriated to North Korea twice. One of the times she was repatriated, North Korea had just entered the period of the North Korean famine, also known as the Arduous March. When she witnessed her younger brother barely living hand to mouth, she ran back to China. Participant C, who finally entered South Korea on her third attempt, returned to China several times to retrieve the child who she had lost touch with after her first repatriation to North Korea. Her in-laws refused to release the child, and it was only once she became a teenager that eventually the child came to Korea. By this time, participant C had had a second child, who was born in South Korea, but having never received child support from the father, she had to work to support them. When she felt that she could not continue as she was, she decided to follow her younger brother who had gone before her to England, saying, "Just leave everything behind there, take it easy, and come to England. Everything will be fine here." Her five-year-old daughter accompanied her. Her first child, however, who after a long separation was already struggling with this reunion with her mother, raising a younger sibling, and adapting to South Korea did not accompany her to the UK. She instead went back to China. Upon arriving in England, participant C was assigned a house in the outskirts of London where she felt isolated. Though there was the Korean community in New Malden, the cost to travel there was expensive even using public transportation, and their visits to New Malden were infrequent. She suffered from severe headaches and anemia and often felt unwell, and once the headache was so painful that she could not even open her eyes. After three years in England, participant C decided in the end that she too would return to South Korea.

Participant D's father was a South Korean soldier captured during the Korean War. North Korea refused to release prisoners of war, instead forcing them to labor in coal mines, a fate shared by participant D's father and her entire family. Her father, who suffered from health problems due to the harsh conditions, managed to escape across the border with her brother and her mother. Participant D at that time was married to a man she had met working in the coal mine with whom she had a son. In the following April, her father sent a broker to guide her and her three-year-old son across a river of melting ice into China. After waiting with her son and her family for a year with other North Korean defectors at a Chinese consulate, they entered South Korea. Her father's status as a former soldier of South Korea and years as a prisoner of war made their case a priority. With her second husband, whom she met in South Korea, she had another son and a daughter. By late 2014, she, her husband and three children booked a flight to Canada. However, once she arrived there, she was disconcerted to discover that so many North Koreans were returning to South Korea that there was a farewell party almost every day. With the help of a local pastor, her children were enrolled in school as the family settle in. After six years of "lasting," participant D received a ticket for a traffic violation that led to background checks and eventually deportation procedures and a return to South Korea in 2020.

Participant E worked as an engineer in North Korea and had a relatively good life. In 2005, his younger brother in China offered to give him a substantial sum of money if crossed over. Participant E hired a broker who helped him cross the border, but when he arrived, he realized that his younger brother had already left for South Korea. Upon hearing that it had been his brother's plan to lure him to South Korea all along, he realized he had been deceived. Accepting that he would settle there, a year later he sent for his son from his former marriage to a North Korean, and they remained in South Korea for ten years. In 2015, he left for England with his son, who was by this time an adult. Participant E had no problem staying employed and earning money in South Korea. However, it was not easy to save, and he was worried about retirement. His envy of "advanced countries" was his main reason for going to England, but life there was not what he had expected. He and his son could not get a job without a visa. His son couldn't go to school as he was already an adult. He endured three years in England out of the vague hope that "A refugee visa will be granted soon." He hired a lawyer and appealed again through interviews, but the lawyer warned, "We can't guarantee that you will get a visa in 10 years or 15 years." Participant E decided to return to Korea after three years, tired of the uncertainty and of not knowing whether a visa would ever be issued.

2. Categorization analysis

(1) Determinants of resettlement in South Korea

In the mid-2000s, when the number of North Korean defectors migrating to the UK surged, the refugee visa issuance rate was on the high side. Despite the high rate of refugees being accepted, interviewees F and G estimated that 20 to 30 percent of defectors who arrived during that period either returned to Korea or left for another country. People who had fantasized about life in England without understanding the real-life challenges such as language barriers would become disillusioned. Those who came alone and remained single as well as the elderly struggled most to adapt and were often the ones to return to South Korea. Some of the difficulty to adapt can be attributed to the British Refugee Act and refugee procedures. Once North Korean defectors apply for refugee status after arriving in the UK, they are dispatched to cities where they are to remain until they receive refugee visas. During this period, North Korean defectors are provided with a place to stay and the minimum living expenses, but if they attempt to relocate on their own, they are automatically denied a visa. These early stages of settlement are the most difficult due to language barriers, cultural differences, and racism. If visa issuance is delayed, prolonged stay in residential areas that do not have a North Korean defector community can have a negative effect on North Korean defectors' psychological and emotional adaptation especially in the absence of other family members. In fact, overall fewer families of defectors choose to return to South Korea as cases of family defection have exhibited greater success rates in adaptation. This can often be attributed to parents' resolve that their children grow up in a less discriminatory environment and have the advantage of English education. They viewed surviving the waiting period for a visa as a trial to be passed to arrive at the stable settlement period. Once a refugee visa has been acquired, however, defectors may choose where to live. Many relocate to the New Malden area, which is the largest Koreatown in the UK with a well-represented North Korean refugee community.

This study, however, focuses on the North Korean families that decided to leave other countries to resettle in South Korea. Factors that played a large part in their decision to leave were economic well-being, visa status, lack of community support, health issues, and family dissolution. Defectors' economic well-being was at least initially determined by the host country's provision of benefits and the refugee policy on placement and employment. In the case of the UK, refugee claimants are allotted a basic living space and minimum living expenses, whereas in Canada, these benefits are provided but for a limited time. Employment, however, is more difficult to find in the UK due to the policy that places refugees in residential areas. In Canada where Koreans are allowed to settle in multicultural cities like Toronto rather than just in the suburbs, it is not difficult to find a job in a Korean business. While the factors affecting economic adaptation differed by country of settlement, the decision to re-enter South Korea based on difficulties attaining a quality of life was the same.

The factors regarding the visa application of defector families with children under the age of 18 differed by country as well. In the UK, deportation of parent with minor children was suspended until those children reached the age of majority. In Canada, the presence of minor children did not postpone a decision to deport a family. Due to the agreement between the Canadian and South Korean governments, North Korean refugees' fingerprints were shared. If it was discovered that they had obtained refugee status in South Korea first, they would be deported even if they already obtained permanent residency in Canada. Verification of refugees has since become a major factor in permanent settlement such as economic benefits, status acquisition, and employment. Those families that do not qualify in the country where they have landed either carry on to another country or return to South Korea.

Lack of community has been related to psychological problems such as loneliness and depression as well as financial difficulties in an overseas destination country. These issues have been reported to a greater extent in cases where there is no North Korean refugee community. As it has been mentioned, in the UK, a refugee's place of residence is assigned until legal refugee status is granted. Without a network of other North Korean refugees, defectors miss out on emotional support but also legal advice in navigating the application system and financial assistance from community groups. Feeling isolated and dejected, many North Koreans return to South Korea.

Health issues are often a deciding factor in North Korean defectors' decision to return to South Korea. North Korean defectors' health problems have become a major factor in re-entering South Korea if they are dissatisfied with the medical services of the destination country, need surgery and have chronic diseases that require detailed explanations in a foreign language. One, all or a combination of these complaints could see a North Korean returning to South Korea where the medical system is familiar and the common language is Korean.

Finally, the main reason North Korean refugee families return to South Korea is family dissolution. In the case of North Korean defectors, there have been cases in which existing family conflicts were aggravated by the move abroad or the move created new conflicts. If there was a dispute among these family members, without external resources such as extended family, neighbors or communities to mediate, the disputes could escalate and cause rifts. There were cases in which some family members returned to South Korea alone and the rest of the family eventually disbanded.

In some situations, just one of those five factors discussed could provoke the departure of North Korean families. However, in most cases several of the factors were involved in the decision to return to South Korea.

(2) Adaptation of North Korean defector families

A. Disconnection

North Korean defectors have experienced disconnection in various areas of life since settling in the UK. In the case of participant B and her family, they felt as if they had been abandoned after the family was assigned a home in a residential area. Participant B said that there was "no one about who the family knew, and they themselves could not speak the language, so there were days of tears." In addition, she felt thoroughly disconnected and isolated from the medical and social systems. This was especially important to her as she suffered from chronic illnesses. The distance to proper health facilities meant she struggled to receive essential medical treatment or even medicine when necessary. The most difficult part was the psychological impact of migration to foreign country had on her children. Since the children were already teenagers when they migrated to the foreign country, they had more problems with language acquisition than younger children would. One day, her second child went missing. Fearing that he, because he could not speak the language well, he would not be able to find his way home, she spent the entire day searching for him. By the end of the day, luckily, a policeman returned him to her, but this incident traumatized the family and made them fearful for their safety. This fear and sense of vulnerability was aggravated by racial discrimination and exacerbated their feelings of disconnection from the country and/ or society in which they had put their trust.

> Racism was everywhere. I heard that situation in New Malden was okay. But we lived in OO. So, it is that we got investigated in the immigration office ant they found a place to settle down for my family. They allocated OO area . . . in the middle of nowhere. As I did not know the language, I was alone, totally abandoned . . . (participant B)

Participant C had health problems which was made worse by the anxiety that "she may not be able to acquire a visa" because she pursued her refugee claimant suit without a lawyer. This left her feeling "too lonely" in her struggle. She did receive advice from North Korean defectors who had arrived in the UK earlier than she and her family had. They emphasized that during the refugee application interviews it was important to claim political persecution as her reason for defection. In the first interview, however, she had to "create a crime" that she had not in fact committed in North Korea. And it became ever more difficult to explain why she should come to UK, not South Korea in the interviews.

> My body ached and I argh . . . I couldn't live anymore, and I was lonely and I cried a lot on my own . . . Being sick and being lonely . . . Proceeding with a lawsuit was too lonely . . . I, in fact, well, in other words, should have said that I went to jail at the immigration office. Nothing but the truth about the experiences I have in North Korea well before, but [they say] I must not say that. I was told to make up a totally new story entailing political issues. To obtain a refugee visa, I have to create a charge that I have never in fact committed before, hmm . . . it was very much so complicated . . . (participant C)

Flustered and distressed by the fabricated tale of political persecution that she had told on the advice other North Koreans, participant C felt ever more disconnected from the country she had hoped to call home.

Participant A's disconnection was the consequence of a series of misfortunes. It started with the death of her child and the negative associations that attached to the neighborhood where they lived. That was followed by the loss of their lawsuit and a sense that the legal system had favored an influential person over their child's life. Now the country had not only become an inhospitable place but the "enemy." The final breaking point came when she herself was hit by a car while riding her bike and the country's medical system failed her. So "on the spur of the moment," she and her family left the country.

> At that time . . . when I lost the lawsuit, it was as if the country became the enemy. And did I tell you that I was hit by a car in February as well? I was riding a bike when the car hit me. I fell and hurt my head, and when I went to the hospital [the medical staff said to me] "Just go home, everything is fine." (participant A)

Participant E felt "disconnected" due to the language barrier and "frustrated" by his pending status prohibiting employment and "not being able to go anywhere." His child, who was an adult, could not speak the language either and since they were in a district without other Koreans could not make friends. Disheartened, he stayed in his room and played computer games day and night. Participant E was also disillusioned with the health care system in the UK.

> [In British hospitals,] They go back and forth between the wards like they did in North Korea in old days. Once you made an appointment with the doctor, you would receive a [confirmation] letter . . . At the private hospitals, [procedures are] faster and they may treat me well. But I have to pay money. But the government hospital system itself is so slow that people die when they get sick. If one is sick, they die. (participant E)

According to participant E, the quality of care the National Health Service (NHS) provide was poor and the system was far too slow. Unlike the private hospitals where one could receive treatment quickly for a price, he said in public hospitals "if one gets sick, they have no option but die there."

The disconnection North Korean defector families experienced was caused by refugee policies that placed people in areas where they felt isolated, confusing legal systems, and deficient medical systems. As individuals, they grapple with language problems, litigation problems, and racial discrimination issues. The growing disconnection eventually leaves the family feeling that best option would be to return to a country where they at least understand the language if not the culture. However, arriving in South Korea for a second time is in sometimes harder than the first time. When those North Korean defector families left South Korea, they surrendered the housing provided by the government and therefore had no place to live and any financial support. Until they could find a residence for themselves, most of the families lived in the homes of other relatives temporarily. Often families would out of necessity split up and stay in different places, for instance taking rooms in a boarding house or cheap inn only large enough to accommodate a single bed and a desk. Though the aforementioned factors are associated with defectors stressful adaptation in the destination country, in the end a version of this adaptation is replicated upon North Korean defector families' return to South Korea.

B. *Psychological distress of the parents of North Korean defect*

Upon reviewing the personal information participants in this study shared during interviews, it became evident that the psychological trauma North Korean refugee parents suffered before, during and after defection was severe. After crossing into China, participant C was discovered by Chinese police and sent to the North Hamgyong Province camp in North Korea. She endured harsh interrogations before being released to work from 5 a.m. until late at night, which was when her physical ailments first started to develop. The psychological and physical traumas she experienced to in North Korea and China affected her overseas migration and adaptation to a destination country.

> The fear [that I had felt when I left North Korea] is different from this fear [that I've felt in the UK]. The fears I experienced before crossing the border from North Korea were like, would I die or live after crossing the river? The fears I experienced in a foreign country were coming from unknown people, different skin color and different language. I was afraid of the people . . . I . . . I was afraid that they would harm me. I was so scared of that. And it is okay if a child is grown big, but my child was young. It was so scary that I had to protect my own child from them . . . I, I, now, will go back there [to South Korea] to live, that fact itself scared me . . . Here we had nothing with us, no one to rely on and that I have to start all over again, so I, I was so scared. So, I knew I should go but then many times I thought about what I had to do and how to do it . . . (participant C)

This interviewee repeated "I am too scared" several times during the interview, and at some points it seemed as if she would relive the fear from her past. She said "I was so scared that strangers would hurt me," and "I was afraid to go back to South Korea, where I had to start all over again with no one to rely on."

Participant A's continuing troubles, such as her own accident after the death of her child and losing money in a South Korean investment scam, left her unable to function as she normally would. The strain on the family that this series of incidents caused created tension, resulting in daily arguments.

Her husband who grieved for those losses they had endured as a family also faced constant discrimination against North Koreans at work. She explained that the tension had created a stressful environment and he suffered from insomnia so severely that he could not sleep without medication.

> What he got at that time was insomnia. He couldn't sleep without medications . . . He filed for bankruptcy. There was NO WAY that we could repay it. My husband was committed to a psychiatric hospital. [He] seriously hurt himself and almost killed himself. He was really having a hard time due to the psychological problems. To, that, OO hospital, that . . . um . . . he was committed for several months. He couldn't just take it and face it. (participant A)

Their troubles did not end with their return to South Korea. Once back, they discovered the unlawful loan they took out through broker before they left had grown to an unmanageable amount with extortionately high interest rates. Her husband was willing to submit to bankruptcy proceedings. Yet despite his determination to be practical in the face of overwhelming debt, the overseas hardships and the death of his child took a toll and he was hospitalized for trauma.

C. Psychological distress of the children of North Korean defectors

Not only the repeated migration but also the experiences in the destination countries have inflicted psychological distress on the children of North Korean defector families. When participant B's family arrived in the UK, her family's unconfirmed status meant British schools did not recognize her children, forcing them to attend alternative schools and immediately marking them as different. Once her children were allowed to attend regular schools, her second child found it particularly difficult after being put ahead to the second year of middle school. This widened the achievement gap between the child and the class. The area where participant B's family resided did not help with her children's adaptation either. Though there were immigrants from diverse backgrounds in a neighborhood they lived, none were from Korea, and her children struggled to establish social relations even with peers experiencing similar resettlement issues. Unable to make friends that would help them adjust to school resulted in frequent absences and both children abandoning their studies. Although her first child attended college in the UK, he became discouraged when the lectures proved too challenging due to the language barrier. The child withdrew into his room, playing computer games and drinking alcohol every day until eventually he became so despondent that he harmed himself. Even so, participant B was unable to fully comprehend her children's emotional difficulties due to her own emotional and physical health issues.

Living there was really difficult. I was living in pain. What you are experiencing was not physical pain but psychological pain. The children were struggling . . . "Mom, let's go back to South Korea. You should have brought me here earlier. I was too old" . . . Mentally . . . I was having a hard time because of the issues with the children. But when I think about it now, I was not my whole self, and as it was too hard for me even to care about myself, I couldn't afford to care about my children at all . . . they said they had a hard time too. The eldest child just hurt himself. You know, he had a knife. He cut his arms all over . . . (participant B)

The family's pain did not end with participant B's or her elder son's mental health issues. When the second son began to suffer from hallucinations and visions for the first time while in the UK, he was diagnosed with an incurable mental illness. He cut off all the social connections and closed himself off in his room. Participant B became too anxious to sleep, terrified what harm her children would do to themselves each and every night as her second son's repeated acts of self-harm and suicide escalated. The children said, "My mother took (us) and made it like this," and they "vented their frustration" out on her. After returning to South Korea and witnessing her children's continuing daily hardships, she blamed herself for everything that had gone wrong and thought, "I shouldn't have gone to the UK." Her first child was aimless after returning to South Korea and began a part-time job making deliveries on a motorcycle. He suffered frequent accidents, and his physical injuries were compounded by psychological pain and financial hardship of compensating the accident victims of the motorcycle accidents.

Participant A's children too were traumatized following the loss of their brother and have received psychological treatment after being diagnosed with depression and post-traumatic stress since resettling in South Korea. Participant A explained that her children are like "a seedling that was just starting to grow is picked and planted in different soil" but could not take root and so withered. Since they had never considered returning to the South during the time they lived abroad, the children were "really confused" about every aspect of Korean society.

A seedling that was just starting to grow is picked and planted in different soil. It could not take root. It becomes withered. That is my children's situation at the moment. So, I had a really . . . [the children] had a hard time. Seriously. [They] came for the first time, the children lost, well, stress, umm, frustration, depression, showed disorder, well, lost, hair loss they had, I'm not kidding. For both of the children, that . . . I mean because of the shock, to begin with, that they had lost own brother OO, [one of the children], became violent, □□, [the other child], became silent. He literally did not express himself at all. This has been diagnosed. I had him all checked out, properly. He suffers from depression, □□, turned out to be sensitive to everything. For OO, whatever comes across he has to kill them first, showing no emotion, being silent. (participant A)

Participant C's child was diagnosed with social anxiety and like participant A's children received psychological counseling after arriving in South Korea. The primary problem was that the child had literally "shut up." At school, the child refused to talk with peers and teachers. When asked the reason for this refusal, the child admits to a hatred of being laughed at should his/her answers be deemed ridiculous and he/she would rather not reply. Participant C is heartbroken and blames herself, believing that by taking her child to the UK seeking an easier life she has exposed the child to a ridicule that has scarred him/her permanently.

> The child is mentally unstable . . . shows anxiety. With me, the child keeps on talking but never talks to people outside. That hurts me a little . . . "How come you don't answer when the teacher asks you a question?" I asked. "Mommy, if I give a wrong answer I shall be laughed at." The child hates that so much. (participant C)

If the waiting period to obtain refugee status becomes protracted, children suffer as much as the adults if not more so since they have not developed skills to cope. Children and young adults feel helpless to change that circumstances that stop them from getting a job or attending school. The period of enforced inactivity has long-term effects too. For example, after re-entry to South Korea, these children are often behind children their own age educationally and developmentally. In the cases of the participants A, B, D, and E, the youths exhibited symptoms of psychological and emotional distress through drinking, game addiction, and self-harm.

The destination itself as well as the frequency of migration influenced the ability of North Korean defector families' children to adapt to their new environment. Most of the participants in this study did not recognize that their children struggled to adjust to the new environment after migration to a non-Korean speaking country. Older children, like those of participants of C and E at the time of overseas migration, failed to acquire the target language and form social relations, resulting in a pattern of maladjustment. Even when parents did realize there were issues, however, more often they could not provide the support their children needed. The frequency and rapidity of migrations also tested the children's resiliency. In some cases, the child was taken from North Korea to China to South Korea then on to a Western country before returning to South Korea in a disconcertingly short time. The parents' lack of mediation for the maladjustment children suffered due to rapid changes caused by frequent migrations to vastly different environments can partially be attributed to their own mental fatigue. In struggling to adapt to a new environment themselves, there is a limit to recognizing and understanding their children's emotional problems and difficulties.

D. *Adaptive behaviors power to disconnect and reconnect relationships*

The adaptive behaviors of participants in this study have influenced their relationships some for the better and a few for the worse. Participant A, upon her return to South Korea, felt as if she was falling into "endless abyss" due to financial difficulties, her husband's hospitalization, and the mental health issues of her children. Nevertheless, she first sought for psychological counseling for her children to soothe and console their broken hearts from the loss of their brother. She also had ample time to restore the relationship between the parents and children. And she enrolled in computer, accounting and beauty-related courses to earn licenses so as to make a living. She said, "Even if I spend money, I'm more grateful actually that I am able to go out and meet people and live an active life."

After a long period of solitary confinement to house, the second child of participant B, one day all of a sudden, took an identification photo in order to sit for the high school certification exam. And he passed the exam, even though he could not manage to study the certification course properly. Participant B is, now, hoping for an optimistic future. She is with her mother who never feared to be repatriated to North Korea to rescue her children several times. And she is also with her children who have faced the hardships in a foreign country, and who are now standing firm against challenges together as a family back in South Korea for resettlement. Though life is tough, she says, "there is nothing like family in times of trouble."

Participant C, who had been estranged from her first child for most of that child's life, had been planning to visit her and her boyfriend at their home in China. Unfortunately, her plans were upended by the COVID pandemic. Participant C regrets that she had not spent more time with her eldest child after bringing her from China to take care of her second child. Even when she did spend time with her older daughter, she could not seem to connect with her. However, she has offered to help her child if she decides to come to South Korea to work.

It may have been different if I didn't work and stayed at home and spent time with my child, but I'd been working all the time, so she didn't feel she was attached so much to me as mom. A baby grows in my arms shall be my baby . . . (Some lines omitted.) Now that I think about it, I've done a lot wrong. (participant C)

Participant C recognized that she might have done more for her elder child and attempted to make amends and re-open the lines of communication as best she could. She had also continued to care for her family in North Korea and sent what money she could afford to spare despite the ongoing migration process. After re-entry to South Korea, however, she became "exhausted" and unable to send money any longer. Her "disconnection from North Korean society" and her family left her with feelings of guilt and so she sent money. The suspension of sending remittances, however, can be seen as an adaptive act that she changed her mode of conduct.

> How could I . . . could I do that. They said they are dying of starvation . . . So, I make a little bit of money and send them a little bit of that money . . . I am now so exhausted, reality bites, now my life is bitter. Now North Korea is not making any sense to me, argh . . . just hearing the words 'North Korea' gives me a head-ache. Now I am sick and tired of everything about North Korea. (participant C)

After returning from a trip to the UK, participant E resolved not to marry participant C. Thinking of his retirement and financial stability, he decided that he would be better off single while exploring the UK freely. Participant E had come to embrace the value South Korean society placed on financial success during his time living there. His changed behavior style from a North Korean focus on marriage and family to economic considerations are indicative of an adaptive act.

Many North Korean defectors made the effort to reconnect family relations and interpersonal relations. These efforts included reestablishing the parent-child relationship and communication with estranged family both in North and South Korea. North Korean defector families that re-united showed growth in their relationship as parents, children, and members of society. These efforts to reconnect can be viewed as an attempt to undo some actions taken in their adaptation to a new environment in order to maintain what they value most: their family. The fact that the behavior of participant C who cut off remittances to her family in North Korea could be seen as an adaptive act to focus on her current life with her child.

She has suffered psychologically and financially as a result of sending remittances, which is the opposite of a healthy growth-fostering relationship that the relational-cultural theory emphasizes. While parental participants had to adapt their behaviors by each country, this made it difficult for them to guide their children through similar experiences.

RESETTLEMENT AND RE-ADAPTATION
IN SOUTH KOREA

North Korean defectors' involuntary resettlement in and adaptation to South Korea was usually due to deportation if their refugee claim was denied. A voluntary decision to return, however, was their solution to unexpected adversity or negative events that made it difficult to continue their lives in other countries.

The positive consequences of resettlement in the South included the security of a familiar environment, ease of communication, and reunions with family members. However, there were drawbacks too. These include financial difficulties from debt incurred to pay for migration brokers, interrupted academic and professional lives, need to find housing without governmental assistance, and loss of contact with the North Korean refugee network. Although returning to South Korea was viewed as a viable alternative to a problematic situation, North Korean defector families' process of resettlement and adaptation is different from their previous experience. This time, North Korean defector families must adjust to South Korean society with fewer social resources available to them.

Yet the North Korean defector families themselves were different. During transnational migration, some families experienced a disconnection of relations that could affect all members' mental health and their resettlement in South Korea. Feelings of alienation during the overseas migration process could cause psychological distress that even the act of resettlement in familiar South Korea could not erase. The parents, in particular those who had been traumatized in the process of defecting from North Korea, suffered from fear-related disorders that intruded on the family's voluntary and planned migration. There were cases where the parents' emotional disorders impaired their ability to recognize their family's need for emotional support in the process of transnational migration, straining an already difficult experience. When parents experience psychological difficulties and physical ailments during frequent migration and repetitive adaptations in new environments, they struggle to understand and take care of their children's psychological needs in overseas settlements. Though these difficulties may manifest during settlement outside the Korean peninsula, they become part of the adaptation process even after returning to South Korea.

The psychological and emotional difficulties of overseas migration often create a fracture in North Korean defector families' identities. For instance, when North Korean defectors create identities so they may pass as refugees in other countries, they are disassociating themselves from South Korea. When they return, the stigma that they failed leads them to cut ties to the other country as they attempt to resettle and adapt again to South Korea. The efforts to adapt to South Korea again include younger children learning or relearning Korean, psychological adaptation, creating new community connections, attempting to blend in, and debt rehabilitation. Many North Korean defectors do their utmost to appear to adapt to South Korea and avoid discrimination. However, many do it for themselves too because they want to eradicate the memory of their migration to foreign countries of which they are not proud. Some North Korean defectors almost seem to replicate the alienation and isolation they experienced abroad in their resettlement to South Korea by becoming reclusive and avoiding the social support of North Korean defectors' communities.

Aversion or distrust of others may also be related to the parents' lives in North Korea and their experiences during defection. As for the youths of the North Korean defector family, other research shows that many embody hybrid characteristics or develop a dual identity that in some cases lead to confusion about their identity. In this study, the reported cases of children's and adolescents' identity formation and development during migration have been fraught with psychological difficulties as well as issues with identity formation. This calls for further research that specifically examines the identity formation of North Korean children who have experienced resettlement in South Korea after transnational migration. This research could be the key to understanding the role of identity in social adaptation of the younger generation of North Korean defectors.

As North Korean defector families adapt to their new environment, they absorb characteristics of that new society into their identities. Yet a "North Korea" identity has formed on the basis that North Korea exists as a space that though cannot be revisited continues to influence North Korean defectors in the process of transnational migration. North Koreans' status as refugees is an example of a "North Korea" identity. When North Korean defectors conceal their South Korean citizenship and promote their disenfranchisement as refugees, the decision to choose their identity during transnational migration has already become a pattern of behavior. The process of removing the traces of the former country of residence before migration is tightly intertwined with disconnection and connection experiences. From the moment of defection, North Koreans attempt to shed characteristics of their previous home.

Once they reach China, they strive to phase out North Korean traits, and in South Korea they continue to moderate North Korean traits but now those they picked up in China too. They continue this practice in countries like the UK or Canada where they purposely remove all traces of South Korea so that they may qualify for refugee status. In the process of transnational migration that connects North Korea, China, South Korea, Britain, and Canada, North Korean defector families have been choosing an identity. They shift through the traits of each country, keeping those they find desirable while desperately trying to eliminate any ones they deem to be negative. The process of disowning previous experiences and concealing aspects of one's identity presupposes a form of relationship blocking that not only affects their migration but shapes their resettlement and adaptation to South Korea.

CONCLUSION

This study conducted in-depth interviews with two groups of North Korean defectors: one group that resettled in South Korea after leaving and another group that remained in the destination country. The first group made up of five defectors who had settled in but then left South Korea for either Europe or Canada only to return to the South was asked about their transnational migrations. This included discussions on their overseas settlement experience and the experiences of resettlement in and adaptation to South Korean society. The other group made up of two defectors still residing overseas was asked their views on what forced defectors to return to the South based on their knowledge of North Korean defectors who had resettled in South Korea.

The data collected offered insight to the adaptation of North Korean defector families to South Korea by focusing on their experiences of relational disconnection during transnational migration. Migration often involves a partial or sometimes complete disconnect from interpersonal and social relationships formed in the residential state prior to migration. As refugees, North Korean defectors have experienced complete social and structural disruption. In this study, North Korean defector families in their adaptation changed their behavioral style and underwent disconnection until finally some experienced a reconnection of their relationships after their resettlement in Korea.

To understand individual suffering, it must be considered together with the society and culture to which the individual belongs in a "relationship and cultural connection" according the relational-cultural theory. The North Korean defectors in this study experienced separation, trauma, discrimination, disconnection, alienation, and pain before re-entering South Korea, as well as struggling to adapt at every stop in their transnational migration. The relational-cultural theory employed in this study provided the framework to make associations North Korean defector families' experiences during repeated migration and examine their adaptation and changing identities as North Korean refugees.

During the interviews, it became evident that the children of North Korean defector families were also negatively impacted by repeated migrations. After their time abroad and even on their return to South Korea they suffered from identity crisis, educational and developmental delay, and psychological trauma due to repeated migration. There is a qualitative difference, however, from the identity confusion and academic difficulties of those children of North Korean defector families who stayed in South Korea and those who resettled there. It is worth noting that the instability children of North Korean defectors experience appear to be intensified for those who have resettled in South Korea after moving abroad. The children's maladaptive behaviors often were exacerbated by the parents' psychological and social difficulties after resettlement in South Korea. Parents that withdrew or were alienated from the network of North Korean defectors or social support for whatever reason frequently could not provide the emotional support their children needed. Therefore, social attention and support should be provided to families of North Koreans who are struggling with accumulated psychological and emotional difficulties due to their traumatic experiences both in defection and repeated migration.

Supports could include outreach programs for families resettled after emigrating abroad, help re-adapting that takes into account the defector's stage of life, and family counseling. There is existing psychological counseling for families of North Korean defectors, but this study has uncovered a need to tailor the counseling for families of North Korean defectors who have resettled in South Korea. To truly help, it would be necessary first to understand the identity of repeated and newly reproduced "people who left North Korea," the disconnection and connection they experience, and the trauma and adaptation within a socio-cultural context.

Despite the above-mentioned the significance of this research, the relatively small number of research participants limits the conclusions drawn by this study. The focus on the UK, Belgium, and Canada does not include the current situation in which about 1,200 North Korean refugees are have been turned away by Russia, Netherlands, Germany, France, Australia, Norway, the United States, and Japan. To have a more complete survey, it would be necessary to examine the experiences of North Korean refugee families who resettled in South Korea after relocating to other countries in the future.

REFERENCES

Chin, Meejeong, and Kim Sangha. "The characteristics and types of family migration of North Korean defectors." *Korean Home Economics Association* 56, no. 3 (2018): 317–330.

Jeon, Hyeong kwon. "Theoretical review of international migration: An integrated model approach for diaspora phenomenon." *Korean Northeast Asian Journal* 49 (2008): 259–284.

Jordan, Judith V., and Linda M. Hartling. "New developments in relational-cultural theory." In *Rethinking Mental Health and Disorder: Feminist Perspectives*, edited by M. Ballou & L. S. Brown, 48–70. New York: Guilford Press, 2002.

Jordan, Judith V. "Recent developments in relational-cultural theory." *Women & Therapy* 31, no. 2–4 (2008): 1–4.

Kang, Chae Yeon. "A study on the migration paradigm of the identity of North Korean defectors." *Multicultural Society Studies*, 11, no. 2 (2018): 5–36.

Kim, Seongnam, Yang, Okkyung, Yoo, Gahwan, and Yoon, Jihye. "Re-entry North Korean defectors' resettlement experience." *Future Social Welfare Research* 10, no. 1 (2019): 39–75.

Kim, Young-kwon. "Reasons of defection seen as a result of the deportation of North Korean defectors in Canada: Anxiety about discrimination and education of children," *VOA*, April 17, 2021. https://www.voakorea.com/korea/korea-social-issues/4965819

Kwon, Soo-young, and Choi, Jeong-heon. "A qualitative study on the experience of North Korean defectors' counseling with professional counselors." *Counseling Research* 12, no. 5 (2011): 1683–1702.

Lee, Ji-yeon. "Transnational movement of North Korean refugee women and the contrast of flexible citizenship: Focusing on cases of re-entry to South Korea after experiencing refugees in Western countries." *Korean Women's Studies* 36, no. 4 (2020): 33–69.

Mandelbaum, David G. "The study of life history: Gandhi." *Current Anthropology* 14, no. 3 (1973): 177–206.

Miller, Jean Baker. *Toward a New Psychology of Women*. Boston: Beacon Press. 2012.

Park, Myung-gyu, Kim, Byeong-ro, Kim, Su-am, Song, Young-hoon, and Yang Woon-cheol. "North Korean Diaspora." The Institute for Peace and Unification Studies Seoul National University. 2011.

Son, Myungah, and Kim, Seokho. "A study on family migration of North Korean refugees: Focusing on the serial migration phenomenon." *Korean Demography* 40, no. 1 (2017): 57–81.

Song, Jay Jiyoung., and Bell, M. 2019. "North Korean secondary asylum in the UK." *Migration Studies* 7, no. 2 (2019): 160–179.

UNHCR. "Global Trend forced displacement in 2018." Accessed February 9, 2022. https://www.unhcr.org/globaltrends2018/

Yi, Soonhyung, Soocheol, Cho, Changdae, Kim, and Meejeong, Chin. 2007. *Adaptation and psychological integration of North Korean refugee families*. Seoul: Seoul National University Press.

Yoo, Soo-young. "A narrative exploration of the experience of North Korean defectors fighting tuberculosis." PhD Diss., Seoul National University, 2020.

Chapter 3

"I Opened My Eyes"

Female North Korean Defectors' Journey from Precarity to Empowerment

HaeRan Shin

This chapter[1] examines how female North Korean defectors' reactions to both economic and political precarity, a state of ongoing insecurity, have occasioned unexpected empowerment. For the purposes of this study, empowerment results from the development of self-confidence through one's accumulating contribution to and ownership of the improvement of one's subordinate position (Parmar, 2003). Empowerment together with the concept of agency have been at the center of growing interest in migration research largely due to their theories of change and engagement (Fischer and van Houte, 2019). This research focuses on the empowerment of female North Korean defectors who after living for some years in South Korea relocated to settle in the Korean ethnic enclave in London, England. The precarity that develops from the uncertain situations created by their repeated migrations test these women's flexibility and the strength of their ethnic networks and social navigation skills. In this case, 'social navigation' involves freeing themselves from restrictive social forces to secure better positions in a changing setting (Vigh, 2009, 419). Arbitrary immigration policy changes, geopolitical shifts, and conflicts within the North Korean community are some of the situations creating precarity that these women have had to negotiate. In demonstrating how women's adaptation to their circumstances or adoption of new approaches lead from precarity to empowerment, this study highlights a relatively under-researched group in the fields of gender and migration studies.

Precarity and social navigation form the theoretical framework for this study since, unlike migrant and refugee women's agency, the shifting social forces and the ontological experiences of precarity (Wee et al., 2014; Ettlinger, 2007) have been studied more thoroughly. Existing discussions on precarity and the precariat[2] (Butler, 2006; Standing, 2016; Waite, 2009; Woon, 2014) have focused on rising insecurity and unpredictability caused by the economic and social changes of contemporary society in general. Those debates that mainly view precarity as a threat and danger to the populace's economic and psychological well-being, however, discount people's adaptation as social navigation (Vigh, 2009). To give these debates balance, Paret and Gleeson (2016) suggest the precarity-migration-agency nexus. In this chapter, female North Korean defectors' agency is evident in their choice to employ social navigation as a coping mechanism (Wall, 2019) in overcoming economic and political precarity, which gives rise to empowerment. It is because of this choice that this study argues that the responses to precarity should be re-evaluated in respect to female defectors' empowerment from wholly negative to partially positive.

For this case study, I pose two questions: How have female North Korean defectors' gendered roles inside and outside the home equipped them to respond to their precarity? How has their social navigation led them into empowerment?

Focused on female North Korean defectors living in a suburb of London's Koreatown, this ethnographic fieldwork revealed that while they might have personal strategies for survival, many find support from their everyday activities within ethnic social networks. As these women strengthen their social and economic positions by interacting with others, they are both reconfiguring traditional gender roles and practicing agency. Their empowerment has been an unintended outcome or by-product of pragmatic survival strategies and only on rare occasions a result of women engaging in a calculated process with anticipated results. Those women's traditional gender roles as caregivers have oddly enough prepared them to assume responsibilities outside their purview, accustomed as they are to multitasking the many jobs required to run a household. Their experiences as first caregivers and then breadwinners in North Korea prepared them to endure defection to and resettlement in South Korea and a second migration and resettlement to the United Kingdom. Their willingness to take on any task, focus on educational and cultural activities and optimize every opportunity helped them withstand precarious situations. The determination to not only survive but thrive saw North Korean female defectors take a leading role both in the household economy and in the Korean ethnic community.

For the above arguments, the rest of this chapter is organized as follows. The next section discusses in general terms the concepts of precarity and social navigation and suggests reconsidering those notions in terms of opportunities and empowerment. This is followed by an introduction of the specific case of female North Korean defectors in London. The first finding section focuses on how these women's gendered mobility helped them cope with the phasing down of refugee benefits at the same time as raising their status in their families. The second finding section outlines women's empowerment outside the home through their activities in the Korean ethnic community and the networks they built around their children's education in particular. The conclusion discusses academic and practical implications of the findings of this study.

THEORETICAL FRAMEWORK: PRECARITY AND SOCIAL NAVIGATION FOR EMPOWERMENT

Discussions on precarity and the precariat have had significant implications for studies on migrant women including female defectors. In earlier discussions on precarity, Bourdieu (Waite, 2009) focused on how the progressively flexible job market (Anderson, 2010; Fudge and Owens, 2006) is creating insecurity, instability, and uncertainty. As welfare decreases and financial difficulties increase (Neilson and Rossiter, 2008), this impacts a society's already marginalized people's way of life, creating what Guy Standing (2012, 2016) has designated the precariat. Standing (2012, 2016) argues that since precarity is steadily on the rise eventually everyone will be affected and become a member of the precariat to some degree. He also argues that if overburdened the precariat suffering from emotional turbulence caused by a lack of security could be inclined to volatile political action (Butler, 2006; Waite, 2009; Woon, 2014).

Despite criticism of Bourdieu's and Standing's oversimplified approaches (Mosoetsa et al., 2016), these earlier discussions on precarity have contributed to a comprehensive understanding of the relations between the global political economy and individuals' lifestyles and emotions. Current debates on precarity have expanded to include growing insecurity of life in general and changing use of time and space. Delving deeper into the drawbacks but touching somewhat upon the new opportunities in individuals' lives too (Lewis et al., 2015; Standing, 2012), these debates also examine the mixed feelings that these changes evoke.

Women and migrants as well as youths, the elderly and the disabled, welfare claimants, and criminals (Standing, 2016) primarily compose the "precariat." Migrants who can be categorized under multiple classifications of vulnerability experience precarity in multifaceted ways (Paret and Gleeson, 2016; Worth, 2016). For instance, precarity in the job market is exacerbated by discrimination, disrespect, and abuse for migrant women of different ethnicities (Wu, 2016) due to their sex, race, and lack of citizenship. Defectors, including North Koreans, who escaped their home countries immediately become members of the precariat in the host countries. According to Butler (2006, 20), they are "socially constituted bodies, attached to others, at risk of losing those attachments, exposed to others, at risk of violence by virtue of that exposure." They have arrived illegally, which leaves them highly vulnerable and at risk of deportation to a homeland they fled, and therefore entirely reliant on the benevolence of the host nation-state (Paret and Gleeson, 2016). Migrant workers' hyper-precarious status is compounded not only by lack of job security but also by their precarity of place and deportability (Wee et al., 2014).

This study does not dispute the emergence of the precariat and of female defectors as an articulated example of precariat. It does, however, question the wisdom in disregarding the significance of agency's responses to precarity. Based on the results of this ethnographic fieldwork, this study criticizes previous literature on precarity as follows.

First, by solely focusing on the bigger picture, previous literature has not paid an enough attention to the interaction between agency and precarity in daily life. Resistance to precarity and the resultant empowerment are found in commonplace undertakings (Ncube et al., 2019) and not the media-worthy events such as protests and rallies. Resistance that demands notice such as protests receives ample attention because it takes such a highly visible form. Waite (2008) holds a limited view of precarity as nothing more than a political concept and identifies the san papiers movement in France or the spring 2006 migrant uprisings in the United States as agency (Paret and Gleeson, 2016). Gradually, though, the wide-ranging implications of migrant women's organizational activities are beginning to attract attention and being acknowledged as empowerment (Caggiano, 2019; Eijberts and Roggeband, 2016). Christopoulou and Leontsini (2017) studied the organizations in Athens arising from the collective action of migrant women suffering double marginality (female and migrant). They noted how through associational activities in work, motherhood and the culture of migration, women have forged connections to support their strategy to be recognized.

Unlike those debates that examine associational activities, I suggest considering social navigation functioning as an everyday response to precarity. In doing so, this facilitates the simultaneous and interrelated assessment of social changes and agency's changes as "motion within motion" (Vigh, 2009: 420). The purpose is to illustrate how a person's active life is set within moving environments (Vigh, 2009: 433). Social navigation, from this perspective, encompasses the assessment of both the risks and opportunities of one's present position as well as the process of plotting and attempting to actualize routes to an uncertain and changeable future (Vigh, 2009: 425).

In fact, migrant women's struggle against the effects of precarity has becomes a consistent component of their everyday life. By virtue of their femaleness and foreignness as well as their precarious legal status, their job options are limited. They are left with no other choice but to seek employment in low-income, contract-based, flexible job markets (Netto et al., 2020; Wang et al. 2017). Neilson and Rossiter (2008) argue that precarity has been the norm in a wider historical and geographic scope for women and migrants long before these socio-economic changes in established societies attracted scholarly interest (See Bastia, 2015 for migrants and urban informality). People that fall into these demographics of female and migrants, however, had to develop flexible coping mechanisms (Shin, 2008, 2011) before the terms precarity and the precariat were ever applied to them. Migrant laborers have adjusted to precarity and learned how to take advantage of the flexibility that these new forms of employment offer. Their willingness to accept low-wage jobs that others may view as beneath them for example, is in fact a coping mechanism. Even inferior jobs can be viewed as empowering when they secure a family's livelihood (Uekusa and Lee, 2018).

Second, previous literature that has not factored in agency's responses offers a rather unbalanced account of the effects of precarity. Standing (2016), for instance, doubts the collective capacity of migrants within the precariat capable of moving beyond concerns for basic survival to push for social change. This belief entirely disregards migrants' agency. But there are several scholars who view the adaptive conformity as the basis for survival and power (Elster, 2016; Kabeer, 1999; Lewis, 1966). Various findings of previous studies confirm the complexity of adaptive conformity and prove that it is not the submissive construct Standing deems it to be.

It is true that even those migrants who ambitiously pursued upward mobility and strategically used precarity to their advantage still ended up being caught in the precariat (Wang et al., 2017). However, the interaction between precarity and people's reaction to it does on occasion culminate in rather accidental activism. One study on Vietnamese marriage migrants in South Korea (Kim and Shin, 2018) documented just such a case of accidental activism. Some marriage migrants that sought to support newly arrived brides and share their knowledge took it further and became activists for marriage migrants' rights.

This study responds to Paret and Gleeson (2016)'s call for the study of broader political and economic shifts and how they reshape the relationships between individuals and groups within historically and geographically specific contexts. Those female North Korean defectors whose proactive coping strategies in reaction to precarity that included accepting lowly positions set in motion the revision of their sphere of family, politics, and the economy (Ettlinger, 2007) before migration. With the advent of the economic crisis in North Korea, North Korean women's function as active economic agents started to emerged (Kim SK, 2014, 2020).

This study suggests approaching female defectors as an articulated example of the empowerment dynamics during precarity. Specifically that in uncertain circumstances these women engage in social navigation to find or even offer security but not with the conscious intention to empower themselves (Hoang and Yeoh, 2011; Vigh, 2009). The fact that their activities in the destination society do empower them is a fortunate by-product (See Parmar, 2003 for the opposite by-product effect). Their adaptive attitudes towards engaging in the informal economy in North Korea and the United Kingdom prove their resilience (Kim SK, 2020). That they also continue to be the main caregivers for their children gives them access to ethnic networks based around their children's education (Kim SK, 2020), networks that assist them in navigating precarious situations. Their adaptability and social navigation of ethnic networks with other North Korean women are critical to their survival (Krajewski and Blumberg, 2014). As Ehrkamp (2013) argues, in the case of migrant women their compliances and resistance are complicatedly entangled.

CASE BACKGROUND

The case study focuses on those female North Korean defectors who live with their families in New Malden, a suburb of London and the location of the city's Koreatown. This Koreatown has the greatest concentration of North Korean defectors (700) outside of South Korea and a number of South Korean migrants (10,000–15,000) in the UK. Their residency permits range from refugees and asylum seekers to permanent residents and UK citizens.

Korea has been divided into North and South Korea since World War II, and the two sides are technically still at war. Though there have been overtures of peace in the last few years, relations between the two countries remain distrustful at best. They are on opposing developmental tracks: North Korea has adopted Juche, a socialist self-reliance, and South Korea has committedly embraced capitalism. Although they share a language, Korean, there is now a discernable difference in their accents and after over fifty years of segregation new words have been introduction that they do not share. Since they view each other as hostile, letters, emails, phone calls, internet communications and telegrams are forbidden between the two countries. It is still illegal for South Koreans to contact North Koreans even outside the Korean peninsula. In theory, if a South Korean happens to encounter a North Korean in the UK, s/he is expected to report it to the nearest South Korean embassy.

The majority of the women in this study resided in those regions in North Korea that border South Korea and made a circuitous escape through China before making their way to South Korea. Despite their shared ethnicity and language, many North Korean defectors have found it difficult to adjust to life in South Korea. The North Korean education system is different from the South Korean one, so North Korean defectors' skills and education do not translate well in the South Korean job market. This creates barriers to finding gainful employment. Additional issues have arisen from the circumstance that anything related to North Korea is still considered politically dangerous in South Korea. Due to North Korea's tightly controlled borders, the lack of communication and information lends itself to supposition and unsubstantiated rumors. Preconceived notions from the time of military regimes in South Korea linger, and as a result, North Korean defectors are often viewed suspiciously as possible spies sent to report back to their government.

Though many genuinely attempted to adjust to and settle in South Korea, after some years many moved again, usually to countries like the United Kingdom. Regarding their reasons for leaving, they explained that, despite their willingness to assimilate to the society, they were tired of the pressure to adopt South Korean ideals. But more than that, they were exhausted by the unrelenting discrimination. That people with whom they shared ethnicity and a language would be so intolerant cut deeply. Many admitted that they could better bear discrimination by people of different ethnicities than from their own kinsfolk. They were quickly disillusioned of any idea that they were the same. "Co-ethnic employers may facilitate access to secondary labor markets for new migrants, but can also exploit these social networks for their own economic advancement, thus debunking assumptions about ethnic solidarity (Rosales, 2014)" (Paret and Gleeson, 2016).

There are two reasons so many North Koreans primarily chose the UK as their next destination. The first reason was the liberal welfare system in place to support refugees had few restrictions or regulations. Unlike some other countries that demanded proof that defectors had come directly from North Korea, the UK did not. Therefore, defectors that had lived in South Korea first could still qualify for refugee status[3] simply by vowing they had come directly from North Korea. Eventual changes to the UK's migration policy and welfare system that reduced financial support for refugees prompted North Koreans to seek jobs. These changes coincided with the UK government's revocation of international students student work permits, leaving a void in Korean ethnic businesses that North Korean defectors quickly filled (Shin, 2018, 2019).

The second reason was the UK's neutrality in regards to North Korea. This is in sharp contrast to the United States where North Korea is often regarded as an axis of evil and defectors felt they were viewed with suspicion. In the

US and South Korea especially they were also considered to be a valuable resource of information about North Korea. They would be repeatedly asked to share their stories of life ruled by tyranny in North Korea with the media, in church, and at various meetings. As far as financial benefits and a generally accepting environment, the UK was one of the most hospitable destinations.

The arrival of North Korean defectors to the UK peaked around 2007 into 2008. The UK government was attentive to the needs of larger families, allocating houses with more rooms to accommodate their numbers, which motivated some North Korean couples to start having more babies. As children born in the UK were growing up in an English-speaking country, their parents started to be anxious about the lack of exposure to the Korean language. Acting on their concern, a group of parents established a Korean language school for the 2nd generation.

While there are only a few North Korean organizations such as their language school, there are quite a number South Korean ones. South Korean organizations have increasingly integrated North Koreans and come to rely on North Korean defectors' active participation and attendance. Those ethnic associations organized by men from either of the Koreas, however, inevitably devolved into conflicts and struggled to stay afloat, whereas associations that primarily involved women such as the South Korean Seniors Association were thriving. Of the North Korean dance group, South Korean dance group, and South Korean singing groups, the South Korean Seniors Association was most active, having 104 members, including 10 North Korean women.

RESEARCH METHODS

An ethnographic and interview-based approach revealed the micro-dynamics that empower those subject women arise from their social navigation (Paret and Gleeson, 2016). Based on mixed ethnographic research methods, this study cross-checked its findings with results from different methods. The research methods included participant observation, in-depth interviews, and archival analysis.

The participant observation and the face-to-face in-depth interviews were conducted during a concentrated period of time from August to December 2017 and January 2019. Upon seeing my ten-year-old son was of a similar age to their children, the parents at the North Korean language school in New Malden suggested he attend, which he did in 2017. I had the advantage of being an insider of sorts during my participant observation there, but as an observer, it was imperative that I explained the academic purpose of the observation and research ethics without delay, which I did. I established close relationships and was invited to informal gatherings and a birthday party as well as organizational activities. As a parent, I could attend various parents' meetings and observe the mothers who are the main actors of the school. As someone welcomed into their acquaintance, many were quite willing to confide how their duties had evolved from the time of the famine to after their defection when I asked them to describe their lives. I also attended a North Korean dance group's practice, as well as several events organized by South Korean or North Korean organizations. All the events included a mix of North Koreans and South Koreans. I also conducted in-depth interviews with several key actors.

There were additional in-depth interviews with nine key actor women in January 2019 that focused on women's roles. The interviews included questions on the extent of their involvement in decisions on the family's defection and resettlements, their participation in organizations in the UK, and their career development over the past ten to twenty years. Although the interviews were tape-recorded to provide official records, the semi-structured format of the interview invited confidences and unexpected stories.

From my first observations in 2011 up to this time, I have become well acquainted with almost all the key actors in the North and South Korean organizations in New Malden. My previous research has contributed to an accumulation of data that includes the examination of women's activities to combat the famine in North Korea, attempts to resettle in South Korea, and involvement in organizational activities in the UK. Over a decade of women sharing their experiences and retrospective interpretations with me, I have come to understand how women's roles inside and outside the home have changed. I have analyzed the data using an interpretative and comprehensive approach to sift through the information to discover women's shifting responsibilities have had the accidental outcome of empowering them.

Empowerment inside and outside the household: Economic and political turbulence and adaptation.

Precarity is not new to North Korean women. They suffered through the economic and political turmoil in North Korea that precipitated the Arduous March, a period of famine and general economic crisis from 1994 to 1998. They endured precarity in the uncertainty of resettlement and the difficult job situations in South Korea and the UK. They adapted to reduced welfare benefits in the UK that compelled them to seek jobs once again to be able to feed their families. Regarding their experiences in North Korea, South Korea, and the United Kingdom, the interviewees commonly described their struggle to find work and out of necessity resorting to accepting low-wage jobs in all three countries. That they accepted low-wage jobs in North Korea indicates that they were already tailoring their adaptive responses as social navigation to cope with precarious situations before they ever defected.

In North Korea, women were accustomed to being recruited to work during labor shortages. The need for women in the workforce was once so great that North Korea passed a law in 1946 that declared men and women equal and established wage parity to encourage women to work outside the home. In fact, women with children received more benefits than men. For example, according to one interviewee, women with three children aged 13 or less would be paid eight hours for six hours of work. Despite legislated equality, when the need for women in the workforce ended in the late 1980s, they were expected to exit the labor market and accept the traditional domestic division of labor that consigned them to being homemakers.

Our interviewees recognized that life in a staunchly patriarchal society that places men as the head of family had prepared them to accept secondary positions. While it is true that many single women had jobs in North Korea, one interviewee explained that after marrying, most women quit their jobs. Since the centralized distribution system that existed previous to the economic crisis in the 1990s apportioned necessities like food to the male head of the household, married women were entirely dependent on their husbands. This became a problem should a woman want a divorce.

It was only after North Korea suffered a serious economic crisis lasting from 1994 to 1998 that caused the collapse of the public distribution system that economic empowerment became a possibility for women. Since food rations had all but stopped and men were forced to continue to work unpaid or face punishment, it was up to women to find alternative sources of income to survive the famine. As married women did not work outside the home, they started selling items (Kim, 2020) to earn money to support their families. They launched an unofficial market called *Jangmadang* (Choe, 2015), an umbrella term that covers everything from farmers' markets to informal local markets to black markets. These markets have developed significantly since the 1990s, and currently the majority of North Koreans depend on them for their survival.

Witnessing the development of the unauthorized economy, people realized the importance of flexible and informal survival strategies. One interviewee explained,

> We used to live inside a bubble. The government protected us and provided everything, even underwear. Then, the public distribution stopped, so people had no idea what to do but sit and starve. Now people are different because of their Jangmadang experiences. I don't think that they would just starve if a similar crisis happens again. (A North Korean woman in her 40s, 8 January 2019)

North Koreans were ill-equipped to cope with the deprivations of the economic crisis, but this interviewee believes that they had since learned how to be flexible and could adapt to survive future disasters.

As Kim (2020) indicates, the economic collapse freed North Korean women to become active economic agents, and that required a dramatic shift from their traditional status as wife and mother to breadwinner. The answers given during the interviews for this study aligned with the findings in Kim's study. The interview subjects confessed that through their transactions in Jangmadang they came to appreciate the need for flexibility and mobility in capitalizing on economic opportunities.

While the crisis itself obliged women to adapt and develop coping mechanisms, the satisfaction women experienced as they contributed to the household economy through selling wares at Jangmadang empowered them. Their empowerment was primarily practiced in relations with their family members, but especially husbands. Regarding women's empowerment based on economic activities, another woman surmised,

> Women especially learned how to survive without the state's protection during the crisis. Before the crisis in North Korea, men were prioritized because the national distribution was in the man's name only. It's called a distribution ticket. Those tickets became redundant as national resources became limited. After women began to go to Jangmadang, their experiences opened their eyes to a new modern society where everybody is making money. (A North Korean woman in her 40s, 9 January 2019)

Women's changing status through their experiences in Jangmadang has attracted attention. Other studies (Jung and Dalton, 2006; Kim SK, 2020) have examined the evolving status of women since the economic crisis and the impact their actions have had on the emerging capitalist processes within North Korea.

The consequences of their actions on a country's trajectory notwithstanding, most women were not consulted by their fathers or husbands when they determined the family would escape to South Korea. Even though women were not involved in the decision, they seemed to find it acceptable nonetheless. Indeed, the majority of the female interviewees did not express a consciousness of unequal gender relations in either North Korea or South Korea or both. Their focus was on their resettlement process and acceptance by South Koreans, and in fact what bothered them most was the implied hierarchy that put North Koreans at the bottom. According to my interviewees, the discrimination they found to be truly injurious was committed by co-ethnic South Koreans. One interview subject clarified,

South Korea is like a foreign country but one where I didn't have a language problem. I even thought that facing discrimination in a country that is in fact foreign would be less awful. (A North Korean woman in her 30s, 11 January 2019)

This was a common sentiment among our interview subjects, and many felt nothing was worse than the contempt of South Koreans. They were deeply disappointed when their expectation of friendly and sympathetic attitudes based on common ethnicity and history was met with prejudice. Many of the interviewees relayed recollections of being treated disdainfully when they acted in a way that revealed an ignorance of the cultural code in South Korea.

Due to their shared language, they fully understood the discriminatory and hurtful remarks that South Koreans directed at them. The antagonistic and complicated relations between North Korea and South Korea made them extra sensitive to every slight. The feeling that they were scorned at every turn was one of the reasons they left South Korea. For many of them, South Korea had not been their first choice in any case. Originally, and quite apart from the discrimination they experienced after arriving, that was due to the difficulty in sending remittances to their families left in North Korea from South Korea. But since South Korea is closest, relocating there was easier and faster than most anywhere else.

Although they felt disempowered by these experiences, it motivated them to discover ways to improve upon their relations with South Koreans even once in the UK. This was in part due to North Koreans reliance on South Korean businesses on the UK for jobs. The refugee welfare that North Korean defectors had relied on had been repeatedly reduced during the years of the Conservative Party's governing. Previous to these cuts in benefits, some had opted to work chiefly in a Korean migrants' job market to earn extra cash. After these cuts, the majority of defectors had to start working outside the home in the official job market. They found work in South Korean shops, restaurants, grocery stores, cleaning companies, and on construction sites. The timing of certain events facilitated a successful job search. First, North Koreans seeking jobs fortuitously coincided with Korean Chinese migrants returning to China, leaving vacancies that need to be filled in South Korean businesses. Second, many North Koreans' children were old enough to be enrolled in nurseries, affording women the opportunity to have full-time jobs.

Once North Korean women started working, they quickly became the primary bread-winners in their households. North Korean men held out for jobs they felt reflected their station in life, while women were willing to take the low-income and less-respected jobs their husbands shunned. As a result, many North Korean men were periodically employed at best, whereas women worked consistently. One woman reasoned that because of the gender hierarchy ideology, men believe that they should hold important positions, relegating women to lowlier jobs. During the famine, women did whatever was necessary to survive, even daring to embark on capitalism-styled selling that could be considered subversive. She outlined the gender difference in the attitudes towards a job with an example from her own life:

> My husband often stopped working, and my brother switched jobs several times. They would say, "Should I really do this kind of job? I can become something important." So I told my husband that, even if you do cleaning, the money you get from the labor is precious. I am thinking of running a food-delivery truck. I know I will do anything for my children. But my husband said that he can't do physical labor because he has a slight physique. And he is looking for a good job for him. (A North Korean in her 40s, 14 January 2019)

Their approaches to precarity had both negative and positive outcomes. On the one hand, willingness to accept low-paying job constrains opportunities to seek better-paying jobs and restricts the time they can invest in their personal improvement, limiting their long-term empowerment. On the other hand, this same willingness to take any job to financially support their families puts them in a position of power in the household. One female interviewee confessed,

> When I stayed at home, I felt guilty because I was dependent on my husband's income. I don't feel guilty any longer because I am making money. (A North Korean woman in her 40s, 8 January 2019)

This woman enjoyed her job and spent time during the interview passionately discussing her ideas for improving workplace procedures. She attributed the confidence she felt in her capabilities in the workplace to the physical and mental hardships she endured during her defection. Traversing two rivers to cross into China to then seek out the German embassy to petition for passage to South Korea had made her feel strong and unbeatable. Her husband's view of her transformation was slightly different. He informed her that her boldness hurt his pride, which discouraged her from continuing to seek solutions for their family's difficulties outside the home. Despite resistance, these women's unrelenting determination to find any job to support their families was akin to their efforts to save their families from starvation in North Korea. This was for them a second awakening of their power. They faced down foreign surroundings, low-wage jobs, and the lack of a family network and rose to the challenge, discovering their strength in the process.

Foreign surroundings and exposure to British culture and attitudes to gender roles challenged and influenced North Korean defectors' views on marriage. One leader in the North Korean community disclosed that, of 100 households, thirty-two couples were divorced by 2016. While the reasons given when filing for divorce included affairs, domestic violence and finan-cial difficulties, this interviewee disclosed that defectors had noticed and mimicked the permissive attitudes to divorce in the UK. He argued that since the UK courts usually accepted women's testimony unreservedly, this left men on the defensive and in a weaker position, sometimes unfairly.

Allocation of housing in the UK further empowered North Korean women even if inadvertently. The UK government automatically put the house granted to the defector family in the mother's name. Some couples pretended to separate so each could have a house. Since it was assumed the children would remain with their mother, the woman would retain the larger house. If the UK government discovered the ruse, the smaller house assigned to the husband was repossessed, but the family was permitted to retain the house where the children resided. Women were now not only the breadwinners but the officially recognized heads of their households.

Outside the home, their jobs and status as the official head of the household granted empowerment. But within their household, North Korean women's personal empowerment developed for two reasons: the presence of North Korean female defectors' networks and the absence of parents-in-law. These women built strong networks that were a source of information on jobs for example and companionship in their daily lives. The interviewees explained knowledge of who worked where ensured that when that person gave notice, news of the vacancy quickly spread through the network. These networks replaced the extended families that women depended on in North Korea in a way that was most favorable to them. As the philosophy of Confucianism still dominates North Korea society, women are obliged to follow the dictates of their husband's parents. Several admitted that since their parents-in-law were no longer a part of their daily lives, they finally have the freedom to follow their own desires.

Emerging power in the ethnic Korean community through educational and cultural activities

Female North Korean defectors' social navigation was facilitated by the transnational ethnic networks that would offer some stability to their precari-ous lives. The networks played a critical part in assuaging collective concerns about their children's education while in exile from their homeland. Due to their gender-related role as primary care-givers, they were more inclined to get involved in organizations of community activities associated with the fam-ily structure. Involvement in organizations such as their children's language school, cultural organizations, and politically neutral organizations, such as the Korean Seniors Association, was purely for the good of the family. In the Korean ethnic enclave, North Koreans' and with South Korean women's lives revolved around shared networks for child care and jobs, creating a sense of community. Women were not consciously seeking empowerment through these activities, but that is exactly what came of their participation.

Though North Korean men established an ethnic association as well, opposing political groups argued regarding the leadership and almost any other point raised until many tired of the struggle, and the association almost collapsed. Unlike the struggling men's associations, the women's cultural and educational activities were thriving since their activities were founded on concern for their families, which precluded political conflict. Appropriately, cultural and educational organizations became the hub of the Korean ethnic community. For example, the most popular and best-attended affairs were organized by the South Korean Seniors Association. Their events, such as the Traditional Korean Costume Fashion Show and the Korean Thanksgiving festival, had a universal appeal and attracted South Korean and North Korean women alike.

North Korean women actively participated in almost all the events in Koreatown. Moreover, even when women had to bring their children along, more attended the North Korean Ethnic Association than men. At the events hosted by South Korean organizations, North Korean women were often the majority and regularly outnumbered South Koreans. To my question why they are so active, one female North Korean defector laughed and said,

> We are just so used to participating in group activities. We were all involved in some organizational activities because not participating in organizational activities would be like betraying North Korea. There was a serious conflict within the North Korean community for the leadership of the ethnic association. But once there is an event announcement, we just call each other and everybody will join. (A North Korean woman in her 40s, 14 January 2019)

She explained that, in North Korea, women were required to participate in associations, so the social activities in London's Koreatown were almost familiar and, in a way, comforting. In North Korea, however, it was customary for women to join organizations according to their marital statuses. The activities themselves were often for the greater good and included collecting trash or iron for economic resources or holding self-criticizing/reflection discussions.

During community participation in New Malden, though, their encounters with South Korean migrant women required delicate handling and truly tested their social navigation skills. Interactions usually took place in their children's schools or events hosted by ethnic organizations, and though the atmosphere was not overtly unfriendly, it was fraught with tension and complicated by underlying discord and discrimination. Those female North Korean defectors were quite aware of the hierarchy that exists in the ethnic Korean community. They were in a secondary position within the community and they knew it. Smiling knowingly, one North Korean woman stated,

> We are the bottom of the bottom in the food chain. (A North Korean woman in her 40s, 8 January 2019)

She was speaking of the unique combination of their status as refugees, their country's lack of geopolitical power, and their gender, all stereotypical of the ultimate minority. She understood that in the eyes of the world they were in every way marginalized, but had difficulty accept that was also the case in the eyes of South Koreans, their co-ethnic neighbours.

If one considers ethnicity as a glue that binds people together, then North Koreans' settlement in South Korea should have been successful. The failure of shared ethnicity to bring people together in this case needs to be viewed as a product of geopolitical tensions. For instance, South Koreans' instead of treating North Korean defectors as their equals were openly condescending. One of the school mothers complained,

> They [South Koreans] have told us [North Koreans] that they are our big brothers. I can't tolerate listening to such ridiculous comments any longer. Why are they big brothers to us? Is it just because they are richer than we are? (A North Korean woman in her 40s, 12 January 2019)

This woman was proud to be North Korean and could not fathom why South Koreans would feel superior for any reason, least of all because they were wealthier. Of those South Koreans that behaved as if North Koreans were inferior, many would refuse to attend community events that might include North Koreans. South Korean women's barely disguised disrespect for North Koreans played out in cultural or social rather than political forums. One North Korean interviewee accused South Koreans of insincerity and seemingly incapable of being candid. She elaborated that since North Koreans were expected to make public confessions regularly, they are accustomed to straightforward answers and blunt honesty. A South Korean woman did not comment on North Korean women's bluntness but admitted that she was annoyed by their fashion and makeup styles. She declared that North Korean women looked old-fashioned and appeared too North Korean to South Koreans' eyes.

Despite their differences, they will dedicatedly work together to develop an organization's capacity, unlike the men who have proved themselves to be combative. One South Korean interviewee admitted to petitioning the headquarters of the South Korean Seniors Association to request that North

Koreans and Korean Chinese that contributed to the organization be awarded official membership. These are just a few examples of the complex and various replies we received explaining the dynamic relations between South Koreans and North Koreans living in the UK.

It should be pointed out that these relations were impeded by South Koreans' misconception of North Korean defectors. A misconception that led them to the expectation that North Koreans would embrace every part of South Korean culture. In point of fact, it is quite the opposite as evidenced by North Koreans' organizational activities that indicate a wish to preserve and develop their culture. One North Korean woman said,

> I feel positive about the relational change between North Korea and South Korea but at the same time I'm worried. We are refugees, but we are North Koreans. People are confused and think that we [North Korean defectors] all hate our country. We can miss our hometown but hate the North Korean government. When we say we don't like North Korea, it is only because of the difficulties in daily life . . . I expect North Korea to become more affluent and powerful so that people do not have to defect to other countries. (A North Korean woman in her 30s, 15 January 2019)

She was addressing the misconception that equated escaping from North Korea with rejecting everything to do with North Korea.

The social navigation of organizational activities was not just North Korean women's response to political precarity but an attempt to preserve their culture. For example, several North Korean women had joined the amateur dance group that I observed in my participant observation of early-morning dance classes. Here, they learned the steps to folk dances such as the rainbow dance, which owing to the swirl of shawls it appears as if the dancers' dresses are continually changing throughout. Since any display of their culture is rare, they were invited to events such as the Kingston Korean Festival even though they are in no way near so skilled as a professional group.

This case demonstrates the social activities that develop from North Korean ethnic networks in destination countries. Unlike their men, North Korean women reject political activities and in doing so skirt political precarity. As a consequence, women transitioned from precarity to empowerment smoothly even during times of political turbulence.

Truth be told, women were considerably less concerned about politics than the circumstance of their children speaking English in the home rather than Korean. They worried that this would create a language barrier and impede communication with their children, but worse than that, they saw it as their children losing their North Korean identity. One North Korean couple started inviting other children to their house and organized a children's Korean language study group. Thanks to donations from a lawyers' office, the study group developed into a North Korean language school that holds classes on Saturdays in a space rented from a local church. Their social navigation skills already so essential to building a life despite political precarity were now crucial to ensuring the success of the North Korean language school.

As North Korean mothers coordinated to rotate the supervision of children before classes and arranging snacks for the breaks, ethnic networks formed from their efforts to assure their children's education. Those North Korean women who had children around the same age could and often would share their concerns with each other. They knew that they could rely on this support system of mothers, and even if all they received was empathy, to discuss their worries with others would alleviate some of the stress.

Except for a few members in positions of management in the school, men were not involved in the discussions on educational decisions. In most cases, fathers would drop their children off at the school and then leave without stopping to speak with either the other fathers or the mothers. That women were making connections in the community as mothers and based on their caregiving occupations provided them with a lifeline that their husbands didn't have. Involvement with the Korean language school had the unanticipated outcome of women emerging as key actors in the North Korean communities. Though they vowed that their actions had nothing to do with an interest in leading, their participation in school activities nonetheless contributed to individual women's empowerment. By virtue of their attendance, women took the lead in community events simply by being visible and this was a significant factor in the reversal of gender roles.

The school contributed to the empowerment of the women teaching there too. One teacher admitted that after she came to the UK and started making money, her life improved financially but she felt that it was empty. It was only when the teaching job in the language school in New Malden came available that she realized that teaching had always been her dream. She reminisced about her literature teacher who taught that the revolution was not fought to please Kim Jong Eun but to give all Koreans a better life had inspired her to teach. She was so impressed by this teacher's concept of a better life that she has pondered the possible implications ever since. The teaching position provided the fulfillment that she had been missing. Though she had expected teaching would give her a sense of completion, she had not anticipated the feeling of empowerment that came from participation in a network supporting children's education.

Participation in a network, however, was something North Korean mothers in their capacity as caretakers were well accustomed. They accompanied their children to any Korean occasion they were invited to attend. In a spirit of affiliation and out of a realization that their clothing choices and general appearance were viewed rather negatively, North Korean mothers dressed themselves and their children in the *Hanbok*, Korean traditional clothes. Rather than attempt to change minds through participation in the community, they allowed their children's performances of Korean songs and dances to build up a positive image.

Despite North Koreans' efforts to create a rapport, some South Koreans still opposed the performances by children from the North Korean language school at South Korean language school events. This open hostility did not provoke North Korean mothers to retaliate nor would they be drawn into a conflict, and if anything, they became more determinedly diplomatic. In fact, North Korean mothers and teachers resisted criticizing the South Korean language school in return and went so far as to welcome South Korean children's membership. Neither striking back nor backing down, North Korean mothers held their ground with dignity, diffusing the situation and taking the power for themselves. When they attended meetings to discuss school matters, they concentrated on business and would not allow themselves to be distracted by personal issues. Their composed diplomacy and the source of their empowerment has roots in their experiences in North Korea. There, it is almost mandatory for women to be involved in organizational activities and attend public meetings, and from these involvements they learned how to comport themselves in professional settings. Remarkably, the hardships of their homeland had equipped these women with the social navigation skills to overcome financial and political precarity, build ethnic networks and face adversity with grace.

According to intersectional theory, North Korean female defectors are discriminated against for multiple reasons but specifically due to their ethnicity, gender and immigration status. It can even be argued that the subject women's own adaptive strategy reinforces restrictive gender roles rather than challenges them. But the findings of this research demonstrate that North Korean women's adaptive attitudes are vital not only for their survival but for their empowerment. Understanding that they have to be flexible to survive, North Korean women collaborate to build transnational ethnic networks (Lo, 2016), without which they would not have access to much-needed information or receive support and inspiration (Ryan, 2007; Teorell, 2003). Though these women may not appear empowered when compared to those people generally deemed to be successful or powerful, they have found a strength within themselves to make a difference in their lives.

This research has implications for the debate on precarity and women and migrant groups as members of the precariat. It also has implications for literature on gendered roles in contemporary society. This includes a juxtaposition of female defectors' adaptability and their male counterparts' adherence to convention. This study contributes to discussions on social navigation as

a coping mechanism for migrant minorities in a host society and the consequences of their responses to their new environment. This study's theoretical
contribution to future research lies in its discussion of the multiple forms of
agency's empowerment and the double-edged nature of precarity.

NOTES

1. This chapter is based on the previously published article, Shin, HaeRan.
"Precarity to empowerment: The consequences of female North Korean defectors'
coping skills and social navigation." *Gender, Place & Culture* (2021): 1-22.

2. Precariat refers to those people who face and/or suffer from escalating precarity.
The term is the combination of precarious and proletariat, indicating an emerging
class in the contemporary society (Standing, 2016). They are those workers who
lack the basic securities of the mid-twentieth century (Standing, 2012; Paret and
Gleeson, 2016).

3. The refugee status has not been given since 2009, when the UK government
strengthened its immigration control. http://www.spnews.co.kr/news/articleView.
html?idxno=1017 accessed on August 4, 2020.

REFERENCES

Anderson, Bridget. "Migration, immigration controls and the fashioning of precarious
workers." *Work, Employment and Society* 24, no. 2 (2010): 300–317.

Bastia, Tanja. "Transnational migration and urban informality: Ethnicity in Buenos
Aires' informal settlements." *Urban Studies* 52, no. 10 (2015): 1810–1825.

Butler, Judith. *Precarious life: The powers of mourning and violence.* Verso, 2006.

Caggiano, Sergio. "Migrant women and politicization of experience: The place of
gender in three social organizations in Buenos Aires and La Plata (Argentina)."
Revue europeenne des migrations internationales 35, no. 3 (2019): 217–238.

Christopoulou, Nadina, and Mary Leontsini. "Weaving solidarity: Migrant women's
organisations in Athens." *Journal of Intercultural Studies* 38, no. 5 (2017):
514–529.

Ehrkamp, Patricia. "'I've had it with them!' Younger migrant women's spatial practices of conformity and resistance." *Gender, Place & Culture* 20, no. 1 (2013):
19–36.

Eijberts, Melanie, and Conny Roggeband. "Stuck with the stigma? How Muslim
migrant women in the Netherlands deal—individually and collectively—with
negative stereotypes." *Ethnicities* 16, no. 1 (2016): 130–153.

Elster, Jon. *Sour grapes.* Cambridge University Press, 2016.

Ettlinger, Nancy. "Precarity unbound." *Alternatives* 32, no. 3 (2007): 319–340.

Fischer, Carolin, and Marieke van Houte. "Dimensions of agency in transnational
relations of Afghan migrants and return migrants." *Migration Studies* (2019).

Fudge, Judy, and Rosemary Owens, eds. *Precarious work, women, and the new economy: The challenge to legal norms.* Bloomsbury Publishing, 2006.

Hoang, Lan Anh, Theodora Lam, Brenda SA Yeoh, and Elspeth Graham. "Transnational migration, changing care arrangements and left-behind children's responses in South-east Asia." *Children's geographies* 13, no. 3 (2015): 263–277.

Jung, Kyungja, and Bronwen Dalton. "Rhetoric versus reality for the women of North Korea: Mothers of the revolution." *Asian Survey* 46, no. 5 (2006): 741–760.

Kabeer, Naila. "Resources, agency, achievements: Reflections on the measurement of women's empowerment." *Development and change* 30, no. 3 (1999): 435–464.

Kim, Sung Kyung. "'Defector,' 'Refugee,' or 'Migrant'? North Korean Settlers in South Korea's Changing Social Discourse." *North Korean Review* (2012): 94–110.

Kim, Sung Kyung. "'I am well-cooked food': Survival strategies of North Korean female border-crossers and possibilities for empowerment." *Inter-Asia Cultural Studies* 15, no. 4 (2014): 553–571.

Kim, Sung Kyung. "Mobile North Korean Women and Long-Distance Motherhood: The (Re) Construction of Intimacy and the Ambivalence of Family." *Korean Studies* 44, no. 1 (2020): 97–122.

Kim, Yulii, and HaeRan Shin. "Governing through mobilities and the expansion of spatial capability of Vietnamese marriage migrant activist women in South Korea." *Singapore Journal of Tropical Geography* 39, no. 3 (2018): 364–381.

Krajewski, Sabine, and Sandra Blumberg. "Identity challenged: Taiwanese women migrating to Australia." *Gender, Place & Culture* 21, no. 6 (2014): 701–716.

Lewis, Hannah, Peter Dwyer, Stuart Hodkinson, and Louise Waite. "Hyper-precarious lives: Migrants, work and forced labour in the Global North." *Progress in Human Geography* 39, no. 5 (2015): 580–600.

Lewis, Oscar. *La vida; a Puerto Rican family in the culture of poverty, San Juan and New York.* Random House, 1966.

Lo, Marieme S. "En route to New York: Diasporic networks and the reconfiguration of female entrepreneurship in Senegal." *Gender, Place & Culture* 23, no. 4 (2016): 503–520.

McIlwaine, Cathy. "Migrant machismos: Exploring gender ideologies and practices among Latin American migrants in London from a multi-scalar perspective." *Gender, Place & Culture* 17, no. 3 (2010): 281–300.

Mosoetsa, Sarah, Joel Stillerman, and Chris Tilly. "Precarious labor, south and north: An introduction." *International Labor and Working Class History* 89 (2016): 5.

Ncube, Alice, Yonas T. Bahta, and Andries Jordaan. "Coping and adaptation mechanisms employed by sub-Saharan African migrant women in South Africa." *Jàmbá: Journal of Disaster Risk Studies* 11, no. 1 (2019): 1–13.

Neilson, Brett, and Ned Rossiter. "Precarity as a political concept, or, Fordism as exception." *Theory, Culture & Society* 25, no. 7–8 (2008): 51–72.

Netto, Gina, Mike Noon, Maria Hudson, Nicolina Kamenou-Aigbekaen, and Filip Sosenko. "Intersectionality, identity work and migrant progression from low-paid work: A critical realist approach." *Gender, Work & Organization* (2020).

Paret, Marcel, and Shannon Gleeson. "Precarity and agency through a migration lens." *Citizenship Studies* 20, no. 3–4 (2016): 277–294.

Parmar, Aradhana. "Micro-credit, empowerment, and agency: Re-evaluating the discourse." *Canadian Journal of Development Studies/Revue canadienne d'études du
développement* 24, no. 3 (2003): 461–476.

Ryan, L. 2007. Migrant women, social networks and motherhood: The experiences of
Irish nurses in Britain. *Sociology, 41*(2), 295–312.

Shin, HaeRan. "Extra-territorial nation-building in flows and relations: North Korea
in the global networks and an ethnic enclave." *Political Geography* 74 (2019):
102048.

Shin, HaeRan. "The territoriality of ethnic enclaves: Dynamics of transnational practices and geopolitical relations within and beyond a Korean transnational enclave in
New Malden, London." *Annals of the American Association of Geographers* 108,
no. 3 (2018): 756–772.

Standing, Guy. "The precariat: From denizens to citizens?." *Polity* 44, no. 4 (2012):
588–608.

Standing, Guy. 2016. *The Precariat: The new dangerous class*. Bloomsbury
Academic.

Teorell, Jan. "Linking social capital to political participation: Voluntary associations
and networks of recruitment in Sweden 1." *Scandinavian Political Studies* 26, no.
1 (2003): 49–66.

Uekusa, Shinya, and Sunhee Lee. "Strategic invisibilization, hypervisibility and
empowerment among marriage-migrant women in rural Japan." *Journal of Ethnic
and Migration Studies* (2018): 1–18.

Vigh, Henrik. "Motion squared: A second look at the concept of social navigation."
Anthropological Theory 9, no. 4 (2009): 419–438.

Waite, Louise. "A place and space for a critical geography of precarity?" *Geography
Compass* 3, no. 1 (2009): 412–433.

Wall, Melissa. "Social Navigation and the Refugee Crisis: Traversing 'Archipelagos'
of Uncertainty." *Media and Communication* 7, no. 2 (2019): 300–302.

Wang, Hao, Wei Li, and Yu Deng. "Precarity among highly educated migrants:
College graduates in Beijing, China." *Urban Geography* 38, no. 10 (2017):
1497–1516.

Wee, Kellynn, Charmian Goh, and Brenda SA Yeoh. "Chutes-and-ladders: The
migration industry, conditionality, and the production of precarity among migrant
domestic workers in Singapore." *Journal of Ethnic and Migration Studies* 45, no.
14 (2019): 2672–2688.

Woon, Chih Yuan. "Precarious geopolitics and the possibilities of nonviolence."
Progress in Human Geography 38, no. 5 (2014): 654–670.

SECTION 2

Life Outside the Korean Peninsula—North Korean Defectors' Settlements

Chapter 4

Do They Get Along?

Interactions between North Korean Defectors, South Korean Migrants, and Korean Chinese Migrants in London

HaeRan Shin

This chapter[1] focuses on the political dimension of a Korean ethnic enclave, how their interactions, collaborations, and conflicts shape their community, in a suburb of London comprised of North Koreans, South Koreans, and *Joseonjok* (Korean Chinese).[2] The research discusses geopolitical perspectives[3] to explain the politics of community, space, and territory that constitute the complicated territoriality of ethnic Korean transnational migrants within their community in New Malden, London. Territory refer to both materially-bordered area and socially and psychologically-formed belongingness. Territoriality in this research is defined as the dynamics of lived experiences and discourses that constitutes the territory of migrants' belongingness either physically or mentally.

I use the concepts of translocalism and transnationalism to elaborate on their relational approaches to one another, and the concept of territoriality to outline the transformations of an ethnic enclave over time. Translocalism concerns the significance of localities in migrants' lives (Brickell and Datta, 2011), while transnationalism refers to multiple ties and interactions linking people or institutions across national borders (Katila and Wahlbeck, 2012).

Territoriality or social belongingness is formed through the affective attachment to kindred groups, connections to home societies, and cooperation with other migrant groups, as well as the temporal dynamics of ongoing negotiations over those territories. While the term "ethnic enclaves" is generally used, I prefer "transnational enclaves" to stress the multiple belongingness and connectiveness of their concentrated community. By approaching transnational enclaves as relational as well as contested spaces, this research challenges the concept of ethnic enclaves as a bounded, solitary, homogeneous, and static area, and contributes to the understanding of ethnic enclaves and inter-group relations in the destination.

This case study focuses on the post-settlement experiences of the three ethnic Korean groups in the transnational enclave in New Malden, London, the largest Koreatown in the UK. South Korean migrants started to arrive to the area in the 1970s, followed by an influx of *Joseonjok* in the late 1990s and North Korean defectors in 2004. An estimated 8,000–20,000 South Korean migrants reside in this Koreatown, the figure varying depending on the area that is being taken into account.[4] The South Korean and North Korean ethnic associations and a number of interviewees approximate there to be 4,000 South Koreans, 400 *Joseonjok*, and 400 North Koreans living in New Malden. Though the ratio of North Koreans to South Koreans (1:10–15) is low, when compared to the 1:1,083 ratio of the Los Angeles enclave, it is quite high. This relatively high concentration of North Koreans posed opportunities for regular interactions with other North Koreans, more likely than even in South Korea where the ratio was 1:1,800.

As an empirical case study, this chapter asks: How have the geopolitical relations of South Korea, China, and North Korea been reflected in the daily interactions in New Malden? How have migrants' attachment to their diverse home societies influenced life in this ethnic enclave in the UK? How do migrant groups' interactions with each other reproduce a hierarchy that reflects the geopolitical standing of their origin countries?

Based on longitudinal mixed ethnographic research, this chapter argues, first, that migrants' lives in the transnational enclave should be understood as the transnational flows of various groups and the geopolitical relations among their origin societies. The transnational flows have spanned three countries for both the both *Joseonjok* and North Koreans. Though originating the countries are different, *Joseonjok* and North Koreans travelled to the same destination countries, first to South Korea and then to the UK. Similar experiences of South Korean society familiarized them with and prepared them for those aspects of cultural and social life that had been transplanted in New Malden.

Second, the transnational enclave is being constantly reterritorialized, a process that refers to the influx of new arrivals and ideas to the territory. The reterritorialization is created through conflict between longer-settled South Korean migrants and newcomers, resolution of the conflict, and finally adaption to arrive at civil interactions at minimum. The newcomers, Joseonjok and North Koreans, are at a disadvantage in terms of legal status, linguistic abilities and economic capital. The power relations of their origin societies have infiltrated individual migrants' lives in part by means of different religious and ethnic organizations.

To demonstrate the dynamics of a transnational enclave, the rest of this chapter is organized as follows. The next section critiques previous studies on ethnic enclaves and suggests revisiting the concept in terms of geopolitical thinking. The section following discusses research methods, and addresses the reasons so many Joseonjok immigrants and North Korean defectors refuse to consent to interviews. A brief synopsis of New Malden's background is provided followed by the first finding section that discusses the transnational networks that have influenced migrants' identities and lives and become part of the landscape of the transnational enclave. The second finding section illustrates how the three Korean ethnic groups' encounters, composed of conflict and adaptation, have constituted a reterritorialized enclave. The third finding section focuses on local agencies such as ethnic and religious organizations and their role in the continued reproduction of inequalities and power relations among the three groups. The conclusion discusses the implications of a geopolitical approach to home and transnational enclaves in the geographies of migration and the future relations between South Koreans and North Koreans.

THE TERRITORIALITY OF TRANSNATIONAL ENCLAVES: GEOPOLITICAL THINKING FOR MIGRANTS' IDENTITIES AND POST-MIGRATION LIVES

The common limitation of previous literature that ethnic enclaves are either a positive or negative space is reviewed here to make an argument for the notion of 'transnational enclaves' as a preferable approach. The concept of ethnic enclaves, as a visible, articulated community, has been quite prominent in studies on urban spatiality of migrant belonging (Collins, 2011). Ethnic enclaves as a place where defectors, refugees, and migrants converge have received significant attention from both academics and policy-makers. Academic studies have largely concentrated on the distinguishing features of ethnic enclaves and effects of segregation from the mainstream of the destination society (Murdie and Ghosh, 2010). Though when compared to ghettos ethnic enclaves have been considered as relatively positively, scholars and policy-makers still struggle to decide whether ethnic enclaves should be viewed positive or harmful (Hack-Polay, 2019; Varady, 2005).

An enclave based on voluntary tenancy is generally regarded as positive especially as sources of urban variety and multiculturalism that introduce diversity to a society that may otherwise be homogenous and unique cultural experiences and possible tourist attractions (Pang and Rath, 2007). Murdie and Ghosh (2010) argue that spatial concentration does not necessarily indicate a lack of integration. The assumption that ethnicity can be reified as an ontological category is a product of viewing the enclave through an ethnic lens. Initially the ethnic lens was employed to gather information to understand the working lives of migrants (Wilson and Portes, 1980), but since then its focus has expanded to address the various issues regarding ethnic enclaves, including ethnic entrepreneurship (Wang, 2012), and ethnic churches and multiculturalism (Kurien, 2007; Portes and Shafer, 2007). In recent years, dynamic factors of ethnic enclaves (Qadeer et al., 2010) and the newer trend of ethnic suburbs (Li, 2006; Li, 2009) have garnered more attention than ever before, but the ethnic lens continues to view an ethnic enclave as a place of being, rather than one of becoming (Schiller and Çağlar, 2013). Debates on the roles of ethnic enclaves, however, have been controversial especially those from the perspectives of the destination society's that tend to distinguish migrants from the main society thereby marginalizing them.

There are those who would argue that enclaves are harmful and a threat to the social cohesion of destination societies (Peach, 2003; Varady, 2005). Yet it is the harm caused by the isolation of the migrants in this limited space (Schnell and Yoav, 2001) that has raised concerns. Many view segregation as a stricture on migrants' jobs and earnings (Xie and Gough, 2011) and the possibilities for upward mobility (Wang, 2010). The limiting effects of segregation not only restricted the first-generation migrants' but second-generation's lives (Gibson and Miller, 2010) as well. Assimilationists believed that as immigrants became assimilated[5] to their receiving country ethnic enclaves would eventually disappear (McPherson, 2010; Brubaker, 2001) and with them the issues of segregation. The arguments advocates made for assimilation were criticized as perceiving transnational flows as an intrusion on the mainstream space of the destination (Werbner, 2001) that needs to be diluted and absorbed.

Despite their different standpoints on enclaves, both perspectives on ethnic enclaves consider them as separate from the rest of the city as places of bounded territories, continuity, and solidarity (Cutler et al., 2008). This limited interpretation can be attributed to the ethnicity-based framework, the so-called ethnic lens. Until recently, migration studies have been too occupied with policy needs and political pressure for social problems (Nagel, 2009) to consider value-laden interpretations of ethnic segregation (Phillips, 2007, 2015). Since the debate on ethnic enclaves has not actively embraced geopolitical insights (Smith and Ley, 2008), "the local" remains a discernible space that is distinguished from transnational flows (Smith, 2001).

To broaden the scope of these perspectives, Collins (2011) suggests a relational-territorial approach that involves both material and mental territorialization of specific spaces in cities. I suggest the concept of transnational enclaves as not existing in a vacuum but evolving through geopolitical changes and individual migrants' continuing interactions in everyday life. To further develop this approach, this study undertakes a transnational/translocal and territorial approaches to better understand the dynamics of the transnational enclave.

A relational-territorial approach proposes a dialogue between urban geography and migration studies (Collins, 2011). This approach focuses on the power relations between people, between people and place, and between people and different places, as well as the constant negotiations over their territories. It contextualizes social relations within an enclave and then re-structures them within the process of post-migration settlement.

This approach can also explain transnationalism and territoriality. First, transnationalism perspectives have argued that transnational migrants develop multiple identities and multiple senses of belonging (Vertovec, 2009; Katila and Wahlbeck, 2012; Smith, 2005; Guarnizo et al., 2003) through engagements with two or more countries (Mazzucato, 2008). Integration and transnationalism are not so distinct as some might believe and in fact are often constitutive of complex relations that combine elements of both (Erdal and Oeppen, 2013).

Transnational practices (Waldinger, 2008) occur in multicultural settings, not necessarily in close interrelation with the majority populations of destination countries (Liu et al., 2012). While social interactions with natives can facilitate migrants' integration into society (Vervoort, 2012), previous studies have increasingly demonstrated that the greater part of interactions are with other migrants rather than with the native speaking majority (Wang et al., 2015: 2). It should not be assumed, however, that interaction among different groups of migrants will necessarily result in integration (for example, Wang et al., 2015) within the enclave. In fact, it is likely that the different migrant groups would continue to reproduce cultural boundaries and stratifications, particularly in the job market where there is a formal hierarchy of bosses and employees.

Geopolitical power relations of origin states are transformed into occupational hierarchies and social stratifications (Li, 1998) in the ethnic enterprises that function within ethnic enclaves (Wang, 2012). As Yoon (2013) demonstrates in a study in Beijing, those cases where South Koreans and Joseonjok (Korean-Chinese) have settled in the same enclave, the disparity that exists in terms of their network resources and financial capacities between their respective origin country are perpetuated in the enclave. An ethnic enclave encompasses complex, transnational relationships that, in turn, intersect in multiple ways with local labor market processes and residential developments and patterns.

Multifaceted as they are, can these enclaves be considered home? Contemporary migration patterns bring about territorially complex attachments and aspirations. Increasingly, migrants have lived in multiple countries (Bashi, 2007; Erdal, 2013; Lee, 2011; Olwig, 2007; Sperling, 2014) and maintained the reality of multiple loyalties as they formed an identity of betweenness (Potter and Phillips, 2006) that is part home country and part adopted countries. Some criticize transnationalism for the methodological nationalism that focuses on the unit of nations anyway (see Halilovich, 2011; Schiller, 2009, for example), but the transnational and the translocal are not exclusive.

Second, to capture the open, meaning-giving, relational process of theoretically space formation (Collins, 2011), I offer the concepts of territoriality to discover how dynamic relations among migrant groups and changing immigration policies reterritorialize ethnic enclaves. Due to Deleuze and Guattari's 1972 study of the process of territoriality, the concept has received further attention (see Carling, 2008; Collyer and King, 2015; Yamazaki, 2002) and initiated studies that contextualize specifics instead of the homogenous narratives of globalization that Mitchell (1997) has criticized. As reterritorialization transpires in neither a unilinear direction nor a borderless way, but in flexible and power-laden ways (Novak, 2011), a processual approach is necessary to satisfactorily discuss a place constructed from social relations.

Later discussions built on debates about territoriality and place, focusing on everyday practices and lived experiences to develop geopolitical perspectives on transnational daily places. An enclave is not only a geographically territorialized space, but also a social field (Levitt and Schiller, 2004) produced through transnational practice, contacts, materials, and religious and affective practices (Müller and Wehrhahn, 2013; Dahinden, 2009; Carling, 2008; Levitt and Schiller, 2004; Levitt, 2001). Everyday practices, lived experiences, social relations, and emotional significance shape migrants' territories that are both transnational enclave and home society.

This chapter focuses on ethnic churches (Min, 1992) and ethnic associations as transnational agencies (Ehrkamp and Nagel, 2012). The transnational agencies anchor daily life, maintaining and reproducing boundaries, as well as de-territorializing and re-territorializing boundaries. They play the role of mediators and are barometers of relations between people and place and between different migrant groups, often influencing one another (Kurien, 2007). By sharing and enhancing cultural belief, ethnic churches play a "dual role of facilitating assimilation and of its members preserving ethnicity" (Yang and Ebarough, 2001: 270). It could be the simultaneous embeddedness or the simultaneous disembeddedness in both societies, the origin and the destination (Western, 2007) that make for a situation where such institutions play two contrasting roles.

RESEARCH METHODS

Mixed ethnographic methods (Bailey et al., 2002) with particular focus on in-depth interviews and participant observation were used in the collection of information for this research. Eleven North Koreans and twelve *Joseonjok* agreed to one or more sessions for a total of thirty-one in-depth interviews. In addition, eight South Koreans who had regular contact with *Joseonjok* or North Koreans as employees, customers, or members of the same Christian groups consented to give interviews. This longitudinal study that started in 2011 and lasted until 2014 revisited the same organizations and interviewees in 2011, 2012, and 2014 to document how geopolitical shifts changed the community over time.

Interviews were conducted in Korean and all answers were usually recorded in writing, with only a few being tape-recorded. Some of the interviewees stipulated that they would consent if I listened but did not write anything down. In those cases, I committed essential content to paper as soon as I left the interview locations. Each in-depth interview lasted one to three hours, which allowed for a reasonable amount of time to share their immigration experiences. Interviews were semi-structured within a loosely structured frame of questions. North Korean and *Joseonjok* interview subjects were asked to explain their migration route and experiences; their interactions with other groups of ethnic Koreans in the community; how their lives changed over time; their social and religious activities; and their views on the development of the transnational enclave and the influence of home societies. South Koreans were asked to share their opinions on the emergence of *Joseonjok* and North Korean immigrants in the job market and describe their relationship with them as employees, customers, and members of the same community.

Convincing North Korean defectors and *Joseonjok* migrants to participate, however, required a sensitivity for their predicament. Since most North Koreans were in the UK had refugee status, their hesitation did not stem from concerns about deportation. Rather they feared that any information they disclosed might endanger the safety (Choi, 2014) of their extended families left behind in North Korea or China. Many *Joseonjok* migrants, however, were in the UK without a visa[6] and anxious about deportation. The *Joseonjok* migrants who were legal residents were still reluctant, choosing not to expose themselves to scrutiny after the Korean media had portrayed them unfairly in the UK. I was often refused interviews outright and those who did schedule interviews would quite frequently neither attend nor give notice of the cancellation. Attempts at snowball sampling, that is being introduced by acquaintances, also had only limited success. Despite assurances their privacy would be protected by a researcher's ethical commitment, their inherent distrustfulness and the knowledge that they could not be protected by law prevented greater participation.

In addition to the in-depth interviews, I also conducted participant observation, site-visits, seventy-six informal interviews, informal focus groups, and qualitative archival analysis to supplement quantitative information gathering. A total of nine occasions afforded opportunities for participant observation at a North Korean ethnic association meeting, at a North Korean church, and at Sunday ceremonies of a *Joseonjok* church. The main thoroughfare of the Koreatown was the primary location for approximately 170 hours of site-visits that focused on people involved in commerce. The informal interviews were ongoing informal interactions that could occur in ethnic restaurants and social gatherings at a sauna, churches, and coffee shops.

For analysis, I cross-checked and analyzed the results of the fieldwork in by interpreting the results of the fieldwork. The analysis focused on both the evolution of the ethnic formation of the transnational enclave and the relationship between the groups of Koreans, and how the roles that ethnic churches and ethnic associations played changed over time.

Case Background

New Malden is situated almost entirely in the Royal Borough of Kingston upon Thames and partially in the London Borough of Merton in south-west London. The community of New Malden emerged in 1846 after the railway was extended from Waterloo to the area and a community grew around the new railway station. In the intervening years the community has developed and changed and now in 2021, New Malden has the largest Korean ethnic population estimated at 20,000 and the highest number of South Koreans and North Koreans in Europe.

Once South Korea and the UK began a formal relationship in 1949,[7] a South Korean ambassador was appointed and an embassy was established for the first time in the UK in New Malden. Koreans settled in the area to be close to the embassy, but as housing prices rose, they migrated to nearby New Malden. The fact that Korean tech giant Samsung was headquartered in New Malden from the 1950s through to 2005 acted as a magnet for other Korean enterprises[8] as well as Korean migrants.

The UK, with 630 North Korean refugees, most of whom live in New Malden, has given refuge to almost half of the 1,282 North Korean refugees living outside South Korea and China. Although South Korea has the largest number of accounted-for North Korean refugees, interactions between South Koreans and North Koreans remain strictly prohibited by both governments. Since the division of the Korean peninsula in 1948, any contact by mail, telephone, or electronic communication such as e-mail, has been forbidden by the National Security Law of South Korea. Contact with North Koreans is a transgression, and as such South Koreans are expected to report it by law. The law in fact demands that South Koreans living in other countries, such as the UK, continue to comply both in avoiding North Koreans and reporting any interactions. This creates confusion as to how avoid interactions with the increasing number of North Koreans who have defected to South Korea since the late 1990s and New Malden since the early 2000s.

Joseonjok are neither North nor South Korean having crossed into China before the Korean War began, and therefore may interact freely with the peoples of both Koreas. Geopolitically speaking, however, their adopted country China had issues both nations. Though an ally, China had land disputes with North Korea, and it was 1962 before the two countries signed a treaty that designated the official border. Relations with South Korea, however, were quote strained by opposing ideologies especially during the Cold War. It was only in 1992 that a Memorandum of Understanding (MOU) between South Korea and China affected significant changes to the relationship that in many ways opened the border between the two countries. China's treaty with North Korea had little effect on *Joseonjok* migrants, but the MOU in 1992 lifted restrictions not only on South Korean trade but on *Joseonjok*'s freedom to migrate, which they did. *Joseonjok* out-migrated from their enclaves in China to more than ninety countries (Park, 2008). While the majority of *Joseonjok* migrants in New Malden lived in South Korea first, many arrived in the UK without their South Korean documents. They chose to arrive without passports or visas to purposely conceal their time in South Korea so as to qualify for the economic benefits available to them in the UK as recipients of refugee status.

While *Joseonjok* and North Koreans arrived in New Malden from different places, once there their experiences meshed as they worked for South Koreans in Korean restaurants, markets, and houses for manual labor jobs. There were approximately fifteen Korean coffee shops and restaurants on the main commercial thoroughfare through the neighborhood, and large Korean grocery markets throughout. In the last decade, these stores have hired and later been primarily run by *Joseonjok* immigrants and North Korean defectors.

This chapter now moves into its analytical sections. The following three sections analyze how the experience of the transnational enclave and "home society" structures the lives of Koreans living in New Malden.

Transnational Enclave Reterritorialized by Geopolitical Relations of Origin Societies

This study's relational and processual approaches highlight the geopolitical relations of the home societies to help illustrate how they reterritorialized the transnational enclave. Though in a new land, the origin society had a presence through news from home. South Koreans and *Joseonjok* found it especially easy to remained tied to their origin society through communication technologies, but North Koreans could not openly contact family and friends at home. North Koreans maintained their connections through illegal telephone calls (Erdal, 2013: 993) usually made in conjunction with a cash remittance sent to kin remaining in the home society. While the primary goal of remittances by North Koreans and *Joseonjok* too was to narrow the income gap that exists between the two countries,[9] this came with the additional benefit of feeling connected to their families. One North Korean explained that it is not necessarily a financial transaction but an act of connection. He illustrated his point with the example that some defectors living in London still sent remittances to family members living in South Korea even though they did not need the money. Many *Joseonjok* interviewees had no families left in China because they had all migrated to South Korea.

While they missed their families, North Koreans and *Joseonjok* seldom sought to replicate lifestyles characteristic of their origin countries. As stated, *Joseonjok* and North Koreans in this study had formerly lived in South Korea for at minimum three and up to ten years. For these North Koreans and *Joseonjok*, the reterritorialization of New Malden began in South Korea and cultural assimilation there. Inevitably their accent, fashion, and manner of speaking had come to resemble those of South Koreans to some degree. Although the three groups share a language, over the almost seventy years of separation and longer in the case of *Joseonjok* migrants changes in vocabulary have created noticeable differences in speech. Though the basics of Korean are unchanged, North Koreans adapted to South Korea more easily than *Joseonjok* who grew in China. During that time, they underwent a mix of emotional experiences as they became accustomed to South Koreans' society and lifestyle, coming to appreciate the culture and developing acceptance of South Koreans. These experiences in South Korea, which some *Joseonjok* and North Korean interviewees had come to think of as their second home, prepared them for South Koreans' social order in New Malden's Koreatown.

One of the main reasons the majority of North Korean defectors left South Korea was to move their children to a less discriminatory environment. Despite a willingness to adjust, many North Korean defectors felt the effort was not reciprocated and were concerned that the constant discrimination would harm their children. Holding South Korea's education system up as a benchmark, North Korean defectors searched for countries with comparable education systems and preferably English-speaking. While still in in South Korea, North Korean defectors witnessed the zealous pursuit of education and the advantages of the popular but expensive private tutoring sessions. While they could not afford private lessons in South Korea, in the UK the financial and cultural disparity between North and South Koreans was diminished and North Koreans could finally offer their children the same or similar advantages.

A North Korean man who has a wife and two children in London disclosed that his wife closely observed what South Korean mothers did to benchmark her children's education against South Korean children's. He said,

> My wife is an advanced mum like South Korean mums. She's arranged so much private tutoring for our children. She was hanging around with South Korean mums and started teaching our children golf, swimming, English, ballet, and so on.

The suggestion that his wife is "advanced" refers to her adoption of South Korean lifestyles. Mimicking South Korean behaviors included not only the observable and quantifiable ones but also ones North Koreans imagined were true of South Korean life. Since they had experienced only a small part of South Korean society, some pursuits and activities they attributed to South Koreans were based on the soap operas and sitcoms they saw on TV rather than reality.

Another interviewee noted that the effort being expended on pursuing the ideals of their second homeland has detracted from adaptation to British society in terms of language and social involvement. This North Korean interviewee in her 40s compared her family's life in Bradford to their life in New Malden as an example of how the origin society, even a secondary one, still influences life in the enclave. She explained that in Bradford there were only a few Koreans, and as a result, she and her family actively engaged with English community members, playgroups for her children, and English churches. She admitted that her English improved significantly while she attended college and interacted with people in the context of community activities organized in Bradford. However, since moving to New Malden, her husband has become involved in a North Korean association and her family has been surrounded by South Koreans and other North Koreans. Since this move, they have been socially and culturally distant from the general population, and she feels as if she has been absorbed by Korean society. While the transnational enclave in part makes for a multicultural UK (Nagel, 2009), through ties to origin societies and assimilation to the second home, the

Koreans of New Malden seemed to view UK society at large as external to their own living circumstances.

Encounters at Work and the Reterritorialization of the Community

Three ethnically similar Korean groups have come to live in enclaved circumstances in a segment of space that is discrete from the host society. South Koreans were the earliest migrants and established businesses that profited from the labor of those North Koreans and *Joseonjok* who struggled to adjust to their new home due to language barriers and cultural differences. The transnational enclave to some degree formed around the interdependence of South Korean businesses owners and North Korean and *Joseonjok* employees in the Korean job market in London. Certain businesses such as Korean restaurants that were frequented primarily by North Koreans, South Koreans, and *Joseonjok* in fact needed no other than Korean speakers as neither the customers nor the owners generally spoke English fluently. The North Korean defectors and *Joseonjok* immigrants were also a source of cheap labor for domestic jobs such as babysitting, cooking, house cleaning, as well as construction (painting, floor-building, and assorted kinds of assembly).

Some of these jobs had been previously held by South Korean students studying in the UK, but new restrictions on student visas significantly altered the work relations in New Malden. As stricter laws that limited non-EU residents from working in the UK were introduced (McGregor, 2008) in 2014, foreign students studying English in the UK who once were permitted to work up to twenty hours a week were suddenly ineligible to work. Only full-time students were still allowed to work according to the new law, but the allotted hours had been reduced by half to ten hours. The same year changes to student visas were legislated, the UK government also reduced benefits for refugees from 1,350 pounds sterling to 500 per month. The same year availability of South Korean students to work in Korean-owned business in the UK plunged, North Koreans' need to work to make up for the financial shortfall of reduced benefits rose. North Koreans and *Joseonjok* filled the vacancies left by students until eventually there was only one Korean restaurant left that hired only South Koreans. These revisions in 2014 to two areas that directly impacted many Koreans in the UK combined to strengthened the encounters of North and South Koreans in New Malden.

The inter-reliant nature of the transnational enclave that creates relationships built on cooperation is also a source of conflict. Although South Korean employers needed North Korean and *Joseonjok* workers, a hierarchical employer-employee relationship exists partly influenced by Confucianism and a military culture in South Korea. *Joseonjok* and North Koreans admitted that they struggled to be the compliant and ceaselessly hardworking employees their South Korean bosses demanded. One North Korean interviewee described South Koreans as authoritarian and exploitative:

> South Korean bosses are very good at exploiting workers as much as possible, breaking the UK labor laws and taking advantage of North Korean and *Joseonjok* workers' vulnerable positions.

As an example of the UK labor laws being broken, this interviewee told of a grocery market that paid North Korean workers with store vouchers instead of money. The workers could either use their vouchers to buy food for in the store or attempt to sell them to other people for cash or trade them. Perhaps expecting that North Koreans would be unfamiliar with the labor laws or that the language barrier would stop them from complaining to proper authorities, this South Korean market took advantage of their vulnerability and limited English.

One South Korean employer (male, 50s) who had six to seven years of experience with *Joseonjok* and North Korean workers declared that neither North Korean nor *Joseonjok* workers had any idea how to operate in a capitalist society. Becoming agitated by the topic, he became strident as he stated that they had a poor work ethic and were inefficient, as well as unwilling to learn or adapt. He admitted that he often resorted to yelling, claiming that was the only way to motivate *Joseonjok* and North Korean employees to work. Despite pronouncing them as unreliable, quick to switch jobs without notice or simply disappear, he explained that South Koreans businesses were short of labor and had no other choice but to hire them due to the new regulations. It was also noticeable that South Koreans' criticisms of *Joseonjok* and North Koreans were quite like how *Joseonjok* described North Koreans.

As time went on, changes in the economic and geopolitical power relations of the origin countries have influenced inter-group hierarchies in the transnational enclave. Since the 1990s, China has emerged as a global economic and political power, and the financial reasons *Joseonjok* once had for working in the UK are no longer quite so relevant. As a result, a number of *Joseonjok* have left the UK and New Malden and returned to China or South Korea. North Korea too has started to receive attention in the UK and globally, creating political tension through nuclear weapons testing. Though their origin country's activities have raised awareness of North Koreans' existence, that was not the reason for the changed dynamics in the transnational enclave. It was the North Korean defectors themselves who affected change. As they settled down and became as one interviewee described as "advanced," South Korean migrants admitted that they felt threatened by North Koreans "catching up" to South Koreans. The hierarchy was no longer quite so clear, and this was very likely to bring about a new phase of de-territorialization and reterritorialization. In the end, the UK through changing regulations regarding visas and refugee status mediated the national hierarchies and the political relations between the three nationalities involved, as well as their employment relations.

Continued Reproduction of Hierarchy And Differences

The convergence of the increasing encounters and experiences with each other had the effect of binding the similar yet disparate groups. However, despite or possibly because of the plentiful interactions that have taken place within the transnational enclave, national sedimentation based on power relations among the three groups have been reproduced rather than reduced. Their status based on the relationship between the current UK environment (Sealey, 2016) and their home state also significantly influenced their positions in the enclave as well as in wider UK society. Even ethnic churches and ethnic organizations have played a role in reinforcing each group's position in the enclave through relations with other groups.

This section focuses on the role the two ethnic institutions of the church that reflected the hierarchy and ethnic associations that formed from a group's different motivations for being in New Malden. First, is an examination of how the role the geopolitical context of the origin societies played in the formation of churches and how this reproduced the hierarchical arrangement of the enclave. Since North Korea prohibits religion and only allows government-approved organizations, the North Koreans have neither formed a church nor an organization nor voted before. As people who had broken the laws of their country by defecting, they could not expect the North Korean consulate in the UK to help them form a church. *Joseonjok* as an in-between population (Shin, 2021) essentially without a homeland could not apply to the South Korean embassy or from the Chinese for support. Since North Koreans and *Joseonjok* had little to no experience in establishing a church, they adopted the South Korean models to form their own churches.

There were approximately eighty South Korean Christian churches in London, and most of them were concentrated in New Malden.[10] However, during my fieldwork, there was one North Korean church and one *Joseonjok* church. The North Korean and *Joseonjok* churches without clergy of their own had to rely on South Korean pastors to give sermons and other South Koreans to help pastors with Sunday rituals. Dependence on South Korean models, clergy and citizens re-produced the hierarchy that placed South Koreans in leadership roles in the enclave. Both churches relied on South Koreans to get space. They rented the same building, a part (the second hall) of a facility used primarily as a Taekwondo studio. The *Joseonjok* church had a ceremony in the morning, and the North Korean church in the afternoon, on Sundays.

Although North Korean defectors had expended effort to form their own church, some wondered whether they would become devoted Christians. Regarding this point, a South Korean leader of the North Korean church pointed out that though religion was illegal in North Korea, the format of Christianity is familiar to North Koreans. One interview subject stated if Kim Il Sung, their national hero, were put in place of God, the Juchesasang[11] would resemble the Christian doctrine. North Koreans were surprised to realize that the ten behavioral rules of North Korea were loosely based on the Ten Commandments. Many were disturbed, though, by the Christian church rituals and gatherings that were reminiscent of the harsher forced gatherings and public confession North Koreans had been subjected to in their homeland. Some North Koreans refused to join the church for this reason alone, saying that escaping from those rituals was what they wanted to gain out of their defection.

Though the South Koreans dominated through their model, their religious leaders, and sheer number of believers, these churches played an important role in the transnational enclave by providing informational, institutional, and mental support to transnational migrants' everyday lives (Kurien, 2007; Levitt, 2003; Sheringham, 2010; Vásquez and Knott, 2014). Participant observation of the *Joseonjok* church and the North Korean church on Sundays found that the congregation usually included the pastors, his or her spouse, and eleven to twenty North Koreans (more women than men), across various age groups. During the ceremony, the pastors emphasized the importance of the whole Korean community including South Korea, North Korea, and *Joseonjok*. After the ceremony, an intimate gathering for tea followed afterwards was to say that they were "like a family." Through such process, those religious leaders reinforced the hierarchy in the enclave.

Second, ethnic association activities reflected the differences in each group's connection to New Malden. Some North Koreans expressed quite strong attachments to New Malden, equating the transnational enclave to an affective country. One North Korean interviewee put it as such:

> South Koreans might return to their country. *Joseonjok* came here for money and will go back eventually. We [North Koreans] cannot go back. We will take care of New Malden.

In acknowledging the unlikelihood of a return to North Korea, this interviewee explained that their community was now in essence their country. It was also a place of many firsts for North Koreans, he added, such as voting in their first election for the chair of their association. Though they started this

group effort to remember their roots and empower themselves, as this interviewee implied, North Koreans are learning democracy from South Koreans
in terms of organizing associations. This indicates a willingness to assimilate
to broader Korean ethnic society of the enclave and a commitment to stay.

In contrast, the *Joseonjok* association focused on mediating a conflict with
South Korean bosses. In general, however, the association suffered with the
lack of financial resources and consistent participation as members were so
busy to survive that they lacked time and interest in bonding. Compared to
North and South Koreans, Joseonjok's fragile status made them only focus on
making money and going back as soon as possible. As time went on, conflicts
between South Korean bosses and *Joseonjok* workers became less about fair
wages or untenable conditions and more about personal discomfort or cultural
differences such as speaking manners, problems that have become systemic
and are now harder to resolve.

Though the origin country continued to have some form of influence on the
hierarchy and relations in the transnational enclave, there was one significant
difference. In London, South Koreans were also migrants. One North Korean
interviewee, who had lived in South Korea for some time, compared his
experiences interacting with and working for South Koreans in South Korea
with those in the UK:

> It's different. In South Korea, there was an attitude more of looking down
> on North Koreans. Here [in the UK], South Koreans are friendlier [to
> North Koreans].

He continued,

> But, there is always a distance with South Koreans anyway. I guess it is because
> there are a lot of cultural and ideological differences. I've become quite close to
> some South Koreans, but the distance still exists.

Even as they learned to live with each other, South Koreans in leadership
roles in North Korean and *Joseonjok* churches reinforce the hierarchy is
prevalent in workplaces and the geopolitics of the origin countries. In the
ethnic associations, however, North Koreans and South Koreans motivations
come quite close. Despite a growing closeness, the awareness that differences
exist still lingered.

The findings of this chapter demonstrate that transnational practices and
geopolitical relationships beyond transnational enclaves have a bearing on
the territorialized and relational space of migrant communities. First, the
geopolitical hierarchy and discord among North Korean, *Joseonjok*, and
South Korean migrants that reflect the origin societies has contributed to

the reterritorialization of the ethnic enclave of transnational migrants. The origin society or "the home society" in the case of North Korean defectors and *Joseonjok* migrants included all the territories before arrival in the destination society, which in this circumstance was South Korea. Second, the transnational enclave was a relational place where the three ethnic Korean groups have concentrated on adjustment to some degree to one another rather than to UK society. Third, hierarchies have in some ways been constructed around the geopolitics of their origin countries but as power relations among their original countries shift so too are the power relations within the enclave. Their adaptation process, not only personal conflicts but also institutional challenges, presage what would likely unfold in a future where Korea is reunified or in the context of increasing networks between Korea and China.

In exploring the impact of geopolitical relations on migrant communities, this research contributes to the dialogue on the relationship between the political and the personal in transnational enclaves. The "imagined communities" (Anderson, 1983) of transnational migrants are territorialized and then reterritorialized as even migrants' memories and emotions re-construct the transnational enclave. Examining migrants' affective space offers insight to the complicated ways the emotionally unsettling processes of migration and resettlement lead to assimilation and connection to "home." In cases of serial migration, affective spaces (Faria, 2014b; Conradson and McKay, 2007; Walsh, 2012; Ho, 2009) and home (2005, and Blunt and Bonnerjee, 2013) can be expanded to encompass migrants' lived spaces and affectionate places, or simply put their physical and mental ones.

NOTES

1. This chapter is based on the previously published article, Shin, HaeRan. "The territoriality of ethnic enclaves: dynamics of transnational practices and geopolitical relations within and beyond a Korean transnational enclave in New Malden, London." Annals of the American Association of Geographers 108, no. 3 (2018): 756–772.

2. *Joseonjok* (or Chaoxianzu or Chosŏnjok. 朝鮮族 in Chinese and 조선족 in Korean) refers to ethnic Koreans whose ancestors migrated to China in the 1880s up until the 1950s to escape Japanese colonisation and extreme deprivation. Approximately 70 percent of the *Joseonjok* working population in Yanbian, the largest ethnic enclave of *Joseonjok* in China, has out-migrated within the last ten years (Park, 2008).

3. The geopolitical perspective is based on the world statecraft of critical geopolitics that influences how individuals process their own ideas of places and politics,

which is distinguished from classical geopolitics that focuses on the impact of states, regions, and resources on international relations.

4. If the Koreatown includes the Kingston area, 12 percent of the total population is South Korean (*Observer*, 10 April 2011). One newspaper says that upwards of 10,000 out of a total of 29,000 people who live in New Malden are Korean (Fischer, 2015).

5. Assimilation refers to a migrants' active adoption of the destination society's language and daily culture so that they will eventually begin to behave like the mainstream.

6. Migration for work between China and the UK is not allowed, but emigration from China has increasingly been facilitated by various kinds of specialist agencies (Biao, 2006). A global network of brokers plays an important role in migration as they direct flows of people and resources beyond the scope of what is legally permitted.

7. http://www.mofa.go.kr/ENG/countries/europe/countries/20070823/1_24592.jsp?menu=m_30_40 Accessed on 6 October 2015.

8. The importance of a Korean ethnic enterprise as an anchor for small businesses and Korean churches has been well-noted in cases of other cities, including Los Angeles (Light and Bonacich, 1991; Ebaugh and Chafetz, 2000).

9. Snakeheads consist of networks among South Koreans, *Joseonjok*, Han people who live in China, and North Koreans who have lived in China and moved to South Korea. http://daily.hankooki.com/lpage/society/201411/dh20141115112833137780.htm, accessed on 6 Aug 2015.

10. There are about one hundred South Korean churches in the UK http://www.newyorkilbo.com/sub_read.html?uid=30652, accessed on 23 June 2015.

11. *Juchesasang* refers to the official political ideology of North Korea.

REFERENCES

Agnew, John. "The territorial trap: the geographical assumptions of international relations theory." *Review of international political economy* 1, no. 1 (1994): 53–80.

Anderson, Benedict. 1983. *Imagined communities: Reflections on the origin and spread of nationalism*. Verso Books.

Bailey, Adrian J., Richard A. Wright, Alison Mountz, and Ines M. Miyares. "(Re)producing Salvadoran transnational geographies." *Annals of the Association of American Geographers* 92, (2002): 125–144.

Barabantseva, Elena. "Seeing beyond an 'ethnic enclave': the time/space of Manchester Chinatown." *Identities* 23, no. 1 (2016): 99–115.

Bashi, Vilna, ed. 2007. *Survival of the knitted: Immigrant social networks in a stratified world*. Redwood City: Stanford University Press.

Biao, Xiang. "A sending country perspective." *The Chinese Overseas* 4 (2006): 352.

Blunt, Alison. "Cultural geography: cultural geographies of home." *Progress in human geography* 29, no. 4 (2005): 505–515.

Blunt, Alison, and Bonnerjee, Jonnerjee. "Home, city and diaspora: Anglo–Indian and Chinese attachments to Calcutta." *Global networks* 13, no. 2 (2013): 220–240.

Brickell, Katherine, and Ayona Datta, eds. 2011. *Translocal geographies*. Ashgate Publishing, Ltd.

Brubaker, Rogers. "The return of assimilation? Changing perspectives on immigration and its sequels in France, Germany, and the United States." *Ethnic and Racial Studies* 24, no. 4 (2001): 531–548.

Carling, Jørgen. "The human dynamics of migrant transnationalism." *Ethnic and racial studies* 31, no. 8 (2008): 1452–1477.

Choi, Eunyoung. "North Korean women's narratives of migration: Challenging hegemonic discourses of trafficking and geopolitics." *Annals of the Association of American Geographers* 104, no. 2 (2014): 271–279.

Collins, Francis Leo. "Transnational mobilities and urban spatialities: Notes from the Asia-Pacific." *Progress in Human Geography* 36, no. 3 (2012): 316–335.

Collyer, Michael, and Russell King. "Producing transnational space: International migration and the extra-territorial reach of state power." *Progress in Human Geography* 39, no. 2(2015): 185–204.

Conradson, David, and McKay, Deirdre. "Translocal subjectivities: Mobility, connection, emotion." *Mobilities* 2, no. 2 (2007): 167–174.

Cutler, David M., Edward L. Glaeser, and Jacob L. Vigdor, "When are ghettos bad? Lessons from immigrant segregation in the United States." *Journal of Urban Economics* 63, no. 3 (2008): 759–774.

Darling, Jonathan. "A city of sanctuary: the relational re-imagining of Sheffield's asylum politics." *Transactions of the Institute of British Geographers* 35, no. 1 (2010): 125–140.

Deleuze, Gilles, and Félix Guattari. 1972. *Anti-Oedipus*. Trans. Hurley, Robert, Mark Seem, and Helen R. Lane. 1983. Minneapolis: Minnesota UP.

Ebaugh, Helen Rose, and Janet Slatzman Chafetz. "Structural adaptations in immigrant congregations." *Sociology of Religion* 61, no.2 (2000):135–153.

Ehrkamp, Patricia, and Caroline Nagel. "Immigration, places of worship and the politics of citizenship in the US South." *Transactions of the Institute of British Geographers* 37, no. 4 (2012): 624–638.

Erdal, Marta Bivand. "Migrant transnationalism and multi-layered integration: Norwegian-Pakistani migrants' own reflections." *Journal of Ethnic and Migration Studies* 39, no.6 (2013):983–999.

Erdal, Marta Bivand, and Ceri Oeppen. "Migrant balancing acts: Understanding the interactions between integration and transnationalism." *Journal of Ethnic and Migration Studies* 39, no. 6 (2013):867–884.

Faria, Caroline. "'I want my children to know Sudan': Narrating the long-distance intimacies of diasporic politics." *Annals of the Association of American Geographers* 104, no. 5 (2014a): 1052–1067.

Faria, Caroline. "Styling the nation: Fear and desire in the South Sudanese beauty trade." *Transactions of the Institute of British Geographers* 39, no. 2 (2014b): 318–330.

Fischer, Paul. 2015. "Korean republic of New Malden." *The Independent*, February 22, 2015. http://www.independent.co.uk/news/uk/home-news/

the-korean-republic-of-new-malden-how-surrey-became-home-to-the-70-year-old-conflict-10063055.html (accessed 20 Dec 2015)

Gibson, Chris L., and Holly V. Miller. "Crime and victimization among Hispanic adolescents: A multilevel longitudinal study of acculturation and segmented assimilation." *A Final Report for the WEB Du Bois Fellowship Submitted to the National Institute of Justice.* Washington: Department of Justice (2010).

Guarnizo, Luis Eduardo, Alejandro Portes, and William Haller. "Assimilation and transnationalism: Determinants of transnational political action among contemporary migrants." *American Journal of Sociology* 108, no. 6 (2003): 1211–1248.

Hack-Polay, Dieu. "Migrant enclaves: Disempowering economic ghettos or sanctuaries of opportunities for migrants?" *Journal of Enterprising Communities: People and Places in the Global Economy* (2019).

Halilovich, Hariz. 2011. "(Per)forming 'trans-local' homes: Bosnian diaspora in Australia." In *The Bosnian diaspora: Integration in transnational communities,* edited by Marko Valenta and Sabrina Ramet, 63–81. Surrey: Ashgate Publishing Limited.

Ho, Elaine Lynn-Ee. "Constituting citizenship through the emotions: Singaporean transmigrants in London." *Annals of the Association of American Geographers* 99, no. 4 (2009): 788–804.

Katila, Saija, and Östen Wahlbeck. "The role of (transnational) social capital in the start-up processes of immigrant businesses: The case of Chinese and Turkish restaurant businesses in Finland." *International Small Business Journal* 30, no. 3 (2012): 294–309.

Kurien, Prema A. "Who speaks for Indian Americans? Religion, ethnicity, and political formation." *American Quarterly* 59, no. 3 (2007): 759–783.

Lee, Helen. "Rethinking transnationalism through the second generation." *The Australian Journal of Anthropology* 22, no. 3 (2011): 295–313.

Levitt, Peggy. and Nina Glick Schiller. "Conceptualizing simultaneity: A transnational social field perspective on society." *International Migration Review* 38, no. 3 (2004): 1002–39.

Levitt, Peggy. ed. 2001. *The transnational villagers.* Berkeley: University of California Press.

Levitt, Peggy. "'You know, Abraham was really the first immigrant': Religion and transnational migration." *International Migration Review* 37, no. 3 (2003): 847–873.

Li, Wei. "Anatomy of a new ethnic settlement: The Chinese ethnoburb in Los Angeles." *Urban Studies* 35, no. 3 (1998): 479–501.

Li, Wei. 2006. *From urban enclave to ethnic suburb: New Asian communities in Pacific Rim countries.* University of Hawaii Press.

Light, Ivan, and Edna Bonacich. 1991. *Immigrant entrepreneurs: Koreans in Los Angeles, 1965–1982.* Los Angeles: University of California Press.

Liu, Ye, Zhigang Li, and Werner Breitung. "The social networks of new-generation migrants in China's urbanized villages: A case study of Guangzhou." *Habitat International* 36, no. 1 (2012): 192–200.

Massey, Doreen. 1991. A global sense of place. *Marxism Today* June: 25–29.

Mazzucato, Valentina. "The double engagement: Transnationalism and integration: Ghanaian migrants' lives between Ghana and the Netherlands." *Journal of Ethnic and Migration Studies* 34, no. 2 (2008): 199–216.

McGregor, JoAnn. "Abject spaces, transnational calculations: Zimbabweans in Britain navigating work, class and the law." *Transactions of the Institute of British Geographers* 33, no. 4 (2008): 466–482.

McPherson, Melinda. "'I integrate, therefore I am': Contesting the normalizing discourse of integrationism through conversations with refugee women." *Journal of Refugee Studies* 23, no. 4 (2010): 546–570.

Min, Pyong Gap. "The structure and social functions of Korean immigrant churches in the United States." *International Migration Review* 26, no. 4 (1992): 1370–1394.

Mitchell, Katharyne. "Transnational discourse: bringing geography back in." *Antipode* 29, no. 2 (1997): 101–114.

Murdie, Robert, and Sutama Ghosh. "Does spatial concentration always mean a lack of integration? Exploring ethnic concentration and integration in Toronto." *The Asia-Pacific Journal,* 9, no. 22 (2010): 1–30.

Nagel, Caroline R. "Rethinking geographies of assimilation." *The Professional Geographer* 61, no. 3 (2009): 400–407.

Novak, Paolo. "The flexible territoriality of borders." *Geopolitics* 16, no. 4 (2011): 741–767.

Olwig, Karen Fog, ed. 2007. *Caribbean journeys: An ethnography of migration and home in three family networks.* Durham: Duke University Press.

Pang, Ching Lin, and Jan Rath. 2007. "The force of regulation in the land of the free: The persistence of Chinatown, Washington DC as a symbolic ethnic enclave." In *The sociology of entrepreneurship,* edited by Martin Ruef and Michael Lounsbury, 191–216. Bingley, UK: Emerald Group Publishing.

Piao, Gang-Xing. 2008. *Joseonjok's international migration and social change* [*Segeowha Sidae Joongkook Joseonjok-uei Chogukjeok eedong-gwa Sahwae Byunhwa*]. Korean Studies Information Co. Ltd.

Peach, Ceri. 2003. "The ghetto and the ethnic enclave." In *Desegregating the city,* edited by David P. Vardy, 31–48. SUNY Press.

Phillips, Deborah. "Ethnic and racial segregation: a critical perspective." *Geography Compass* 1, no. 5 (2007): 1138–1159.

Phillips, Deborah. "Claiming spaces: British Muslim negotiations of urban citizenship in an era of new migration." *Transactions of the Institute of British Geographers* 40, no. 1 (2015): 62–74.

Portes, Alejandro, and Steven Shafer. 2007. "Revisiting the enclave hypothesis: Miami twenty-five years later." In *The sociology of entrepreneurship,* edited by Martin Ruef and Michael Lounsbury, 157–190. Emerald Group Publishing Limited.

Potter, Robert B., and Joan Phillips. "'Mad dogs and transnational migrants?' Bajan-Brit second-generation migrants and accusations of madness." *Annals of the Association of American Geographers* 96, no. 3 (2006): 586–600.

Qadeer, Mohammad, Sandeep K. Agrawal, and Alexander Lovell. "Evolution of ethnic enclaves in the Toronto Metropolitan Area, 2001–2006." *Journal of*

International Migration and Integration/Revue de l'integration et de la migration internationale 11, no. 3 (2010): 315–339.

Schiller, Nina Glick. 2009. *A global perspective on transnational migration: Theorizing migration without methodological nationalism.* Centre on Migration, Policy and Society.

Schiller, Nina Glick, and Ayse Çağlar. "Locating migrant pathways of economic emplacement: Thinking beyond the ethnic lens." *Ethnicities* 13, no. 4 (2013): 494–514.

Schnell, Izhak, and Benjamini Yoav. "The sociospatial isolation of agents in everyday life spaces as an aspect of segregation." *Annals of the Association of American Geographers* 91, no. 4 (2001): 622–636.

Sealey, Clive. "Wither Multiculturalism? An Analysis of the Impact on Welfare Practice and Theory of Policy Responses to an Increasingly Multicultural Society in the UK." *Revista de Asistenta Sociala* 1 (2016): 11–26.

Sheringham, Olivia. "Creating 'alternative geographies': religion, transnationalism and everyday life." *Geography Compass* 4, no. 11 (2010): 1678–1694.

Shin, HaeRan. "The Precarity of Strategic Navigation of Choso˘njok Migrants in South Korea." *European Journal of Korean Studies,* 20, no. 2 (2021): 7–35.

Smith, Michael Peter. 2001. *Transnational Urbanism: Locating Globalization.* Malden, MA: Blackwell.

Smith, Robert. ed. 2006. *Mexican New York: Transnational lives of new immigrants.* Oakland: University of California Press.

Smith, Heather, and David Ley. "Even in Canada? The Multiscalar Construction and Experience of Concentrated Immigrant Poverty in Gateway Cities." *Annals of the Association of American Geographers* 98, no. 3 (2008): 686–713.

Sperling, Jessica. "Conceptualising 'inter-destination transnationalism': The presence and implication of coethnic ties between destination societies." *Journal of Ethnic and Migration Studies* 40, no. 7 (2014): 1097–1115.

Varady, David P., ed. 2005. *Desegregating the city: ghettos, enclaves, and inequality.* SUNY Press.

Vásquez, Manuel A., and Kim Knott. "Three dimensions of religious place making in diaspora." *Global Networks* 14, no. 3 (2014): 326–347.

Vertovec, Steven. 2009. *Transnationalism.* London: Routledge.

Vervoort, Miranda. "Ethnic concentration in the neighbourhood and ethnic minorities' social integration: Weak and strong social ties examined." *Urban Studies* 49, no.4 (2012): 897–915.

Waldinger, Roger. "Between 'here' and 'there': Immigrant cross-border activities and loyalties." *International Migration Review* 42, no. 1 (2008): 3–29.

Walsh, Katie. "Emotion and migration: British transnationals in Dubai." *Environment and Planning D: Society and Space* 30, no. 1 (2012): 43–59.

Wang, Qingfang. "How does geography matter in the ethnic labor market segmentation process? A case study of Chinese immigrants in the San Francisco CMSA." *Annals of the Association of American Geographers* 100, no. 1 (2010): 182–201.

Wang, Qingfang. "Ethnic Entrepreneurship Studies in Geography: A Review." *Geography Compass* 6, no. 4 (2012): 227–240.

Wang, Zheng, Fangzhu Zhang, and Fulong Wu. "Intergroup neighbouring in urban China: Implications for the social integration of migrants." *Urban Studies* 53, no. 4 (2016): 651–668.

Werbner, Pnina. "Metaphors of spatiality and networks in the plural city: A critique of the ethnic enclave economy debate." *Sociology* 35, no. 3 (2001): 671–693.

Western, John. "Neighbors or strangers? Binational and transnational identities in Strasbourg." *Annals of the Association of American Geographers* 97, no. 1 (2007): 158–181.

Xie, Yu, and Margaret Gough. "Ethnic enclaves and the earnings of immigrants." *Demography* 48, no. 4 (2011): 1293–1315.

Yamazaki, Takashi. "Is Japan leaking? Globalisation, reterritorialisation and identity in the Asia-Pacific context." *Geopolitics* 7, no. 1 (2002): 165–192.

Yang, Fenggang, and Helen Rose Ebarough. "Transformations in new immigrant religions and their global implications." *American Sociological Review* (2001): 269–288.

Yeoh, Brenda SA., Shirlena Huang, and Theodora Lam. "Transnationalizing the 'Asian' family: imaginaries, intimacies and strategic intents." *Global Networks* 5 (2005): 307–315.

Yoon, Sharon. J. "Mobilizing ethnic resources in the transnational enclave: Ethnic solidarity as a mechanism for mobility in the Korean church in Beijing." *International Journal of Sociology* 43, no.3 (2013): 29–54.

Chapter 5

Communication of North Korean Defector Families through Transnational Migration

Heuijeong Kim

By March 2021, the number of North Korean defectors to have entered South Korea had reached 33,523 (Ministry of Unification 2021). Due to this increasing number, not only have North Koreans' histories as well as their motives for defecting multiplied but also the paths they choose to take after settling in South Korea. One of the paths that has been drawing attention is the phenomenon of North Korean defectors who even after having established a life in the South leave for a third country. As of 2017, 746 North Korean defectors had left South Korea to resettle in any of the twenty-five other destination countries that accept North Korean refugees. Once they arrive in the new country, North Korean defectors apply for refugee status in order to obtain permanent residency and eventually citizenship. According to the United Nations High Commissioner for Refugees (UNHCR 2018), 1,422 North Korean defectors have been recognized as refugees with an additional 533 whose refugee applications are pending, which amounts to 1,995 North Korean defectors.

Migration to a new environment is a life-changing event that inevitably affects the growth and development of family members. Relocating to a foreign country is a stressful time as family members struggle to learn different languages and adapt to different cultures and social systems. How well family members process and adjust to the new environment is closely related to how they communicate with one another. A family that communicates well can alleviate at least some of this stress by providing each other with emotional support that offers a psychological sense of safety. If, however, communication among family members is inhibited for whatever reason, it may increase the psychological strain of migration and negatively impact their adaptation to the new destination. Some defectors upon arriving in the destination country will immediately communicate with family members left behind to discuss plans for their defections or a reunion later. Those defectors who escape alone, however, without family support and help, may become completely disconnected and isolated from the rest of family after their resettlement.

Reestablishing communication with family members in North Korea can be challenging since transnational migration or the accepted movement of people across international borders is not how North Korean defectors cross borders. Even after they have migrated to a third country, North Korean defectors limit their communication with people outside their immediate circle, fearing their status as stateless persons might become known and reported, leading to deportation. Considering that they are defectors and refugees, the uniqueness of their situation, as well as the legality of it, distinguishes them from ordinary transnational migrants in the purpose, method, and process of their migration. North Koreans defectors' initial move at least cannot be described as based on economic logic and strategic choices made for the family that characterizes neoclassical migration (Son and Kim 2017). Families planning international migration generally discuss the economic or strategic reasons for relocation amongst themselves before making the decision to move. The fact that North Korean defectors escaping from North Korea would need to practice secrecy often meant that other family members would not be included in the decision-making.

North Korean defectors' restrained family communication before, during and even after the relocation process is closely related to their social and education systems in the North. A social system called "ho-sahng-vi-pahn," meaning reciprocal criticism, is a daily routine North Korea's citizens practice to check and control other (Lee et al. 2007) family members, neighbors and coworkers. Reminded daily by these checks, North Koreans hesitate to share their political grievances, suspicions, or plans for defecting even with those family members they believe could be trusted not to report them. Due to socio-cultural characteristics taught in schools at the earliest age, this engrained distrust penetrates deeply into the North Korean residents and their society. In the North, their ideology begins in early childhood education and informs residents that "soo-ryoung," the Leader, offers much more love than one's own parents (Kim and Kim 2020). To defect from North Korea, therefore, is a betrayal of "soo-ryoung." It can negatively affect the family left behind, and further cause the collapse of families.

In cases where a family member is known for their strong communist ideology, the possibility exists that if they should hear about a plan to defect that they would oppose the family's escape or report it to the state. Those North Koreans intending to defect must continue to act as they always would and communicate as little as possible about the plan and method of migration to family members to avoid discovery. Most defections that involve a family are kept secret from children and sometimes even spouses right until the last moment. To ensure that family members behave as normally as possible before crossing the borders they are told, "We are going to visit your auntie's home," or "I will take you to see your mom." The time for the defection is decided by the broker's schedule and the ongoing situation in the North. For example, if military controls have increased to stop people crossing into China, the broker might choose to postpone until restrictions ease again.

Arriving safely in China does not mean, however, that the ordeal is over. In some cases, unscrupulous brokers sell North Korean women to Chinese men in a phenomenon known as "bride-buying." In other instances, North Korean women accept the situation because they have no way to survive. In the event that these North Korean women married Chinese men decide to escape, they would not communicate plans to leave for South Korea for fear of being stopped. When the time comes to leave, North Korean brides often defect from China "as if fleeing," much like their flight from North Korea. A small number of the defector women who are on good terms with their Chinese families leave word that they intend to return to take their children to South Korea for resettlement. Those mothers who attempt to leave China with children must be especially careful to conceal the escape from their Chinese husbands and only tell their children what is absolutely necessary until they reach safety (Kim 2018). Whether traveling through China as refugees or escaping from their second family, communication amongst family members in the process of migrating to South Korea is necessarily limited. After having been granted South Korean citizenship, however, communication amongst North Korean defector family members when leaving for Western countries may differ from that occurred in the aforementioned cross-border movements.

The degree of North Korean defectors' communication throughout the migration process determines family relationships after the migration, family reunion and relocation, and their identity formation and adaptation in settlement. This study views North Korean defectors' communication through the lens of family to examine extended family care, family roles and the adaptation patterns that occurred as a result of a series of migration processes. Interviews with five North Korean defector families whose transnational migration from North Korea through China and South Korea to arrive in the UK offer insights to the communication and adaptation of the defector families. When considering the migration of North Korean defector families, how they communicate will determine the success of their migration.

THEORETICAL FRAMEWORK: MIGRATION AND COMMUNICATION OF NORTH KOREAN DEFECTOR FAMILIES

North Korean defector families who have continued to other countries after settlement in South Korea have through their transnational migration become migrants and refugees simultaneously. The process of North Korean defector families' migration from North Korea to South Korea, regarded as forced immigration, is one that generally has the characteristics of seeking refuge. These characteristics include fear of capture and persecution, statelessness, illegal movement across borders, as well as the physical danger of the routes North Korean defector families take to arrive in South Korea (Kim 2018; Yi, Cho, Kim, and Chin 2007). As more North Korean defectors escape, the information that filters back through earlier defectors' social remittances have diversified the method and process of defecting, allowing current defectors to plan their defection in advance (Son and Kim 2017). However, the reality is that even when their preparations and route were meticulously organized, the risk of being found out before or caught during defection still exists. That said, the possible impact that defection may have on the family members not defecting remains the same whether the defectors are caught or escape successfully.

Once North Koreans defectors arrive in South Korea and are granted asylum and eventually citizenship, legally at least they are no longer refugees even if they still feel that way. It is once they migrate from South Korea to another country that the mixed characteristics of migrants and refugees develop. By definition, they are migrants in that they are South Korean nationals voluntarily emigrating, but the fact that they file for refugee status in the destination country reasserts their identity as refugees. The difference in their second application for refugee status lies in their motivations. When they arrived in South Korea, many were escaping terrible conditions as refugees, but when they left South Korea, they were looking for a better life as migrants (Song and Bell 2019).

Studies on migrant families examine the differences between parents and children in how they respond to the host society's culture and how that affects children's identity formation and values as well as the role parents play. Depending on the nature of the parents' conflict resolution through communication, this can decide the cohesion of families and the mental health of the second generation based on communication within the family (Jang 2016). In *Working with Refugee Families*, the role of refugee family is examined as the emotional regulator of children in buffering or exacerbating the effects of recurrent traumatization of children during migration and trauma-specific processes (De Haene, Grietens and Verschueren 2007). According to this book, parents' accessibility and support are key factors in shielding refugee children as much as possible from the impact of forced migration. It emphasizes the need for open communication between parents and children first to heal the psychological and emotional trauma children have endured and second to foster growth and adaption to a new country. However, in most refugee families, the parents are struggling themselves and satisfying both their and their children's emotional and physical needs strains their abilities as caregiver. Due to the physical, emotional, and mental hardships refugee parents have themselves experienced in the process of defection and transnational migration, they often fail to recognize their children's problems and need for personalized parenting.

Issues with communication within families begin in North Korea, but the stress of migration can cause already tense situations to devolve into conflict that may result in traumatic events (Bek-Pedersen and Montgomery 2006). When family violence becomes a form of communication between parents and children, this can manifest as physical or emotional abuse or neglect that extends the child's traumatic experience. In those cases when neglect is involved, the parents often neglect themselves too, leaving the children to care for themselves and their parents, resulting in "parentified children." In a study on North Korean refugee mothers conducted by Kim (2018), there were some who could not meet their children's need for psychological safety due to their own past traumatic experiences and anxiety. Instead of communicating reassurance, they transferred their own anxiety to their children, which in turn amplified their children's anxiety (Kim 2018). When a parent is unable to psychologically overcome or resolve past traumatic events, these painful memories become a part of everyday life through the negative emotions they engender such as ongoing sadness, fear, and anger. This interferes with a parent's ability to offer positive reinforcement and promote a sense of security through their conversations with their children. Further examination of the communication between parents and children could provide insight into the adaptation of North Korean defector families and the development of their children in the process of transnational migration.

Cultural identity is also transmitted and passed on to the next generation through family communication. Studies on children from multicultural families deal with the feelings of duality and confusion they experience in regards to their ethnic identity. Children from multicultural families may face greater challenges adapting to the host society due to the complication of forming an individual identity as well as racial and ethnic identity (Lee 2018; Song and Park 2019). North Korean parents' communication is also significant to the formation of North Korean national or cultural identity of children born in the destination country. When North Korean defector parents living in South Korea imprint their North Korean identity on their children, this influences the children's identity formation (Lee et al. 2020). North Korean refugees who have then settled in the UK often "reterritorialize" or reconstruct that North Korean identity while interacting with British citizens and South Korean immigrants (Kim 2018). As the hybrid identity of these defector parents, who have repeatedly made transnational movements, is transferred to their children, the children may experience identity crises or personal difficulties. This is especially true of North Korean defectors' whose children either settled in the UK at a young age and do not remember the process of defection or were born there. These children grow up to form their identities through a secondhand understanding of their parents' stories of their experiences in North Korea, China, and South Korea. Considering that many parents have experienced stress, loss, and trauma in their transnational migrations, the psychological emotional problems of the parents also transfer to the children through verbal and nonverbal communications (Kim 2018). In addition to the trauma experienced during the migration process, North Korean defectors encounter various stresses and hardships in their daily lives in new settlements. As daily routine challenges have been seen to affect psychosocial outcomes more directly than the enduring trauma from past defection processes (Rasmussen et al. 2010), settlement stressors are more closely related to mental health symptoms (Worthington, Muzurovic, Tipping, and Goldman 2002). Taking all this into account, the establishment of a community-based psychosocial intervention system could provide much-needed support to children from North Korean defector families facing the psychological and emotional challenges of successive migration.

Previous studies on the psychological and emotional challenges of the migration process have focused on the experiences of individual North Korean defectors (Ryu 2014; Lee 2013) or the settlement of defector families but only in South Korea. Although research on North Korean defectors who relocate to other countries after their settlement in South Korea exists, the focus is mainly on the push factors that drive them to leave. These push factors include discrimination against North Korean defectors and the maladjustment of North Korean defectors to South Korean society. Other studies are primarily concerned with North Korean defectors' adaptation to South Korean society.

Two recent studies on North Korean defector families, however, have revealed at least partial motivation for "successive migration with family support" (Son and Kim 2017; Chin and Kim 2018). In one study, Son and Kim (2017) analyze the phenomenon of North Korean defector families' continually expanding serial migration from the perspective of family. The other one by Chin and Kim (2018) explains the migration characteristics and types of North Korean defector families in terms of international migration. What these studies have in common is that they analyze family migration focusing on the process of defection from North Korea and China. They do not, however, include the migration experiences of the defector families in the process of defecting from South Korea. It is presumed that the communication of North Korean defector families in the process of leaving South Korea is much freer and more active than those in the process of defecting from North Korea or China. However, few studies have been done on this topic so this remains an educated guess as little is known as fact.

This raises the question, how does communication within North Korean defector families evolve after they leave South Korea for Europe and/or Canada? Since there are very few studies on this subject, it will be necessary to examine North Korean defectors' communication during the course of the migration process to determine if it does indeed change. To map this possible evolution, this study aims to analyze the communication of North Korean defector families in the process of transnational migration and their settlement in new environments. This study, therefore, will contemplate North Korean defector families' communication during the process of their transnational migration from North Korea through China to settle first in South Korea and then Europe for their second settlement.

RESEARCH METHODS

A noticeable trend of North Korean defectors leaving South Korea to resettle in Europe began in the late 2000s, and for many their transnational migration took them to the Koreatown in New Malden, a suburb of London in the UK. This study examines the communication practices of North Korean defector families who have engaged in transnational migration. To understand the challenges North Korean defectors face, five mothers (Participants A, B, C, D, and E) in their 40s living in New Malden were interviewed. These participants first defected from North Korea, passed through at least one other country, usually China, before arriving in South Korea for their first settlement. As is the case for many North Korean defector families, the wife and mother of the family tends to take the lead in serial migration, evolving the family from the traditional patriarchy to a matriarchal family (Chin et al. 2015). For this reason, the research participants for this study only involved women. The migration experiences of this group of women were similar. They all defected from North Korea between 1995 and 2001 to escape a period of extreme poverty and starvation called the Arduous March, and they all left South Korea between 2007 and 2008. Their transnational migration followed similar routes from North Korea through China to settle in South Korea and then on to the United Kingdom where they currently reside in New Malden with their children.

The purpose of this study was to conduct a qualitative study of North Korean defectors' family communication following transnational migration that ended in New Malden. The interview questions were derived from an analysis of previous studies on the migration and communication habits of migrants and refugee families generally and families of North Korean defectors specifically. The subject of this questionnaire focuses on communication among North Korean defector family members in the UK, as well as with remaining family members living in North Korea, China, and South Korea. The questions were semi-structured to allow for a free exchange of information during the interviews.

This study conducted in-depth interviews from August 21 through to August 26, 2019, with five female North Korean defectors in their 40s residing in the UK. The research participants in this study were contacted through the Association for North Korean Defectors (ANKD) in New Malden employing snowball sampling. The interviews were conducted by the author at the office of the ANKD and scheduled either in the morning or afternoon depending on the participants' availability.

Though the sample size is small and the duration of the fieldwork short, this researcher has been building a relationship with North Korean refugee families in New Malden since 2016 through annual research trips. This study that analyzed North Koreans' communication practices specifically was conducted in 2019 during this researcher's fourth trip to the UK. In addition to the data collected through in-depth interviews, the qualitative method was expanded upon through ethnographic research and the observation of North Korean refugees in everyday-life situations. To establish a rapport and create trust, the researcher shared personal anecdotes with the North Korean interviewees to build a researcher–interviewee relationship that was not confined to New Malden. For example, on those occasions when the North Korean research participants visited South Korea, they resumed the association and would share information on North Korean refugee families in the UK. The ongoing nature of this researcher's research method that would reveal discrepancies in data collected increases the reliability and validity of this qualitative study even though the number of research participants is limited.

Prior to the interview, the purpose of the study and the substance of the interview questions were explained, and only those who volunteered to participate were selected for this research. The author attempted to create a relaxed atmosphere where the participants would feel comfortable answering questions. Before any questions were asked, it was stressed that the participants would neither be pressured to provide information that they were unwilling to share nor penalized for it. Their anonymity was assured by designating an ID number in place of their names for the purpose of protecting their personal information. The author, at all stages of the study, strove to abide by the research ethics pertaining to voluntary participation, informed consent, confidentiality and storage and maintenance of data.

To understand North Korean defectors' patterns of transnational migration and family communication, the data collected from in-depth interviews has been broken down into understandable categories using the Downe-Wamboldt approach. In this case study this approach involves three steps. First, a repeated reading of the interview transcripts to identify the core thoughts and concepts for the main theme. Second, a subtopic was developed to explore the characteristics of the family communication in the process of family's transnational migration. Third, the main theme and subtopic were re-analyzed and then integrated to arrive at the final conclusion. To ensure that the evaluation of the data collected "stays true," the author followed Sandelowski's criteria of reliability, auditability, suitability, and confirmability for this qualitative study. Since there is currently a lack of research on overseas relocation and North Korean defectors' family communication, it is critical that the meaning and characteristics of their communication be as accurately presented as is possible.

MIGRATION DECISIONS AND NORTH KOREAN DEFECTORS' FAMILY COMMUNICATION

When North Koreans make the decision to defect, their discussions or communication with their families about their plans tend to be limited or even non-existent. Family communication about the decision to defect varied depending on other family members' loyalty to North Korea, whether a family member had already defected, and whether they went alone or as a group. Regardless of the individual's circumstances, relationship or level of communication with other family members, the dangers associated with escaping and the need for secrecy forces many defectors to leave without telling their family.

This lack of communication can be attributed in part to the laws in North Korea that decide where citizens will live, denying the freedom to move at will. Planning ahead or having a discussion with other family members about their relocation was something that North Korean families had never experienced. Having no experience and the only examples were defectors who left before that seemed simply to disappear, North Koreans struggled with how much to tell family before they left. In most cases where North Korean defector women became part of a Chinese family through "bride-buying," the decision to relocate to South Korea is not shared with any member of her new family. Their escape from their Chinese family is as dangerous as when they left North Korea. In the process of forced and escape migration, North Korean women are moving illegally across borders and must be extremely careful due to the fact that if caught they could be sent back to North Korea. This also hinders smooth communication among their families.

In the case of participant A, she could not tell her parents that she was defecting due to their unquestioningly loyalty to the country. As for participant B, she told her mother that she intended to defect, arguing that her defection would put her in a position to send money home and financially support their poor relatives. A younger cousin had defected earlier and was sending money to his mother, participant B's aunt and her mother's sister, so the argument was convincing. In the end, she had to escape North Korea without telling her mother when due to her mother's strong opposition to her defection. Participant C's parents died before she decided to defect, so she only had a brother to inform of her defection. Even though participant C also defected with telling her only one family member, her original intention was to go back to North Korea after earning some money in China. Sometimes they kept their plans secret because they just could not persuade their families to accept their decision. Other times they kept the dangerous information to themselves to protect their families so if asked they could honestly deny all knowledge. In some cases, they were aware that they had come to the state's attention due to other family members having fled the country before them and had to exercise the utmost caution.

> To my parents, until then, betraying the state itself is unheard of. As I said before, Mom and Dad are very loyal to the state. That is why I couldn't imagine either of them going anywhere else at all. So, I couldn't tell them anything and just left there alone. If I told my parents, they would have stopped me. (participant A)

> "Shall I go (abroad) and send money to you, Mother?" I asked my mother. But she didn't want me to leave. She said, "Dear, please don't say that . . . " She suddenly burst into tears and said, "I don't need that kind of money, so please stop thinking about defecting." So, from then on, she watched me so that I could not go anywhere. "Okay, Mom, I will not defect from North Korea." Then, in my mind, I thought to myself that I would never be able to tell my mother that I still intended to leave the state. (participant B)

The participants in this study decided to leave South Korea and migrate to the UK almost as impulsively as they decided to defect from North Korea. Participant B briefly informed her husband that she had decided to take their children and move to the UK. Only after she qualified for a visa there did her husband joined her later.

> My husband, well, he doesn't know the specifics. I don't give detailed or lengthy explanations. Not much . . . One night I woke up and said, "I will go to the UK" . . . Even though I wondered how I would get there, but in the end, I just wanted to go, I just wanted to go there with my kids . . . (participant B)

Participant C did not know about North Korean defectors leaving for overseas countries where they applied for refugee status. She just wanted to leave South Korea because she and her husband were not on good terms, but she could not decide where she and her family should resettle.

> At first, I was planning to go to Australia. But what a coincidence uh . . . So [a friend in the UK] told me to come to the UK. I asked my friend if I could live in the UK if I went, and she said I could. My friend didn't give me further information but kept telling me "Just come," so I went. I have no regrets. That . . . I have no regrets. Even if I have to go down the same track again. Because it was a good decision. [Researcher: What did you tell your husband at that time?] [In the end, he allowed it] If he didn't allow it, I would have tried to run away. (participant C)

Participant D was offended and hurt by how the South Koreans she met at her child's day-care center treated her, so without a second thought she decided to desert South Korea. To convince her children to agree to the migration to the UK, she explained that she as a North Korean defector was a social outcast in South Korean society. It may be humiliating for her in South Korea, but when she considered that her children would also have to live with the same humiliation, she thought, "It will kill me." She could not accept that her children would suffer the social stigma of being "North Korean defectors" for the rest of their lives. So, she left South Korea, thinking "I should sacrifice myself for the children."

> I told my children that even if we go abroad, we will be (somewhat) branded with the stigma of being "North Korean(defectors)." Whatever it happens, it won't be as bad as here. So, let's go there. (participant D)

Participant E was in South Korea for only one month before she decided to leave despite her parents' disapproval upon hearing her plan to go to the UK. In participant E's case, as well as the other four cases, the decision to relocate was arrived at in a relatively short period of time almost on a whim. Rather than discuss a plan to move with their families, they stated their intention and then left. Participant B was the only one to engage her children in the type of communication that is akin to negotiation. Life in North Korea had taught them to keep their thoughts to themselves, and their forced migration experiences had reinforced the importance of decisive action and the danger of wasted words. Lessons very much in evidence in their transnational migration.

THE FEAR THAT SHAPES AND LIMITS NORTH KOREAN DEFECTORS' FAMILY COMMUNICATION

The transnational family network of the North Korean defectors in this study spreads from North Korea through China and South Korea to the UK. Actively engaged in multilateral communication, North Korean defectors maintain communication with their families left behind in North Korea as well as any family they have acquired in the countries they have previously transited through. However, without a broker as an in-between, it is difficult to communicate with family members left behind in North Korea. It is perhaps for this reason that the participants in this study admitted that fear limits their communication with their families in North Korea. Before a broker will arrange telephone conversations with the families in the North, North Korean defectors must divulge their families' personal information such as full names and addresses. This puts their families in the North at risk if problems arise, for example, if the broker is caught by the police in China and offers the defectors' personal information for a reduced sentence.

For North Korean defectors, these phone calls are akin to a reunion with their family and inspire happiness and positive feelings. At the same time, however, these phone calls can cause distress stemming from the trauma of defection, fear of being repatriated to North Korea, and concern for family members still in the North. They felt guilty for leaving family members behind and concern about the political persecution they might face, but they also felt responsible for those they encouraged to defect with them.

> We were all caught, on the edge of Dalian in China. Somehow, they found out [that we had defected from North Korea] and the police came to catch us. Seven police officers came rushing in with guns. To catch my father and mother. Because my father's arrest order was issued in North Korea. Because he was blacklisted [in North Korea] . . . My parents couldn't escape. They were caught and sent back to the North. No contact whatsoever, we couldn't communicate with each other. I've called all my relatives. But anyway, according to the broker, they were . . . A bad thing happened to them [implying that the parents were dead]. (participant B)

The participants talk of the terror that governs every aspect of life from childhood to adulthood in North Korea. One interviewee summarized the fear in one sentence, "I can die if I speak recklessly." The sense that to speak out of turn could be deadly was engrained in them by their parents from an early age. They were taught that "there should be secrets within the family" and that some "secrets as such should not be disclosed even among the family members" in regards to what they did to survive. Life during the Arduous March was a time of hardship and starvation for many North Koreans. Participant D, who had just started at university during this time, had to forage for firewood in the mountains and carry loads of coal to help heat their home. One day she asked her father, "Why on earth is the Leader, our father, making our lives so hard?" Her father harshly scolded her for questioning the dear Leader. This fear of saying something wrong that has been instilled since infancy in North Korea interferes with smooth and open communication within the family.

> I thought that if I meet people and talk recklessly, I could die. I think that fear has always been with me. That's why our parents taught us that no matter where we go that we must always watch what we say. I learned from my parents that even within the family there should be secrets. You can't tell even to your family what you heard at your work. So, as there is a proverb [in Korea] that the birds always overhear what you say during the day, and the rats overhear what you say at night [meaning 'walls have ears']. So, I always knew that I must never have a loose tongue. (participant A)

> [In North Korea, children usually] don't ask why the Leader, our father, is giving us a hard time. But I did. So my father told me that I was wicked . . . "If you go outside and say that, our family will all be killed, so shut up and stay quiet." My father told me to make sure to keep my mouth shut [others told me the same thing]. For sure. So, course I haven't talked about it. I haven't said anything. (participant D)

Consequently, this has had a negative effect on the family communication during any kind of migration, and limits the emotional support they might offer each other should a crisis occur during transnational movement. The fear that limits communication among defectors' families starts with the parents' experiences of oppression in North Korea and trauma during the defection process. The politically, socially and culturally repressed communication learned in North Korea seems to accompany defectors in their successive migrations to China, South Korea, and the UK. The anxiety and tension around communication that aggravates the stress of being refugees and stateless persons does seem to diminish, however, with repeated migration. In fact, some positive changes have been observed in their communication with their children after settling in the UK, once a period of adaptation has passed. Not only has the quality of communication improved with their children, but communication with family members in South Korea also appears to be relatively freer.

COMMUNICATION AND MAINTAINING RELATIONSHIPS WITH FAMILIES REMAINING IN NORTH KOREA: REMITTANCES AND TELEPHONE CALLS

North Korean defectors who have settled in the UK stay in touch with their families in North Korea by sending remittances through brokers who usually also set up a telephone call at the same time. Depending on where the family members are located in North Korea determines how easy it is to make contact. This is because, in order to avoid surveillance by the state in North Korea, one must travel to one of the border areas and meet with the broker to receive the cash and calls from their defector families living abroad via a Chinese mobile network. It is during the physical handoff of cash that North Korean family members use the brokers' cell phones to talk to the defectors. For North Koreans to leave their area of residence and travel through different regions to arrive near the border to meet with brokers, they must buy a pass. Not only do they incur financial costs as well as the time and effort to move to the border area, but in buying the pass their movements are documented, which could attract the authorities' notice.

Since brokers arrange the phone calls as proof of payment and for no other reason, to communicate with family remaining in North Korea essentially must include the act of remittance. Given that there are no legal avenues to sending money, North Korean defectors who want to send remittances to their remaining families in North Korea have no alternative but to use brokers. Knowing that North Koreans have few options, these brokers sometimes charge more than 30 percent of the remittance as a commission fee. Maintaining communication through brokers not only puts a financial burden on North Korean defectors but in some cases also adds a psychological strain.

Participant A was both robbed and threatened by brokers in the past. Brokers sometimes charged her for excessive amounts as a commission fee for remittance or rescue of the family members left behind in North Korea. They threatened her that they would report to the National Security Agency all the information of the families remaining in North Korea if the fee was not being paid. Fearing what the brokers could do with all the information she was sure they had on her North Korean family and herself, she was not in a position to argue with them. Deciding that she had to extricate herself from this arrangement, she came to the difficult decision to stop sending remittances to her remaining family members in North Korea. This has resulted in her "deep resentment" of Chinese people, the brokers. Participant D has also recently ceased to send remittances to her family in North Korea as well as her child in China from her "bride-buying" marriage. Participant D explains that she would help her child in China if the child visits her in the UK but only then because she now has another child to raise.

> We send money to the [broker's] account in China. But, then, the money is seized by the broker because they know that we have no lawful identity anywhere. Because the broker knows that we can't complain about it even if they do so. So, I have some resentment towards Chinese people, the brokers . . . Then the brokers, once we start sending remittances through their accounts, they begin to threaten us. Because money comes from abroad. So, the brokers keep encouraging the families remaining in the North to talk to us on the phone [so that we continue to wire them money]. (participant A)

> I told my child's grandmother in China that I did everything that I had to do when I was living with you in your house, and then I came to South Korea, so from now on don't ask me to send you money anymore. When my child in China grows up and visits me some day, then maybe I will do something, but before that, don't ask me for help anymore. After I came to South Korea, I used to, for a year or two, send money to my family in North Korea. But my sister calls me about once every three months, asking for financial help. "Sister, I am not the goose that lays golden eggs." (participant D)

> [We] send money [to North Korea] every month. We only talk to each other on the phone . . . [I] miss them every time it happens. [What do you talk about with them at that time?] Whether living there is better than before and what is life like . . . (participant A)

Since settling in the UK, North Korean defectors have been in contact with their families in North Korea and China by phone or "*kakaotalk*," an instant messaging application on mobile phones. These lines of communication have allowed defectors to help other North Korean family members to defect to South Korea and family members in South Korea to emigrate to England. Those conversations with their families in North Korea and China conducted at the same time as money is sent might be about confirming receipt of funds but they are also an opportunity to encourage their families to relocate. In the case of families in South Korea, family communication also has practical purposes, such as extending invitations to the UK to study or live. Participant B, after receiving her visa and becoming better established, invited her sister's children living in South Korea to the UK so they could have an education in the UK. "Successive migration with family support" that reunites family members whether related by blood or by marriage has through communication become possible.

While a network of transnational communication amongst family members is multilateral, the transnational movement of North Korean refugees and family communication is unidirectional due to North Korea's closed borders. North Korean defector families depend on transnational communication to maintain connections with family members separated by distance and borders, reuniting them virtually if not physically.

NORTH KOREAN DEFECTOR FAMILIES' STRUGGLE TO COMMUNICATE THROUGH THEIR PSYCHOLOGICAL AND EMOTIONAL DIFFICULTIES IN THE NEW SETTLEMENT

Those North Korean defector families that moved to countries where the language was foreign to them faced challenges in the new settlement unlike any of those faced in South Korea. Parents who moved to the UK without other adult family members suffered not only loneliness but the psychological burden of being solely responsible for their children. Yet some North Korean defector mothers proved to be adept at solving life's difficulties on their own, having learned resiliency during the defection process. Even in transitioning to life in the UK, some have exhibited tendencies to solve problems on their own rather than relying on social resources or seeking help within the North Korean community. Others did not do so well, as evidenced by gambling problems, alcoholism and infidelity, as well as incidents of assault and in some extreme cases murder in New Malden's Koreatown.

The participants in this study discussed their psychological and emotional difficulties and how that affected their children's adaptation during resettlement. In the case of participant C, she confessed that when her children were young, she often beat them because she herself was struggling. As a result, her children were withdrawn and tried to hide their difficulties or solve them on their own rather than talking to her. She did not want to talk to her children about their difficult past either and hoped they would not remember.

> For some reason, I don't have many good memories. Back then, I had a hard time just surviving because of my husband, and I took my stress out on my children. So, I beat my kids a lot . . . I don't talk about the old days. So, it seems

that my daughter forgot all about it. And, by the way, she sometimes remembers that I just beat her and . . . (participant C)

Participant D since her early childhood has believed that "if I alone cannot protect my body, I am dead." For this reason, even during resettlement, she would not accept psychological support or emotional comfort from close acquaintances including family members. Rather than receiving support or protection from her family, she has always played the role of protector, taking all the responsibility for her family. It means that sometimes when she should have accepted help to make life easier, she would do it all herself and make life harder and more stressful. It also might affect that she indirectly communicating to her children that it is wrong to accept help even when it is needed.

I had one thing in mind that I would be dead if I alone couldn't protect my body, myself. I guess I had it in my mind since childhood . . . I had something that I had to protect, my family. That dominated my mind. So, someone protects me? I've never had the thought. I've never really turned to anyone when I had a hard time, really. (participant D)

I was lonely at first. I couldn't make myself understood and had no friends. Sometimes when a passerby spoke in English, to me that sounded like Korean. At that time, it was really hard. I found it mentally hard to adapt [to the new environment]. (participant C)

Feelings of isolation, loneliness and pressure to protect the family and make the migration a success was made worse by the learned behavior to not communicate their thoughts and needs. For some parents it was too much and they lashed out at their children sometimes physically and sometimes verbally. Others by not talking about problems or accepting help not only made their own lives harder but set unhealthy examples for their children. These difficulties can be attributed to the trauma of defection, as well as the common difficulties of migrants settling in a new country.

NORTH KOREAN DEFECTOR CHILDREN'S ADAPTATION, IDENTITY, AND COMMUNICATION

When leaving South Korea, North Korean defectors travel on their South Korean passports to cross the border as if they are going on a vacation. After arriving in the UK, however, they hide the fact that they have already lived in South Korea and in many cases obtained citizenship and instead identify themselves as only North Korean defectors. Now, not only is communication within the family restricted but there is active deception to conceal their life in South Korea in order to obtain refugee status in the UK.

Children were often confused by the need to censor their words and essentially forget their South Korean identity in the process of settling as a refugee in the UK. When participant C settled in the UK, her young children could not understand why they had to pretend they had never lived in South Korea and struggled to adapt. Frightened that they would be discovered, she monitored and controlled her children's speech and would scold them harshly whenever one of them mistakenly declared that they had lived in South Korea.

> Every time he made a slip of the tongue, I scolded him a lot. Whenever the children mistakenly said the fact that we had lived in South Korea, and so on and so forth. (participant C)

At first, North Korean defectors actively maintain the refugee identity, but after their application to stay is accepted, they go through a period of adaptation and identity formation. North Korean defector children who have either spent their formative years in several countries or been exposed to the multiple identities of their migrant parents may absorb the most from these experiences. By communicating in their native language at home and the language of the host country in interactions with the destination population, the children form identities that take from both worlds. North Korean parents, apart from the example of their own multiple identities, talk to their children about their backgrounds to remind them of their identities as Koreans, both North and South. Participant D told her children, "Because you're Korean, you're South Korean. Mom and Dad are North Korean, but you're South Korean because you came to such a good country and were born in there." Though participant D tells her children that they are "South Korean," she also tells them that if reunification occurs in the future, they will be expected to go to North Korea to help rebuild the country.

> Yes, you are South Korean. Though Mom and Dad are North Koreans as we both were born in North Korea, as we came to South Korea and you all were born in South Korea, South Korea is your home country. We belong to different countries. Mom is from the North, but you all are from the South. Then, the ones born in South Korea should go to the North and to rebuild once the two Koreas are reunited. (participant D)

Participant E lives in the UK as a North Korean defector, but she tells her children that their "dad and mom are both South Korean" so that her children feel that their roots are in South Korea. She is thinking ahead, however, to difficulties with North Korea and is considering how her children might be able to join the South Korean military.

Once you get discharged from the army, and when you are in South Korea, wouldn't it be good to get help from the state if something dangerous happens in future? Living in the UK is one thing. As Mom and Dad, we are all Korean . . . We always give that image to our kids. Our roots are in South Korea. That's important, but also, when a person leaves home and joins the army for a two-year-long service, it's hard for young men, but then the opportunity provides them to become real adults, just like turning over a new leaf. (participant E)

Although the participants interviewed are pleased that their children are learning English and successfully adapting to the British society, they do not want their children to forget their roots. To ensure that her children speak Korean, participant D sends them to the Korean language school, which is held once a week. This is not just to preserve their culture and language but because she expects them to move to North Korea after reunification. Participant A's children not only speak Korean in the home, but speak it well.

My second child is at ease with the South Korean culture and South Korean language even if she was born in the UK . . . My child tells me that she still likes to speak in Korean. Of course, she speaks English at school, but she speaks Korean well at home. [What if the children want to stay in South Korea? What would you say?] To me, I don't like it. My first child, not the second one, keeps saying that he/she wants to live in South Korea. (participant A)

The children of participant A were born in the UK or have lived there from an early age, but they feel comfortable speaking Korean and admire the South Korean culture. Participant A intends to take her children on a visit to South Korea because she thinks that they need to experience South Korean culture and not just what they see on YouTube or TV. However, she is concerned that her children might decide that they would prefer to live in South Korea. This is because the first child has often said that she wants to live in the South.

If the children are confused by what their parents want for them, that would be due to the mixed messages that their parents send. The parents encourage their children to adapt to the UK society while simultaneously reinforcing their Korean identity through Korean language lessons, speaking Korean at home, visits to Korea, and access to Korean Wave culture. Not only are the parents reinforcing Korean culture in the present but planning their children's return to rebuild a reformed North Korea or a reunified Korea in the future. Children's identities as South Korean, North Korean or just Korean was strengthened through their parents' transferred identity. While this inspired interest in their homelands, it could also interfere with children's organic identity formation, leading to ambiguity or confusion as to what their identity should be.

CONCLUSION

To examine how transnational migration affects family communication of North Korean defectors, this study conducted interviews with five female North Korean defectors residing in New Malden, London, England. The study was broken down into five categories to examine how communication changes during the different phases of transnational migration. First, family communication was discussed in relation to the decision to defect and then the decision to relocate in the process of transnational migration and how it differed in each situation. Second, North Korean defectors' continuing fear of communication as a result of North Korea's oppressive regime was explored as well as the observations that this fear sometimes diminishes after transnational migration. Third, North Korean defectors' remittances and phone calls were considered for their roles in maintaining communication with dispersed or separated family members, in some cases reuniting them. Fourth, the effect of the strain of psychological burdens and difficulties on North Korean defectors' family communication was explored. Fifth, North Korean defector children's identity formation as a result of parents' communication and transfer of their own multiple identities was discussed.

Until recently, most studies have concentrated on the migration characteristics and migration patterns of North Korean refugee families who have settled in South Korea. This study, however, has explored family communication among North Korean defectors who engaged in translational migration. Whether other North Korean defectors take the same route as the interviewees in this study or not, their transnational movement basically leads to the separation/dismantling of the families just the same. Existing studies have mainly focused on the migration process, settlement, and adaptation of North Korean defectors at the individual level. The findings of this study show transnational migration and adaptation of North Korean defectors must be understood in one framework: not North Korean individuals but families.

Though this study has introduced North Korean defectors' family communication to the debate on transnational migration, the small number of participants interviewed presents some limitations. However, by examining the family communication of even a few North Korean defectors, it started the conversation on the dynamics of family relations in the process of transnational migration. This study also identified the fear of communication learned in North Korea that continues to affect defectors throughout their migrations, the 'refugee' identity, and the passing down of the Korean identity to the younger generations. In addition, it was found that the communication of the defector families has had a significant impact on their adaptation, the formation of identity and the mental health of the children of the defectors. The results also demonstrate that policies on North Korean defectors should take into consideration what families need in resettlement when deciding what supports to provide. Further, the study of families of North Korean defectors discloses aspects of migration and adaptation from previous researches on migrants and refugees.

To address the limited scope of this study's sample group to be able to generalize the results, future research will need to include a greater number of defectors at the interview stage. Further, the participants of this study were limited only to the North Korean defectors who had taken a route from North Korea through China and South Korea to settle in the UK. Future studies would need to include North Korean defectors who first, took various routes in their transnational movement, and second, settled in countries other than the UK. Finally, family communication is private and personal in that it is exchanged only with trusted family members especially in the case of North Korean defectors. This study has focused on North Korean defectors' family communication only through the lens of adult defector women and their children. To provide a comprehensive view of the communication of North Korean defector families who have experienced transnational migration, future studies would need to include the perspective of other family members.

REFERENCES

Bek-Pedersen, Kathrine, and Edith Montgomery. "Narratives of the past and present: Young refugees' construction of a family identity in exile." *Journal of Refugee Studies* 19, no. 1 (2006): 94–112.

Chin, Meejung, and Kim, Sangha. "Family migration characteristics and types of North Korean defectors." *Family and Environment Research* 56, no. 3 (2007): 317–330.

De Haene, Lucia, Hans Grietens, and Karine Verschueren. "From symptom to context." *Hellenic Journal of Psychology* 4 (2007): 233–256.

Downe☐Wamboldt, Barbara. "Content analysis: method, applications, and issues." *Health Care for Women International* 13, no. 3 (1992): 313–321.

Jang, Ahn-lee. "Asian-American family communication patterns from the perspective of young adult children." *Studies in Humanities and Social Sciences* 51 (2016): 51–72.

Kim, Heuijeong. "Development and effect of the attachment-based emotional regulation program for North Korean refugees' children born in the third country" PhD Diss., Seoul National University, 2018.

Kim, Heuijeong, and Kim, Jisoo. "Analysis on the characteristics and implementation of the 2013 revised North Korean kindergarten curriculum." *Journal of Early Childhood Education* 40, no. 4 (2020): 61–85.

Laible, Deborah J., and Ross A. Thompson. "Attachment and emotional understanding in preschool children." *Developmental Psychology* 34, no. 5 (1998): 1038.

Lee, Jitaeck, Lee, Seonhee, Kang, Jeongmo, and Yoo, Seoungyeon. "A phenomenological study on the identity of North Korean defectors' mothers and the formation of children's identity." *Korean Journal of Qualitative Research in Social Welfare* 14, no. 2 (2020): 89–115.

Lee, Soyean. "A study of longitudinal changes and relevant factors of multicultural acceptability attitudes amongst multiethnic adolescents." *Studies on Korean Youth* 29, no. 1 (2018): 179–208.

Lyons-Ruth, Karlen. "Dissociation and the parent–infant dialogue: A longitudinal perspective from attachment research." *Journal of the American Psychoanalytic Association* 51, no. 3 (2003): 883–911.

Miller, Kenneth E., Gregory J. Worthington, Jasmina Muzurovic, Susannah Tipping, and Allison Goldman. "Bosnian refugees and the stressors of exile: A narrative study." *American Journal of Orthopsychiatry* 72, no. 3 (2002): 341–354.

Park, Young-Jun. "'We are like international orphans' North Korean defector wandering abroad." *Segye Daily News*, October 11, 2017. http://www.segye.com/newsView/20171010004985

Rasmussen, Andrew, and Jeannie Annan. "Predicting stress related to basic needs and safety in Darfur refugee camps: A structural and social ecological analysis." *Journal of Refugee Studies* 23, no. 1 (2010): 23–40.

Ryu, Jong-hoon. *After defecting from North Korea, Some Korean.* Seoul: Seongan Books, 2014.

Sandelowski, Margarete. "The problem of rigor in qualitative research." *Advances in Nursing Science* 8, no. 3 (1986): 27–37.

Son, Myung-ah, and Kim, Seokho. "Family migration of North Korean defectors: With a focus on the phenomenon of chain migrations." *Korean Journal of Population Studies* 40, no. 1 (2017): 57–81.

Song, Jay Jiyoung, and Bell, M. "North Korean secondary asylum in the UK." *Migration Studies* 7, no. 2 (2019): 160–179.

Song, Sari, and Park, Myungsook. "The effects of dual cultural identity on the satisfaction of life among children in multicultural families: Focused on the mediating effects of self-efficacy and interpersonal relationship ability." *Family and Culture* 31, no. 4 (2019): 30–60.

Yi, Heeyoung. "(Post) Division and actor-network of international migration-case study on the life and human rights of 'traveling' North Korean refugees." *North Korean Studies Review* 17, no. 1 (2013): 355–393.

Yi, Soon-Hyung, Cho, Soo-Churl, Kim, Chang-Dai, and Chin, Meejung. *The Social and Psychological Acculturation of North Korean Defector Families.* Seoul: Seoul National University Press. 2007.

Chapter 6

De-bordering North Korea

Remittances and Global Networks

HaeRan Shin

De-bordering is defined by the "simultaneous processes of boosting cross-border interactions, through the implementation of facilitating mechanisms compatible with the exercise of sovereign power" (Leandro and Duarte, 2019).[1] The concept of a (de-)bordered North Korea is one that this chapter will explore through the "geopolitical ethnic networks" that have developed from North Korean defectors'[2] transnational ethnic networks. In the case of North Korean defectors, their first act of de-bordering was to prove that the border could be breached by escaping. While most North Korean escapees take a similar route that ends in South Korea with a plan to remain there, some will eventually move again to a second and in some cases a third or fourth country. It is through these multiple mobilities that North Koreans have developed the geopolitical ethnic networks (Shin, 2018, 2019) that have been critical in de-bordering North Korea. As the mobility of people, cash, information, narratives, and culture (Amelung and Machado, 2019; Németh, 2017; Tervonen and Enache, 2017) has accelerated, studies have shifted focus to migrants' movements.

While the physical mobility of defection is a significant de-bordering practice in and of itself, but it has become evident that bordering and de-bordering should be understood as both physical and mental constructs (Agnew, 2008; Armbruster, 2011; Krasteva, 2017). Unlike previous geopolitical and border studies that have focused on the physical aspects of bordering such as passport control, this research examines how those defectors' economic and political activities contribute to the theoretical de-bordering of North Korea (see Gelézeau et al., 2013 for de-bordering Korea). There are those studies that have discussed (Newman and Paasi 1998; van Houtum and Naerssen 2002;

van Houtum, Kramsch, and Zierhofer 2005; Rumford 2006) de-bordering as a product of migrants' various social activities and daily narratives in destination countries that have prompted reforms in their home countries. These studies, however, do not include de-bordering practices that outright defy border control as in the case of North Korean defectors' activities.

North Korean defectors' de-bordering activities take two forms: remittances and political activities that re-imagine North Korea (Choi, S., 2014). These two activities were chosen specifically on account of their economic and political impact on the de-bordering of North Korea. Remittances sent secretly to family members provided the money needed to buy necessities or sometimes luxury goods on the black market. The significance of remittances is twofold in that they undermined the government's economic control over the country and they circumvented restrictions on incoming currency with this one act of de-bordering. North Korean defectors' transnational ethnic networks have developed for and from these activities that specifically connect them to their families and friends at home.

Unlike the remittances that only could succeed in secrecy, global and regional political networks openly challenged the North Korean government's right to control the country and by extension the border. North Korean defectors endeavored to create governments-in-exile with the intention to raise awareness and discredit the current regime, or in preparation to rule or advise once the regime collapse. Whatever the approach, these networks allied defectors fighting for political reform in North Korea.

This chapter aims to answer two questions. How has remaining connected to their families, relatives, and friends at home through connections with other North and South Koreans as well as Chinese brokers de-bordered North Korea? How have financial and social remittances (Hoang, 2019; Levitt, 1998; Levitt and Lamba-Nieves, 2011) and alternative political activities challenged the North Korean border and government's authority? Here social remittances refer to the information, ideas, attitudes, and practices that defectors absorb then transmit to their home society through contact with home-based social networks (Levitt, 1998; Rapoport, 2016).

This study investigates the interaction between geopolitical dynamics and North Korean defectors' daily lives using participant observation and in-depth interviews to document de-bordering practices in two different destinations: London and Los Angeles. First, North Korean defectors in both cities maintained contact with their families still in North Korea through remittances and verbal or electronic communications. The transnational networks that allowed money and information to flow in eventually sustained the flow of vital information out. Second, networks of North Korean defectors staged political activities meant to undermine the existing sovereignty. The purpose in selecting these two locations where North Koreans' situations are widely dissimilar is to demonstrate that each group mounts a government-in-exile, their circumstances can influence their approach and the results. These linked political activities across geographical regions though they did not breach border control were vital to the ongoing opposition of North Korea's ruling party.

To answer the two questions that have been posed, I divide the rest of the chapter into six sections. The first section presents the theoretical framework of geopolitical ethnic networks. I demonstrate how transnational ethnic networks for de-bordering activities eventually evolve into geopolitical ethnic networks. This is followed by a summary of my research methods after which comes a comparison of North Korean defectors in the Los Angeles and London Koreatowns. The findings are explained in the two sections. The first finding section is subdivided into two parts. The first part examines the consequence of remittances as geopolitical activities on de-bordering, while the second part outlines how remittances develop into social remittances that together impact de-bordering. The second finding section illustrates first the regional networks in LA and then the global networks based in Europe that connect North Korean defectors living abroad. While these networks have not had a significant impact on moving reforms forward, they suggest alternative approaches to governing a North Korea free of the Kim regime. I conclude by discussing how the geopolitical ethnic networks' activities engage international agents in the de-bordering of North Korea.

GEOPOLITICAL ETHNIC NETWORKS
FOR UNALLOWED CONNECTIONS

To explain the intersection of transnational ethnic networks and geopolitical dynamics, I have suggested the concept of "geopolitical ethnic networks." Although there have been studies on transnational ethnic networks and geopolitics, there are few that bring the two concepts together as they are here. Most previous discussions on transnational ethnic networks (Kim, 2013; Mitchell, 2000; Wayland, 2004) have long deliberated on migrants' daily lives and the implications of their networks within the ethnic enclave but have not considered the impact of social forces such as globalization and geopolitical power on defectors' lives. It is only recently that studies have specifically investigated the effects globalization, the development of communication technologies, and the growth of global organizations on defectors' lives (Leurs and Ponzanesi, 2018).

Focus inward on the ethnic enclave can be in some part attributed to the ground-breaking work by Mark Granovetter (1973) on the importance of interpersonal ties. Building on this premise, several studies began to consider how transnational ethnic networks support ethnic businesses (For example, see Kariv et al., 2009; Rusinovic, 2008; Yeung, 2000, 2008; Etemad and Wright, 2003). Geography and migrant studies argue that asylum-seeker (Barak-Bianco and Baijman, 2015) and refugee entrepreneurship (Desai et al., 2020) rely heavily on social embeddedness, the extent to which human action takes place within social relations (Koelet, 2017), and fellow migrants' patronage to establish themselves (Bagwell, 2008; Katila and Wahlbeck, 2012; Portes, 1999; Wong and Ng, 2002; Muller and Wehrhahn, 2013; Jones et al., 2010; Miera, 2008; Mitchell, 2000; Yeung, 1997).

What these observations infer is that ethnic connections and therefore ethnic networks are invaluable for building trust in transnational entrepreneurship (Chen and Tan, 2009; Portes and Sensenbrenner, 1993). While some support this deduction, there are those that suggest that the significance attached to the relationship between ethnic networks and business has not been adequately justified or proved (Hsu and Saxenian, 2000). Others dispute these proposed deductions on the grounds that those studies did not include transnational ethnic networks developed for political change, knowledge sharing, and religious purposes (Friesen and Collins, 2017; Shin, 2019; Wayland, 2004), or those ethnic networks that offer housing, education, and psychological comforts (Bloch, 2014; Datta et al., 2006) to individuals. In the post-settlement life of defectors, refugees and asylum seekers, transnational ethnic networks play an important role in social bonding (Hanley et al., 2018) as well as finding employment and housing. Refugees' first, second, and even third choices tend towards countries that have historically accepted ethnic and co-ethnic refugees (Rüegger & Bohnet, 2018), with the expectation that an ethnic network will already be in place.

Although ethnic networks provide support for refugees and economic migrants alike, studies have illustrated that without the financial assistance that many economic migrants receive from home refugees depend on ethnic networks more. Some studies in countries including Canada have found that refugees struggle to integrate economically to the host economy and have higher unemployment and poverty rates (DeVoretz et al., 2004) than economic migrants. However, a study of refugees in the US showed many in fact had greater financial success than economic migrants (Cortes, 2004), proof of their determination and self-reliance. Defectors' success could be attributed to their willingness to repeatedly migrate, enticed by the allure of internationalized job markets (Robertson et al., 2016; Vertovec, 2004) relocate until they were satisfied with their situation.

From these multiple migrations, ethnic and multi-ethnic networks have emerged (Wang et al., 2015), connecting refugees, their families and friends, and other supporters across the origin society, the destination society, and successive destination societies (Bashi 2007; Olwig 2007; Lee 2011; Shin,

2018; Sperling 2014). Observing the interactions of North Korean defectors' multi-ethnic networks (Chung 2005; Shin, 2018), it becomes apparent that various ethnic Koreans including Korean-Chinese, South Korean migrants, and Korean-Americans are involved. Due in large part to multiple-destination migration, North Korean defectors' increased encounters connected them to defectors in many other countries as well as to those in their current destination. As a result, they could enlist support for and from networks anywhere in the world until eventually the networks became a worldwide organization.

Despite evidence of their mobility, studies on North Korean defectors in general (Chubb, 2013; Jeon et al., 2005; Gelézeau et al., 2013; Ko et al., 2004, for example) narrowly focus on the Korean peninsula and border areas (Chubb, 2013) or just in relation to North Korea (Lee and Gerber, 2009; Song and Denney, 2019). Other studies on North Koreans (Yoon, 2001) have focused on defectors' traumatic experiences and resettlement (Chung, 2008; Davis, 2006; Eom, 2009; Jeon et al., 2005). In recent years, however, several anthropological studies have begun to examine the experiences (Shin, 2018; Chung, 2014; Jung et al., 2017; Lee, 2014, 2019a, 2020) and political activities (Lee, 2019b) of North Korean defectors who have relocated to the Global North.

Building on this trend, this research focuses on the financial flows and political activities that shape the geopolitical ethnic networks that challenge the existing North Korean border (Shin, 2018, 2020). First, since North Koreans' defection automatically prevents them from communicating with or sending money to those remaining in their home country (Seo, 2019), they need to establish geopolitical ethnic networks to do so informally. As North Korean banks are prohibited from accepting money from Western institutions, networks that include informal actors such as brokers are necessary to relay money to their families (Hastings, 2016: 116). While remittances to North Korea are usually funneled through North Koreans living in Japan, China, and South Korea, Chinese actors also play a significant role in transmitting remittances such as outside information (Ha, 2011) and cash remittances (Lee and Gray, 2017). It is a reasonable assumption that if North Korea can breach the physical border with China, then Chinese brokers should be able to find a way to bank across the border. Although their origin society's borders are almost impenetrable, through transnational networks that at times include Chinese brokers, defectors maintain connections with their family members through remittances (Hoang, 2019; Levitt, 1998; Levitt and Lamba-Nieves, 2011). North Koreans' practice of sending remittances through a network of people over several countries to circumvent North Koreans border has become geopolitical in nature (Su and Cai, 2020, Rafig, 2020, Carbonara, 2019).

Globalization (or technology) has expedited sending the remittances that offer so much aid to the families and communities in the origin countries (Bakker, 2015; Hudson, 2008). Approximately 80 percent of the respondents surveyed send money to North Korea with average remittances ranging between 1.5 and 2 million won a year (1,350 to 1,800 USD) (Haggard and Noland, 2017). The annual sum of money from South Korea was estimated by the country's Ministry of Unification at around 10 million USD.

Since much remains unknown about the outcomes of remittances sent from the displaced to their relatives, however, the assessments of the relationship between remittances and development are not fully formed (Vargas-Silva, 2017). That these practices have mixed results, however, have been demonstrated by studies on the stabilizing and destabilizing effects of remittances and other forms of activities on the receiving country (Lyons, 2007; Horst, 2008). Many studies have found they have a positive effect on economic growth, poverty reduction, and consumption levels (Adams and Page, 2005; Chami, et al., 2005; Stark and Lucas, 1988; Meyer and Sherab, 2017; Taylor, 1992). Lum et al (2013)'s analysis indicates that government policy as barriers to diaspora involvement can provoke opposition to the government and result in estabilizing activities. These estabilizing activities are an extension of the geopolitical ethnic networks started with the remittances sent home by refugees. Seeking to change the regime that excludes them, some members of geopolitical ethnic networks become politically disruptive to unsettle the status quo that in some extreme cases can incite a civil war (Collier and Hoeffler, 2004; Cederman et al., 2009). Should the desired upheaval occur, these defectors' networks are prepared to offer financial assistance and political advice once an armistice is achieved and their homelands begin implementing reforms (Dietz, 2000; Kolstø, 1999; Korobkov and Zaionchkovskaia, 2004; Le Bail and Shen, 2008; Ma, 1993; Song, 2017).

What does tend to hold true is that remittances have a noticeably positive effect on low-income countries, while their impact on upper-middle and high-income countries are not quite so obvious (Issahaku et al., 2018). Studies show that the effects of remittances on a closed economy like North Korea's are having a significant impact on the country's regional economy. Some families have invested the money in long-term business plans, while others financed their economic networking in the *Jangmadang*, Korean for market, located between Hamgyung region in North Korea and Jilin Sheng in China. The remittances have also been used for the less practical purchases such as luxury items and cell phones (Kim, 2014).

As financial remittances have been increasing in recent years, so too have social remittances, and together their combined effects on the de-bordering of North Korea have been noticeable (Bansak and Simpson, 2019). Migrants and defectors embrace the information, attitudes and practices in the destination society that define social remittances (Luttmer and Singhal, 2011) they then export to their home societies through contact with their families and other social networks (Levitt, 1998; Rapoport, 2016). Both types of remittances are instrumental in de-bordering North Korea as they disobey the regulations that prevent the flows of money and communication. This is an example of political bottom-up activism that challenges the existing regime and identity (Hartnett, 2020; Rapoport, 2016).

Second, geopolitical activities by like-minded refugees united for political change create geopolitical ethnic networks to raise opposition to the ruling party de-border North Korea intentionally. Previous literature on Tibetan (McConnell, 2016) and Polish (Engel, 1993) governments-in-exile demonstrated that defectors' political activism can lead to alternative sovereignty such as in the case of North Korean governments-in-exile (Song, 2017). To effectively challenge the existing sovereignty of North Korea, political activities had to be coordinated, which involved the establishment and the development of regional and global networks by North Korean defectors.

De-bordering is not constituted solely by policy and laws (Nikiforova and Brednikova, 2018) but socially and symbolically through narratives and practices that reconstruct the national border (Agnew, 2008; Amelung and Machado, 2019; Chouliaraki, 2017; Rumford, 2006; Krasteva, 2017). While Gelézeau et al. (2013)'s book on North Korea acknowledges that de-bordering has occurred, this research concentrated only on events within the Korean peninsula and the Sunshine policy, which aims to soften North Korea's attitudes towards the South rather than to absorb the North. What this pinpoint focus on one location disregards is the physical, mental, and institutional construction (Agnew, 2008; Armbruster, 2011; Krasteva, 2017) and social and cultural practices and narratives of (de-)bordering that can occur anywhere and in any form (Amelung and Machado, 2019; Németh, 2017).

RESEARCH METHODS

The research methods of this study of North Korean defectors in two cities include in-depth interviews, focus groups, participant observation, and archival analysis. The fieldwork was conducted in December 2018 and January 2019 in London and in November 2019 in Los Angeles. As I have conducted fieldwork in London before, portions of the data and insights from previous studies (Shin, 2018, 2019) were also used here.

The subjects interviewed include key actors in organizations such as North Korean ethnic associations, North Korean defectors' global network, North Korean churches, the South Korean elderly association, and a North Korean language school for the second-generation. I carried out eighteen in-depth interviews (two North Korean defectors and five South Korean migrants in Los Angeles and nine North Korean defectors and two South Korean migrants in London). Each interview lasted one to two hours, they were semi-structured and usually tape-recorded, and all were in Korean. Those who worried about their status in the country refused being part of the interviews. It was especially difficult to access North Korean defectors in Los Angeles for this reason, but the interviewees were those who played a critical role in the nation-building.

I bolstered those interviews with participant observation, focus groups, and interviews with South Koreans who had at some time been involved in North Korean–related activities. Participant observations were made in a North Korean church in Los Angeles, and a North Korean children's school and at a social gathering in London. Any information that I acquired through participant observations and in-depth interviews was cross-checked. I conducted two focus groups with key actors in ethnic Korean community activities (one in LA and one in London). I also collected archival data from various sources including newspaper articles and the conversation.com. For the data analyses, I employed an interpretive approach and categorized the interview data according to the key themes of the study, compiling the interviews and finding sequences of spoken events.

NORTH KOREAN DEFECTORS IN LOS ANGELES AND LONDON

As approximately 30,000 North Korean defectors settled in South Korea, tales of human rights violations (Hong, 2014), human trafficking (Choi E, 2014; Kim et al., 2009), and life under a harsh dictatorship (Sung, 2019) have emerged. Many took a harrowing circuitous route through either China or Thailand to arrive in South Korea, intending to settle there permanently. Although quite a few interviewees disclosed that they had planned to remain in South Korea in the beginning, their disappointment with the treatment they received made some reconsider. During the in-depth interviews, I was told that even some members of the National Intelligence Service team, assigned to help North Koreans assimilate, expressed their resentment of the escapees. Usually, the fact that North Koreans' resettlement came at the expense of South Korean taxpayers was at the root of the animosity. Of those North Korean defectors[3] to leave South Korea, 746 defectors dispersed to twenty-five different countries including the US, the UK, Germany, and Israel, with twenty-eight defectors returning to North Korea.[4] Once they decided to relocate, their preference was for economically advanced countries such as the UK and the US. They explained that they preferred to move to a country like the UK, believing it to be a less discriminatory environment and have a better welfare system than many other countries.[5] They also cited a superior education system as one of their criteria, their children's education being one of their chief concerns.

Out of approximately 130 North Korean defectors to settle in the US, 50 of those live in the Los Angeles Koreatown[6] at the time of this study. Considering there were only 50 North Koreans in Los Angeles compared to the 700 to 1,000 North Koreans in and around New Malden, a suburb of London, their experiences were quite different. The ratio of North Koreans to South Koreans in London is 1:10–15, while in Los Angeles it is 1:1,083. Without the strength that comes from numbers, Los Angeles defectors are hesitant to interact and therefore socially isolated. Rather than stand out by establishing a place for themselves in the enclave, they attempt to blend in almost to the point of disappearing. North Korean defectors in London, however, are well adjusted and approach their daily encounters with South Koreans more as equals, collaborating with them on events, joint sponsorship, and committee memberships. The similarities and differences of each group's experiences are as follows.

Their similarities being few are quickly summed up in one paragraph. The language barrier was an obstacle that most shared. Nearly all North Koreans defectors face the challenge of learning a new language regardless of where they settle outside the Korean peninsula. For this reason, most North Koreans settled in or in the vicinity of the Koreatown in Los Angeles and London for easy access to the ethnic job market. For the same reason, most North Korean defectors worked for South Korean business owners, even those who had worked in South Korea and preferred not to work for a South Korean again. The other notable similarity between the two groups was that the majority of North Koreans would send a portion of their earnings home.

As already mentioned, their difference in numbers had a huge impact on their activities. Since there are so few North Koreans in LA, attempts to form ethnic organizations all their own have struggled. Even though they had no or few ethnic organizations of their own, they preferred not to participate in South Korean organizations to avoid the negative reactions to their North Korean-ness. Some North Koreans professed to pretending to come from the Kang Won province of South Korea, which has a similar accent to North Koreans, just prevent encountering prejudice.

Unlike in LA's Koreatown where North Korean defectors attempt to go unnoticed, London's Koreatown is the site of a "North Korean village." Recognized as having the largest concentration of North Korean defectors outside South Korea, their numbers are significant enough to allow North Koreans in London to establish their own ethnic organizations and activities and give them the confidence to join South Korean organizations.

Though the North Korean community in LA has little by way of organizations, there are several small North Korean churches.[7] At the time of this fieldwork there were only a few members in each, but those churches still managed to organize relatively significant activities that were attracting attention. The pastor of the Church of Nazarene, which was established in New York in 2003 and moved to Los Angeles later, was active in the community and even succeeded in establishing a shelter for North Koreans. After the pastor left the city in 2012, the North Korean community was bereft, and without her support and guidance the church's activities and atmosphere deteriorated. That the loss of one person could have a devastating effect on the community exposes the limited scope of their support systems.

The organizational activities of North Korean defectors in London, however, have committees of people to see that they run efficiently and uninterrupted. Furthermore, there is a diversity of choices including North Korean ethnic associations, children's Korean language schools, churches, and unification organizations. Since North Koreans actively participate in events organized by the South Korean ethnic associations, they consolidate their position in the larger Korean community even while identity tensions between North and South Koreans linger (Shin, 2018, 2019; Watson, 2015).

While North Koreans in both cities require assistance and sometimes charity, at least initially, North Koreans in Los Angeles are the recipients of South Korean migrants' charity on an ongoing basis. Individual donors would invite North Korean defectors to special events at Christmas or New Year's, and the National unification advisory committee would extend invitations to the Thanksgiving and New Year's celebrations it hosted. One South Korean lawyer has invited North Koreans to take a tour of Universal Studios every year since 2007. Ongoing charity in LA creates a dependency that reinforces the disparity between North and South Korea, whereas in London the North and South Koreans are building a new future side by side.

DE-BORDERING NORTH KOREA BY
FINANCIAL AND SOCIAL REMITTANCES

While remittances have been discussed for their connection to and support of family members in North Korea, this section focuses on de-bordering through financial and social remittances and their social and political outcomes. First, though, it is important to understand how remittances as transnational obligations (Ives et al., 2014) impact defectors' lives and why they choose or choose not to send them.

Remittances seem to be an unavoidable consequence and a biggest effect of defectors' escape. Some North Korean defectors give the impression that remittances are a form of reparation paid to their families for leaving them behind. Their sense of guilt is sometimes overwhelming. One interviewee in Los Angeles supposed that her main purpose in life and what drove her to continue to work so hard was so she could send remittances to her daughter and niece to alleviate a little of the guilt. She said,

> I send money to my daughter in North Korea and my niece in mainland China.
> (An interviewee in Los Angeles, 5 November 2019)

This interviewee confessed that she regretted leaving her daughter behind in North Korea. Since not all families in North Korea necessarily require remittances to alleviate their lot, some defectors send money simply to maintain a connection and not out of a sense of guilt. One interviewee in London clarified,

> I think every North Korean keeps sending remittances to their families in North Korea. Once a month, or once a year. Usually when we send money, we say hi. Otherwise, people call just to talk without sending money . . . I haven't sent money for a while because my siblings are well-off, probably better than I am.
> (An interviewee in London, 15 February 17, 2020)

Mostly North Koreans send money because there is an expectation that the defectors will be support their extended family. That many defectors do not earn enough to assure their futures in the destination societies makes it difficult for them to send money home too (Ives et al., 2014). An interviewee, a North Korean defector living in London, shared,

> My brother contacted me through a broker to announce his son's wedding. It's been ten years since I sent money. I sent £2,000. They called me back, saying they need more because my nephew's bride is from an affluent family. I refused it. I said that the living expenses and education in the UK are so expensive and I have two children, so I really couldn't send more. (An interviewee in London, 8 January 2019)

Like what this interviewee described, negative consequences have been observed including economic burdens on sending migrants (Kozel and Alderman, 1990; Stahl and Arnold, 1986).

Regardless of why, however, it is the how that is important here. To initiate cash flow and information sharing, transnational ethnic networks that facilitate the transfer of remittances and connect North Koreans inside and outside North Korea had to be established. In creating these networks, defectors challenged the border control and became agents of change by utilizing the following two ways.

First, North Korean defectors created a geopolitical ethnic network. It should be noted that these geopolitical ethnic networks include not only North Koreans and their Chinese brokers but other ethnic Koreans such as Korean-Chinese and South Koreans. However, only a few South Koreans are involved as brokers since they, unlike Korean-Chinese and Chinese, are not permitted to enter North Korea or contact the brokers and families living there. Defectors with the help of brokers would channel remittances into North Korea, eroding the regime's dominion over the country's finances. Often, at the time of the transfer, brokers would arrange a phone call so the families in North Korea could assure the defector that the money had been received. Initially these communications were brief and only about the money transfer, but now the conversations can involve everything from advice on setting up businesses (https://www.voakorea.com/archive/nk-experts-economy-111211129) to updates on their lives. These phone conversations that enable social remittances to flow in and sometimes out strengthen the geopolitical ethnic networks that connect defectors and their families and quietly initiate de-bordering.

That is on the condition that their activities remain undiscovered. One North Korean defector in London explained the penalty should a family be caught receiving remittances,

> There is a video of a North Korean defector's family in North Korea who apologizes for the defector's escape. A rumor among us [North Korean defectors] is that the family was receiving remittances from the defector, and a communist party member was bribed to let it slide. The party member was caught, so the family had to make the video as a punishment. (An interviewee in London, 10 January 2019)

Although the reason for this video is based on conjecture, knowledge of its existence demonstrates that the de-bordering by social remittances is having an effect. North Koreans defectors could not have learned about the video and the rumored reasons for it without their illicit phone conversations.

Second, cell phones have become the universal geopolitical tool for de-bordering. Whether it is financial remittances or the interchange of social remittances, technology is the newest and likely to be the most effective tool for de-bordering. In the case of North Korea, cell phones exacerbate one threat and create a new one. First, they are Chinese brokers' preferred means for transferring money from their accounts to accounts in North Korea (Kim, 2014: 32). Cell phones' convenience are expediting every aspect of the exchange. For example, rather than coordinate a audio conference call complicated by different time zones, North Korean interviewees reported that brokers have started to send videos of their families confirming the receipt of funds.

However, while cell phones simply speed up the existing system of financial and social remittances, they have created a direct line to defectors' family members unimaginable before. Which brings up the second point in how cell phones contribute to de-bordering. The proliferation of technology enables defectors to buy SIM cards that will allow them (Page 54) to access to North Korean's Koryolink network, disregarding the state's ban on communication. When one interviewee mentioned that he made calls to his sister and mother in North Korea, I asked about his sister. His response was "My sister? I talked to her last week," as if this was an ordinary occurrence and not breaking North Korean laws. His nonchalance was somewhat perplexing since even commonplace updates on life and society in general are in fact acts that challenge the borders. Due to technology, however, and the social remittances exchanged through everyday conversations, defectors have normalized de-bordering.

The financial and social remittances combined with technology have tested North Korea's borders and demonstrated that they are more porous than some might have expected. However, despite the geopolitical ethnic networks connecting North Korea to other societies and acts of de-bordering, the economic and political structure has not changed significantly (Connell, 2016). Undeterred, North Korean defectors' financial and social remittances are gradually engaging North Korea in limited globalization and opening the border even if only incrementally.

DE-BORDERING THROUGH ALTERNATIVE POLITICS

When the Moon Jae-In government in South Korea initiated a summit with the North Korean government in 2000, some North Koreans felt this exonerated the atrocities rather than censured them. This second section on de-bordering practices discusses the North Korean defectors' regional and global networks that put forward alternates to the existing political party to govern a country that they believe only North Koreans can.

Though there was a sense of betrayal when the South Korean government attempted reconciliation, most North Koreans had doubted that they had South Korea's fully understanding or supported them before that. Some accused the South Korean government of left-wing tendencies and sympathy for North Korea, while others believed that the South Korean government attempted to control North Korean defectors. One interviewee in Los Angeles criticized the Moon government for revoking financial support for North Korean–related organizations. When a famous North Korean defector celebrated the election of Moon Jae-In, many North Korean defectors withdrew their support for his leadership, another interviewee revealed.

Deciding that they could not trust the South Korean government, they engaged in activities such as those regional political networks in LA, believing it would give them a say in their country's future. North Koreans in LA tended to align themselves with Korean churches and those Korean American organizations that focused on conservative Christian politics and discourses driven by the Cold War politics (Kim, Nami 2016; Min 1996). The networks of churches and organizations that included North Koreans, South Koreans, and Korean Americans were well established by the 1990s and the early 2000s according to all five Korean American interviewees in Los Angeles. Even though the primary purpose of their activities was to liberate North Korea, various events were also organized as fund-raisers that would financially and politically support North Korean defectors. It was during those years that some Korean Americans even volunteered to travel to North Korea for charity work.

The interview subjects explained that as time passed, North Korean defectors' interest in organizational activities declined in every area except for politics, and as a result, only a few charity activities continued. This was partly due to the influence of conservative Christian politics on North Koreans, as well as US actors focused on establishing an exile government. The idea that a government-in-exile would put pressure on the North Korean government and could step in to rule when the regime collapsed was an appealing one.

In 2016, North Koreans based in Los Angeles announced that they would establish a government-in-exile by the following year. Plagued by problems, the project was delayed until 2018. Once they were established, the opposition to the Workers' Party of Korea of approximately twenty North Korean defectors still struggled. One interviewee active in the organization explained that the government-in-exile collapsed within a year or two due to infighting. Not only was there strife within the party but according to this interviewee the North Korean community and liberal South Korean organizations in Los Angeles disapproved. He went on to explain that he would have preferred to coordinate organizations focused on daily needs such as an ethnic association, but his colleagues were anxious to build a government-in-exile. Those people who disapproved of the government-in-exile but still wished to contribute to the improvement of defectors' lives often engaged instead in activities such as the ethnic associations that the interviewee mentioned.

Whether one agreed or disagreed, there was a consensus that if nothing else the government-in-exile's existence and its members' activities raised awareness by attracting media attention. Another active member of the exile government in Los Angeles explained that their main goal was to remind the world the of the Kim Jong-un regime's brutality, stating

An exile government should put pressure on the North Korean government and expose their wrongdoings. (An interviewee in Los Angeles, 3 November 2019)

North Korean political networks produce discourses on how to destabilize the current regime and engage defectors in activities that help them feel by making a difference they are empowered In fact, North Korean defectors' successful escape was the first stage to empowerment as well as an act of de-bordering that defied even if it did not destabilize the state's authority. However, the political aspirations of North Koreans in LA are quite unlike the largely apolitical activities of North Koreans in London. European actors saw themselves as mediators between the North Korean and the South Korean regimes and representatives of North Korean defectors' interests. An interviewee in London discussing the European exile government stated,

> It does not replace the North Korean government, but the presence of an exile government itself is meaningful because many people in North Korea neither like nor trust the South Korean government. (An interviewee in London, 8 January 2019)

This interviewee in London also believed that those North Korean defectors that have experienced the two Koreas and Europe should take the lead in a future united Korea. Unlike the LA exile government that aspired to govern, the European exile government's main purpose would be to advise how best to govern a free North Korea. Though key actors in both cities attempted to mount an exile government, albeit for different reasons, they were not interested in collaborating with each other. According to the European faction, the US actors were incapable of organizing a government and were too easily manipulated by right-wing American politicians. The LA actors struggled to sustain a group and were not interested in being overwhelmed by actors in other networks.

Though the group in London rejected a partnership with the LA government-in-exile, there was interest in forming a 'the North Korean refugees' global network.' In 2013, they held their first meeting in London and elected two chairs for the European network, one based in London and the other in Brussels. While a basis of operation is essential for administration, the far reach of North Korean defectors' geopolitical ethnic networks through repeated mobilities cannot be so easily consolidated. To maintain these worldwide networks and stay informed about goings-on in other countries, North Korean defectors maintain contact mainly through Kakaotalk, a free mobile instant messaging application. Although the European networks were not campaigning against the North Koreans government, unlike the exile government in LA, their activities to unify North Koreans in preparation to return is an act of de-bordering. Both in LA and in London, North Koreans have planned for the day that the Kim regime would fall and how they would respond. They have envisioned a future version of the North Korea that though it may not physically de-border North Korea has begun to do so in their imaginations.

While the approaches of the LA and London geopolitical ethnic networks differed, by suggesting alternative governments or visions of what could be, they redefined the North Korean state in an act of de-bordering. Ironically, while geopolitical ethnic networks re-imagined a North Korea free of the Kim regime have de-bordered the country, by restating the very things they disagree with this has essentially been re-bordering North Korea.

By focusing attention on border-crossers' activities that build these networks rather than the nation states' laws and policies on refugees and defectors, this research contributes to the academic debates on bordering as a process. It examined the capacity of North Korean defectors' geopolitical ethnic networks to de-border North Korea. Geopolitical ethnic networks developed as follows. First, the continued contact of North Korean defectors with their family members in the home country challenged the border control and opposed the regime. Through their defection and their practices of financial and social remittances, they proved that control over the border is physically and conceptually fallible thereby de-bordering North Korea. Second, North Korean defectors developed global and regional networks to plan for a future North Korea freed from the current regime in acts of de-bordering.

Defectors' cultural and ethnic identity emerge in terms of nationalist thought about culture, place, and identity (Eastmond, 1998). Their attachment to their origin society, left less by choice than the need to escape a difficult political situation, combined with their continued or re-established connection to family helped create transnational ethnic networks. This same attachment influenced by the political atmosphere of the home and destination country, as well as the politics within the Korean community, has contributed to the development of the geopolitical networks.

The past few years have witnessed slight changes in the geopolitical economy of the Korean peninsula between South Korea and North Korea, as well as North Korea and other involved countries. When origin countries' situations change, recent studies on defectors (See Song, 2017) reveal that their networks and activities evolve in response. North Korean defectors and their exile governments have been preparing their response to the possible changes in the geopolitical bordering dynamics of their origin society. Regardless of the when these changes might occur, the country's structural development will likely be built with the money individual defectors send to their families to legitimize their defection and assuage their guilt.

In the greater scheme of an entire country's geopolitical and economic situation, defectors' influence might not be glaringly obvious, but their existence and activities have bordering as well as de-and re-bordering potential. This research contributes to the debate and extends understanding of de-bordering but also calls for developing the debate on re-bordering in terms of human agents' discourses and networks. The discussion on remittances and the ease with which funds can now be transferred also has implications for the migration-development nexus (Bailey, 2010; Henry et al., 2004). Financial remittances might or might not have the problematic secondary effect of supporting the sustainability and development of North Korea under the current regime. The long-term consequences are difficult to predict. Whether the remittances continue to simply supplement the North Korean economy and allow the regime to stay in power or they motivate the country to open its door is yet to be seen.

NOTES

1. This chapter is based on the previously published article, Shin, HaeRan. "The Geopolitical Ethnic Networks for De-bordering: North Korean Defectors in Los Angeles and London." *Asian Journal of Peacebuilding* 9, no. 2 (2021): 209–232.

2. I prefer the term "defector" in this study as it refers to those who escaped from their homeland, forsaking everything, and therefore it applies to all North Koreans living in another country. The term refugee is more often associated with the legal status determined by the destination society, and since the interview subjects include refugees, refugee applicants, and permanent residents/citizens it is not an accurate term for the purpose of this study. Migrants, unlike defectors and refugees, are usually free to return to their home countries, and for that reason it is not a designation that would pertain to North Koreans. Kim (2012) discussed the changing and occasionally controversial social discourses of each term and the ways in which they have been related to North Korean defectors in South Korea. In those instances when I have used the terms migrant or refugee in this chapter, it has been in keeping with their use in other studies being discussed such as Kim's.

3. Different sources suggest different numbers of those North Korean defectors who left South Korea after staying for a while. Out of the 30,000 defectors, it was estimated 749 (https://www.mk.co.kr/news/politics/view/2019/10/813016/) to 1,500 (Chosun, 18 November 2019 https://news.chosun.com/site/data/html_dir/2019/11/18/2019111800332.html, accessed on 23 April 2020) to 3,000 (Topdaily, 18 June, 2019. http://www.topdaily.kr/news/articleView.html?idxno=57567, accessed on 23 April 23, 2020) moved to other countries.

4. https://www.koreatimes.co.kr/www/nation/2017/11/103_238860. html accessed on July 28, 2020; https://www.hankookilbo.com/News/Read/

A2020072615120002800, accessed on June 8, 2020, an interview with a South Korean involved in a North Korean church mentioned Israel.

5. https://theconversation.com/why-does-the-uk-deport-north-korean-asylum-seekers-92129

6. https://ubin.krihs.re.kr/ubin/mobile/wurban/maincitynews_view. php?no=1801&thema=, accessed on 22 July 22, 2020.

7. Christianity has been quite strong in Los Angeles, having more than ten thousand big and small Korean churches.

REFERENCES

Adams Jr., Richard H., and John Page. 2005. "Do international migration and remittances reduce poverty in developing countries?" *World Development*, 33(10): 1645–1669.

Agnew, John. 2008. "Borders on the mind: Re-framing border thinking." *Ethics & Global Politics*, 1(4): 175–191.

Amelung, Nina, and Helena Machado. 2019. "'Bio-bordering' processes in the EU: de-bordering and re-bordering along transnational systems of biometric database technologies." *International Journal of Migration and Border Studies*, 5(4): 392–408.

Armbruster, Heidi. 2011. "Bordering, de-bordering, cross-bordering: A conclusion." In *Negotiating Multicultural Europe*, eds. Armbruster, Heidi, and Ulrike Hanna Meinhof. London: Palgrave Macmillan, 185–207.

Bagwell, Susan. 2008. "Transnational family networks and ethnic minority business development." *International Journal of Entrepreneurial Behaviour & Research*, 14(6): 377–394.

Bailey, Adrian J. 2010. "Population geographies, gender, and the migration-development nexus." *Progress in Human Geography* 34: 375–386.

Bakker, Matt. 2015. "Discursive representations and policy mobility: how migrant remittances became a 'development tool.'" *Global Networks*, 15(1): 21–42.

Bansak, Cynthia, and Nicole B. Simpson. 2015. "Asylum seeker entrepreneurs in Israel." *economic sociology the European electronic newsletter*, 16(2): 4–13.

Bansak, Cynthia, and Nicole B. Simpson. 2019. "Updating an ODA policy in Canada: The role of global remittances in development." *The School of Public Policy Publications*, 12.

Bashi, Vilna. 2007. *Survival of the knitted: Immigrant social networks in a stratified world.* Stanford University Press.

Bloch, Alice. 2014. "Living in fear: Rejected asylum seekers living as irregular migrants in England." *Journal of Ethnic and Migration Studies*, 40(10): 1507–1525.

Carbonara, Miriana. 2019. "Border paradox: Crossing, experiencing, and representing borders between Bologna and Modena in the early modern period." *World Art*, 9 (3): 277–302.

Cederman, Lars-Erik, Halvard Buhaug, and Jan Ketil Rød. 2009. "Ethno-nationalist dyads and civil war: A GIS-based analysis." *Journal of Conflict Resolution, 53*(4): 496–525.

Chami, Ralph, Connel Fullenkamp, and Samir Jahjah. 2005. "Are immigrant remittance flows a source of capital for development?." *IMF Staff papers, 52*(1): 55–81.

Chen, Wenhong, and Justin Tan. 2009. "Understanding transnational entrepreneurship through a network lens: Theoretical and methodological considerations." *Entrepreneurship theory and Practice, 33*(5): 1079–1091.

Choi, Eunyoung. 2014. "North Korean women's narratives of migration: Challenging hegemonic discourses of trafficking and geopolitics." *Annals of the Association of American Geographers, 104*(2): 271–279.

Choi, Shine. 2014. *Re-Imagining North Korea in International Politics: Problems and Alternatives.* Routledge.

Chouliaraki, Lilie. 2017. "Symbolic bordering: The self-representation of migrants and refugees in digital news." *Popular Communication, 15*(2): 78–94.

Chubb, Danielle. 2013. "North Korean defector activism and South Korean politics." In *De-Bordering Korea: tangible and intangible legacies of the sunshine policy.* eds. Gelézeau, Valérie, Koen De Ceuster, and Alain Delissen. Routledge, 105–120.

Chung, Angie Y. "'Politics without the politics': The evolving political cultures of ethnic non-profits in Koreatown, Los Angeles." *Journal of Ethnic and Migration Studies 31*, no. 5 (2005): 911–929.

Chung, Byung-Ho. 2008. "Between defector and migrant: Identities and strategies of North Koreans in South Korea." *Korean Studies*: 1–27.

Chung, Byung-Ho. 2014. "North Korean refugees as penetrant transnational migrants." *Urban Anthropology and Studies of Cultural Systems and World Economic Development*: 329–361.

Collier, Paul, and Anke Hoeffler. 2004. "Greed and grievance in civil war." *Oxford economic papers, 56*(4): 563–595.

Cortes, Kalena E. 2004. "Are refugees different from economic immigrants? Some empirical evidence on the heterogeneity of immigrant groups in the United States." *Review of Economics and Statistics, 86*(2): 465–480.

Datta, Kavita, Cathy Mcilwaine, Yara Evans, Joanna Herbert, Jon May, and Jane Wills. 2006. "Work and survival strategies among low-paid migrants in London." In *London: Queen Mary, University of London.*

Davis, K. 2006. "Brides, bruises and the border: The trafficking of North Korean women into China." *SAIS Review of International Affairs, 26*(1), 131–141.

Desai, Sameeksha, Wim Naudé, and Nora Stel. 2020. "Refugee entrepreneurship: context and directions for future research." *Small Business Economics*, 1–13.

DeVoretz, Don J., Sergiy Pivnenko, and Morton Beiser. 2004. "The economic experiences of refugees in Canada." ZA Discussion Papers, No. 1088, Institute for the Study of Labor (IZA), Bonn.

Dietz, Barbara. 2000. "German and Jewish migration from the former Soviet Union to Germany: Background, trends and implications." *Journal of Ethnic and Migration Studies, 26*(4): 635–652.

Eastmond, Marita. 1998. "Nationalist discourses and the construction of difference: Bosnian Muslim refugees in Sweden." *Journal of refugee studies, 11*(2): 161–181.

Engel, David. 1993. *Facing a holocaust: The Polish government-in-exile and the Jews, 1943–1945*. UNC Press Books.

Eom, Tae-Wan. 2009. "A phenomenological approach to traumatic experiences among North Korean defectors." *Korean Journal of Social Welfare, 61*(2), 189–213.

Etemad, Hamid, and Richard W. Wright, eds. 2003. *Globalization and entrepreneurship: policy and strategy perspectives*. Edward Elgar Publishing.

Friesen, Wardlow, and Francis L. Collins. 2017. "Brain chains: managing and mediating knowledge migration." *Migration and Development, 6*(3): 323–342.

Gelézeau, Valérie, Koen De Ceuster, and Alain Delissen. 2013. eds. *De-bordering Korea: tangible and intangible legacies of the sunshine policy*. Routledge.

Gelézeau, Valérie, Koen De Ceuster, and Alain Delissen. 2013. The hard life of North Korean migrants in South Korean society. In *De-bordering Korea: tangible and intangible legacies of the sunshine policy*. eds. Gelézeau, Valérie, Koen De Ceuster, and Alain Delissen. Routledge, 121–135.

Granovetter, Mark S. 1973. "The strength of weak ties." *American journal of Sociology, 78*(6): 1360–80.

Ha, Sunghak. *The Influx of outside information and regime stability in North Korea*. A Master's Thesis, Georgetown University, 2011.

Haggard, Stephan, and Marcus Noland. 2017. *Hard target: Sanctions, inducements, and the case of North Korea*. Stanford University Press.

Hanley, Jill, Adnan Al Mhamied, Janet Cleveland, Oula Hajjar, Ghayda Hassan, Nicole Ives, Rim Khyar, and Michaela Hynie. 2018. "The social networks, social support and social capital of Syrian refugees privately sponsored to settle in Montreal: Indications for employment and housing during their early experiences of integration." *Canadian Ethnic Studies, 50*(2): 123–148.

Hartnett, Lynne Ann. 2020. "Relief and revolution: Russian émigrés' political remittances and the building of political transnationalism." *Journal of Ethnic and Migration Studies, 46*(6): 1040–1056.

Hastings, Justin. 2016. *A most enterprising country: North Korea in the global economy*. Cornell University Press.

Henry, L., Mohan, G., & Yanacopulos, H. 2004. "Networks as transnational agents of development." *Third World Quarterly, 25*(5), 839–855.

Hoang, Lan Anh. 2019. "Young women and girls as providers for households of origin." *SUPPORTING BRIGHTER FUTURES*, IOM UN Migration. 62–111

Hong, Christine. 2014. "War by other means: The violence of North Korean human rights." *Asia-Pacific Journal, 12*(13): 1–30.

Horst, Cindy. 2008. "The transnational political engagements of refugees: Remittance sending practices amongst Somalis in Norway: Analysis." *Conflict, Security & Development, 8*(3): 317–339.

Hsu, Jinn-Yuh and AnnaLee Saxenian. 2000. "The limits of guanxi capitalism: Transnational collaboration between Taiwan and the US." *Environment and Planning A 32*(11): 1991–2005.

Hudson, David. 2008. "Developing geographies of financialisation: Banking the poor and remittance securitisation." *Contemporary Politics 14*(3): 315–333.

Issahaku, Haruna, Joshua Yindenaba Abor, and Mohammed Amidu. 2018. "The Effects of Remittances on Economic Growth: Reexamining the Role of Institutions." *The Journal of Developing Areas 52*(4): 29–46.

Ives, Nicole, Jill Hanley, Christine A. Walsh, and David Este. 2014. "Transnational elements of newcomer women's housing insecurity: remittances and social networks." *Transnational Social Review*, *4*(2–3): 152–167.

Jeon, WooTaek, ChangHyung Hong, ChangHo Lee, Dong Kee Kim, Mooyoung Han, and SungKil Min. 2005. "Correlation between traumatic events and posttraumatic stress disorder among North Korean defectors in South Korea." *Journal of Traumatic Stress*, *18*(2): 147–154.

Jones, Trevor, Monder Ram, and Nick Theodorakopoulos. 2010. "Transnationalism as a force for ethnic minority enterprise? The case of Somalis in Leicester." *International Journal of Urban and Regional Research*, *34*(3): 565–585.

Jung, Kyungja, Bronwen Dalton, and Jacqueline Willis. 2017. "The onward migration of North Korean refugees to Australia: In search of cosmopolitan habitus." *Cosmopolitan Civil Societies: An Interdisciplinary Journal 9*(3): 1–20.

Kariv, Dafna, Teresa V. Menzies, Gabrielle A. Brenner, and Louis Jacques Filion. 2009. "Transnational networking and business performance: Ethnic entrepreneurs in Canada." *Entrepreneurship and regional development*, *21*(3): 239–264.

Katila, Saija, and Östen Wahlbeck. 2012. "The role of (transnational) social capital in the start-up processes of immigrant businesses: The case of Chinese and Turkish restaurant businesses in Finland." *International small business journal*, *30*(3): 294–309.

Kim, Eunyoung, Minwoo Yun, Mirang Park, and Hue Williams. 2009. "Cross border North Korean women trafficking and victimization between North Korea and China: An ethnographic case study." *International Journal of Law, Crime and Justice*, *37*(4): 154–169.

Kim, Harris H. 2013. "Transnational ethnic networks and the creation of immigrant social capital: A multilevel analysis." *The Social Science Journal*, *50*(3): 349–358.

Kim, Nami. "The Impasse of Telling the 'Moral Story': Transnational Christian Human Rights Advocacy for North Koreans." In *Critical Theology against US Militarism in Asia*. Palgrave Macmillan, New York, 2016, 153–176.

Kim, Yonho. 2014. "Cell phones in North Korea." *Washington, DC: The US-Korea Institute at SAIS*.

Koelet, Suzana, Christof Van Mol, and Helga AG De Valk. 2017. "Social embeddedness in a harmonized Europe: The social networks of European migrants with a native partner in Belgium and the Netherlands." *Global Networks 17*(3): 441–459.

Ko, Sung Ho, Kiseon Chung, and Yoo-seok Oh. 2004. "North Korean defectors: Their life and well-being after defection." *Asian perspective*, *28*(2): 65–99.

Kolstø, Pål. 1999. "Territorialising diasporas: The case of Russians in the former soviet republics." *Millennium*, *28*(3): 607–631.

Korobkov, Andrei V., and Zhanna A. Zaionchkovskaia. 2004. "The changes in the migration patterns in the post-soviet states: The first decade." *Communist and Post-Communist Studies, 37*(4): 481–508.

Kozel, Valerie, and Harold Alderman. 1990. "Factors determining work participation and labour supply decisions in Pakistan's urban areas." *The Pakistan Development Review, 29*(1): 1–18.

Krasteva, Anna. 2017. "If borders did not exist, Euroscepticism would have invented them or, on Post-Communist re/de/re/bordering in Bulgaria." *Geopolitics, 25*(3): 678–705.

Le Bail, Hélène, and Wei Shen. 2008. "The return of the 'brains' to China: What are the social, economic, and political impacts." *Asie Visions*, 11: 1 –31.

Leandro, Francisco José BS, and Paulo Afonso B. Duarte, eds. *The belt and road initiative: An old archetype of a new development model*. Springer Nature, 2020.

Lee, Hee Young, and Jurg Gerber. 2009. "'We just do what we think is right. We just do what we are told': Perceptions of crime and justice of North Korean defectors." *Asia Pacific Journal of Police & Crime Justice*, 7: 21–48.

Lee, Helen. 2011. "Rethinking transnationalism through the second generation." *The Australian Journal of Anthropology, 22*(3): 295–313.

Lee, Jong-Woon, and Kevin Gray. 2017. "Cause for optimism? Financial sanctions and the rise of the Sino-North Korean border economy." *Review of International Political Economy 24*(3): 424–453.

Lee, Soojung. 2014. "Social relations and attitudes between South Korean migrants and North Korean refugees in the Korea Town, New Malden, U.K." *North Korean Studies Review 18*(1): 137–174.

Lee, Soojung. 2019a. "From 'North Korea defectors' to 'social patriarchs': The meanings of migration experience and social activities of North Korean migrant men in the United Kingdom." *North Korean Studies Review 22*(2): 8–46.

Lee, Soojung. 2019b. "Homeland politics of North Korean migrants in the U.K." *Korea and World Politics 35*(4): 177–213.

Lee, Soojung. 2020. "A relational understanding of 'senses of well-being' of North Korean immigrants in the U.K." *Contemporary Society and Multiculture 10*(2): 177–213.

Leurs, Koen, and Sandra Ponzanesi. 2018. "Connected migrants: Encapsulation and cosmopolitanization." *Popular Communication, 16*(1): 4–20.

Levitt, Peggy, and Deepak Lamba-Nieves. 2011. "Social remittances revisited." *Journal of Ethnic and Migration Studies, 37*(1): 1–22.

Levitt, Peggy. 1998. "Social remittances: Migration driven local-level forms of cultural diffusion." *The International Migration Review, 32*(4): 926–948.

Lum, Brandon, Milana Nikolko, Yiagadeesen Samy, and David Carment. 2013. "Diasporas, remittances and state fragility: Assessing the linkages." *Ethnopolitics 12*(2): 201–219.

Luttmer, Erzo FP, and Monica Singhal. 2011. "Culture, context, and the taste for redistribution." *American Economic Journal: Economic Policy 3*(1): 157–79.

Lyons, Terrence. 2004. "Engaging diasporas to promote conflict resolution: transforming hawks into doves." In *Working Paper presented at the Institute for Global Conflict and Cooperation Washington Policy Seminar.*

Ma, Shu-Yun. 1993. "The exit, voice, and struggle to return of Chinese political exiles." *Pacific Affairs* 66(3): 368–385.

McConnell, Fiona. 2016. *Rehearsing the state: The political practices of the Tibetan government-in-exile.* John Wiley & Sons.

Meyer, Dietmar, and Adela Shera. 2017. "The impact of remittances on economic growth: An econometric model." *EconomiA, 18*(2): 147–155.

Miera, Frauke. 2008. "Transnational strategies of Polish migrant entrepreneurs in trade and small business in Berlin." *Journal of ethnic and migration studies, 34*(5): 753–770.

Min, Pyong Gap. 1996. *Caught in the middle: Korean communities in New York and Los Angeles.* University of California Press.

Mitchell, Katharyne. 2008. "Networks of ethnicity." In *A companion to economic geography*, ed. Sheppard, Eric, 392–407.

Müller, Angelo, and Rainer Wehrhahn. 2013. "Transnational business networks of African intermediaries in China: Practices of networking and the role of experiential knowledge. *DIE ERDE–Journal of the Geographical Society of Berlin, 144*(1), 82–97.

Németh, Ágnes. 2017. "The immigrant 'Other' and artistic expression: (De) bordering via festivals and social activism in Finland." *Journal of Cultural Geography, 34*(1): 51–69.

Newman, David, and Anssi Paasi. 1998. "Fences and neighbours in the postmodern world: boundary narratives in political geography." *Progress in Human Geography, 22*(2): 186–207.

Nikiforova, Elena, and Olga Brednikova. 2018. "On labor migration to Russia: Central Asian migrants and migrant families in the matrix of Russia's bordering policies." *Political Geography, 66*: 142–150.

Olwig, Karen Fog. 2007. *Caribbean journeys: An ethnography of migration and home in three family networks.* Duke University Press.

Portes, Alejandro, and Julia Sensenbrenner. 1993. "Embeddedness and immigration: Notes on the social determinants of economic action." *American Journal of Sociology, 98*(6): 1320–1350.

Portes, Alejandro. 1999. "Conclusion: Towards a new world-the origins and effects of transnational activities." *Ethnic and racial studies, 22*(2): 463–477.

Rafiq, Samah. 2020. "Linear Borders, Partition and Identity in Postcolonial South Asia." *Geopolitics:* 1–23. DOI: 10.1080/14650045.2020.1757652.

Rapoport, Hillel. 2016. "A democratic dividend from emigration?" Policy Brief, Migration Policy Centre Issue, 2016/07.

Robertson, Zoe, Raelene Wilding, and Sandra Gifford. 2016. "Mediating the family imaginary: Young people negotiating absence in transnational refugee families." *Global Networks, 16*(2): 219–236.

Rüegger, Seraina, and Heidrun Bohnet. 2018. "The Ethnicity of Refugees (ER): A new dataset for understanding flight patterns." *Conflict Management and Peace Science*, *35*(1): 65–88.

Rumford, Chris. 2006. "Theorizing borders." *European Journal of Social Theory*, *9*(2): 155–169.

Rusinovic, Katja. 2008. "Transnational embeddedness: Transnational activities and networks among first-and second-generation immigrant entrepreneurs in the Netherlands." *Journal of Ethnic and Migration Studies*, *34*(3): 431–451.

Seo, Soomin. 2019. "One foot in prison and one foot out: State-appointed local journalistic labor in North Korea." *Journalism Studies*, *20*(12): 1747–1763.

Shin, HaeRan. 2020. "Transnational Ethnic Networks." In *International Encyclopedia of Human Geography*, 2nd edition. vol. 13, ed. Audrey Kobayashi. Oxford: Elsevier, 389–393.

Shin, HaeRan. 2019. "Extra-territorial nation-building in flows and relations: North Korea in the global networks and an ethnic enclave." *Political Geography*, Vol. 74, 102047.

Shin, HaeRan. 2018. "The territoriality of ethnic enclaves: dynamics of transnational practices and geopolitical relations within and beyond a Korean transnational enclave in New Malden, London." *Annals of the American Association of Geographers*, *108*(3), 756–772.

Song, Jay, and Steven Denney. 2019. "Studying North Korea through North Korean migrants: Lessons from the field." *Critical Asian Studies*, *51*(3): 451–466.

Song, Jiyoung. 2017. "Co-evolution of networks and discourses: A case from North Korean defector-activists." *Australian Journal of International Affairs*, *71*(3): 284–299.

Sperling, Jessica. 2014. "Conceptualising 'inter-destination transnationalism': The presence and implication of coethnic ties between destination societies." *Journal of Ethnic and Migration Studies*, *40*(7): 1097–1115.

Stahl, Charles W., and Fred Arnold. 1986. "Overseas workers' remittances in Asian development." *International Migration Review*, *20*(4): 899–925.

Stark, Oded, and Robert EB Lucas. 1988. "Migration, remittances, and the family." *Economic Development and Cultural Change*, *36*(3): 465–481.

Su, Xiaobo, and Xiaomei Cai. 2020. "Space of compromise: Border control and the limited inclusion of Burmese migrants in China." *Annals of the American Association of Geographers*, *110*(3): 847–863.

Sung, Minkyu. 2019. "Balloon warriors for North Korean human rights activism: a critique of North Korean defector-activists' post-humanitarianism." *Critical Asian Studies*, *51*(3): 355–367.

Taylor, J. Edward. 1992. "Remittances and inequality reconsidered: Direct, indirect, and intertemporal effects," *Journal of Policy Modelling*, *14*(2): 187–208.

Tervonen, Miika, and Anca Enache. 2017. "Coping with everyday bordering: Roma migrants and gatekeepers in Helsinki." *Ethnic and Racial Studies*, *40*(7): 1114–1131.

Van Houtum, Henk J., Kramsch, O. T., and Zierhofer, F. W. 2005. *Prologue, b/ordering space*. Ashgate, UK: Aldershot.

Van Houtum, Henk, and Ton Van Naerssen. 2002. "Bordering, ordering and other-ing." *Tijdschrift voor economische en sociale geografie, 93*(2): 125–136.

Vargas-Silva, Carlos. 2017. "Remittances sent to and from the forcibly displaced." *The Journal of Development Studies, 53*(11): 1835–1848.

Vertovec, Steven. 2004. "Cheap calls: The social glue of migrant transnationalism." *Global Networks, 4*(2): 219–224.

Wang, Zheng, Fangzhu Zhang, and Fulong Wu. 2015. "Intergroup neighbouring in urban China: Implications for the social integration of migrants." *Urban Studies, 53*(4): 651–668.

Watson, Iain. 2015. "The Korean diaspora and belonging in the UK: Identity tensions between North and South Koreans." *Social Identities, 21*(6): 545–561.

Wayland, Sarah. 2004. "Ethnonationalist networks and transnational opportunities: The Sri Lankan Tamil diaspora." *Review of International Studies, 30*: 405–426.

Wong, Lloyd L., and Michele Ng. 2002. "The emergence of small transnational enter-prise in Vancouver: The case of Chinese entrepreneur immigrants." *International Journal of Urban and Regional Research, 26*(3): 508–530.

Yeung, Henry Wai-chung. 1997. "Business networks and transnational corporations: A study of Hong Kong firms in the ASEAN region." *Economic Geography, 73*(1): 1–25.

Yeung, Henry Wai-chung. 2000. "Embedding foreign affiliates in transnational busi-ness networks: the case of Hong Kong firms in Southeast Asia." *Environment and Planning A, 32*: 201–222.

Yeung, Henry Wai-chung. 2008. "Perspectives on Inter☐organizational Relations in Economic Geography." In *The Oxford Handbook of Inter-Organizational Relations*. Eds. Cropper, Steve, Mark Ebers, Chris Huxham, and Peter Smith Ring. Oxford Handbooks. 473–501.

Yoon, In Jin. 2001. "North Korean diaspora: North Korean defectors abroad and in South Korea." *Development and Society. 30*(1): 1–26.

SECTION 3

North Korean Identities Reconstituted as They Muddle Through

Chapter 7

Representation and Self-Presentation of North Korean Defectors in South Korea

Image, Discourse, and Voices

Kyung Hyo Chun

This chapter examines how media representations reproduce images of North Korean defectors, and how North Korean defectors' self-presentation contradicts the media with narratives of how they imagine themselves.[1] The media-perpetuated image of North Korean defectors as displaced victims whose identities are mostly formed by life under an oppressive regime fails to grasp the intersection of their aspirations, determination, and agency. The self-presentation of North Korean defectors reveals that they are eager to assume responsibility for the construction and control of their own images, which goes beyond the hitherto nationalized, gendered, and ethicized identities. Self-presentation, despite a certain amount of autonomy, is a product of strategic choices conditioned by social discourse and media representation.

As of the end of 2021, the number of the North Korean defectors residing in South Korea is approximately 34,000, which out of over 51 million people is a very small portion of the country's entire population. This even holds true when their numbers are compared to the approximately 1,600,000 international brides and 1,700,000 long-term foreign visitors living in South Korea. Yet, the unique political circumstances dividing the two Koreas, the aspiration or expectation of unification, and the symbolism of a unified nation combine to render North Korean defectors in South Korea as a group of considerable significance. Since North Korean defectors are not viewed as wholly "other" by most South Koreans, what should be approached as adaptation and integration is instead treated as a reintegration to society.

In addition to having a language in common, North Korean defectors are believed to have an advantage over other migrants as heirs to a shared 5,000 years of history as Koreans and an assumed solidarity with their fellow South Koreans. The notion that a shared language and cultural affinity is enough to unite North Korean defectors and South Koreans is short-sighted. Because of presumed sharedness in historical experience and culture, North Korean defectors are considered qualitatively different from other ethnic groups and are regarded as objects of complete integration rather than that of effective adaptation (Choi, 2012; Choo, 2006; Seo, 2013; Moon, 2010).

This perspective on sharedness also supported the assumption that South Korea would be the final and indisputably optimal destination for North Korean defectors. Following this line of thought, the act of crossing borders to finally arrive in South Korea would be considered the achievement of their ultimate goal. The next logical step would be to become a "normal" South Korean citizen through full integration, if not complete assimilation. Most South Korean policies aimed at the successful adaption and integration of North Korean defectors reflect this widespread assumption. Contradicting these assumptions, however, is the fact that the North Korean defectors live not only in South Korea, but also in other Asian countries, North America, and Europe. Additional evidence refuting these assumptions is the fact that most of those living outside the Korean peninsula were *talnam* North Korean defectors. Talnam is a term that is only applied to those who "escaped" from South Korea after having resided there for an extended period. This further illuminates the existence of a divide between the prevalent popular belief of South Koreans and the real situations of North Korean defectors (Jun, 2012; Lee and Lee, 2014; Park et al., 2011).

Through media coverage and government policies, the majority of South Koreans are aware that North Korean defectors live among them. However, very few of them have encountered a North Korean in person, let alone engaging in meaningful interactions. As a result, South Koreans rely on media representation and policy discourses to construct an image of North Korean defectors. Unfortunately, having very few options, North Korean defectors supply what the media wants to hear as the only way to have their voices heard.

With these circumstances in mind, this chapter asks the following questions: How involved are North Korean defectors in the process of constructing their social images? How often do North Korean defectors have an opportunity to have their voices heard? Are there discrepancies between how the dominant discourse on North Korean defectors and their self-presentation reflect their motivations and intentions? If there is a gap between media representations and self-presentations, doesn't it limit the capacity of North Korean defectors to live as emancipated citizens in South Korea? In answering these questions, the following sections explore how media shapes the images and location of North Korean defectors in South Korean society. A counterpoint is presented in an analysis of the information garnered through interviews with North Korean defectors that ask them to discuss the ways they present themselves. This article also attempts to shed light on the ambivalent state of North Korean defectors who are suspended between not citizens like us but not refugees like them (Chung, 2008; Yoon, 2015), and on the alternative ways for understanding North Korean defectors. As a pilot study rather than a full-fledged research project, this article contains interviews with only a small number of North Korean defectors to illuminate the points being made.

LOCATING NORTH KOREAN DEFECTORS: PREVIOUS RESEARCH AND CONCEPTUAL FRAME

Current scholarship on North Korean defectors can be roughly grouped into three categories to streamline analysis even though the data overlaps considerably. The first, which forms the largest part of current scholarship, centers on the discourse of adaptation and social integration of North Korean defectors within South Korean society (Cho and Han, 2017; Kim, 2016; Lee and Choi, 2017; Seol and Song, 2017). Literatures in this category examine the state of as well as the multiple factors involved in the process of adaptation and integration, including South Koreans' perception of North Korean defectors (Kwon, 2011; Sohn and Lee, 2012; Yoo and Lee, 2014). Studies in this area usually include both quantitative (survey) and qualitative (interview) methods, although the latter is more often than not used as a complementary measure to the former. Research on adaptation and social integration frequently has policy implications and is often funded or even commissioned by the government or government-related institutions. Due to data being primarily collected and managed by the government, the focus on homogeneity to help form policy means that the diverse voices of North Korean defectors are almost undetectable in these studies. Studies on acculturation, on the other hand, exhibit a greater interest in individual cases (Yun and Park, 2016).

While studies on adaptation and integration often approach North Korean defectors as a collectivity, other studies are keen to examine narratives generated by individuals. Given that the majority of North Korean defectors are women, it is not surprising that many studies focus on gender-related issues in storytelling or memory-making processes (Cho, 2015; Kim, 2014; Yang and Lee, 2017). In addition to women, the psychology of the youth is another popular subject because young people, with their presumed malleability, are believed to best demonstrate the journey in which identity and perception of individuals undergo a series of changes (Baek and An, 2016; Jung, 2005; Kim et al., 2018).

Identity politics form a significant part of this research. Identity formation, identity differentiation, identity transformation, and identity disorientations are among the popular subjects (Kang, 2011; Lee, 2014; Oh, 2016). Although stories and memories of individuals can flesh out the skeleton of the afore-mentioned policy-centered discourse, the representation and generalization of North Korean defectors' personalized accounts of their experiences have raised doubts and questions. There is also a concern that over-dramatized and sensationalized portrayals of defection could entrench North Korean defectors as victims.

Recent trends in scholarship on North Korean defectors have situated them in the context of a transnational landscape. In this study, North Korean defectors are located beyond the insulated boundaries of nation-states to account for identity, psychology, adaptation, and so on (Chun, 2018; Kang, 2018; Han, 2015). *North Korean Diaspora* is a seminal work published in Korean that attempts to shed light on the transnational aspect of the North Korean defector issue (Park et al., 2011). In this co-authored volume, the pull-and-push factors for North Korean defectors to relocate to different corners of the world are well explored. Shin (2019) explores the creation of "extra-territorial nation" in a study based on long-term fieldwork observing North Korean defectors' various interactions with South Koreans, other North Korean defectors, and foreigners in New Malden, UK (see also Lee Soojung, 2014, Song and Bell, 2019).

Studies actively engaged in discourses on transnationalism have resulted in a forum that addresses the North Korean defector issue on a global level. And while that is a move forward, these discourses have limitations particularly those that equate geographical location to transnationality. For example, North Korean defectors are regarded as transnational only after they "escaped" from South Korea and resettled in other countries. This stipulation excludes those who have remained in South Korea from discussions on trans-nationalism. This tacit assumption that transnationality primarily involves the physicality of geopolitics omits people's aspirations and worldviews from the conversation.

To go beyond present-day scholarship on North Korean defectors, this chapter juxtaposes analysis of South Korean media's collective image of North Korean defectors with that of individual North Koreans' interviews. In so doing, this not only identifies the gap between media representation and self-presentation of North Korean defectors, but also pinpoints "the third space" where North Korean defectors can be located (Bhabha, 2004).

AMBIGUOUS STATUS OF THE NORTH KOREAN DEFECTORS: LEGAL, CULTURAL, SOCIAL CONSIDERATIONS

The status of North Korean defectors in South Korea is ambiguous on multiple levels. Article Three of the Constitution declares that the Korean peninsula and all the belonging islands are the territories of South Korea, which in principle renders North Koreans as South Korean nationals. In 1997, the Law on the Protection and Settlement Support of the North Korean Defectors was implemented. This law defines North Korean defectors as someone "having residential addresses, direct families, spouses, and jobs on the northern part of MDL (Military Division Line) who defected from North Korea and has not acquired other nationality." Hence, constitutionally speaking North Korean defectors are already citizens, but legally they can only obtain Korean citizenship on the condition that another nationality has not been previously acquired. Should they meet this criteria, North Korean defectors forego the naturalization process and are immediately granted South Korean citizenship, unlike other foreigners.

Although the South Korean Constitution does not recognize North Korea as a nation, international laws do acknowledge North Korea and its right to rule over its territory. Under international law, North Korean residents are officially foreigners in South Korea, and according to the protocols of the United Nations High Commissioner for Refugees, they are even mandated as refugees. However, rulings by the UNHCR are not legally binding and cannot be enforced if the nation-state refuses to obey. This is the case in China where North Korean defectors are dealt with as if they were illegal immigrants, not refugees, and thus subject to deportation to North Korea (Aldrich 2011).

Unlike in China, where North Korean defectors are viewed as either illegal immigrants or economic migrants, most Western countries recognize North Koreans as refugees. As such, they are protected under the UNHCR, which explains the North Korean populations in the UK and other European countries. During their journey from North Korea to South Korea, North Korean defectors undergo a series of transformations in terms of their status. They start out as North Korean citizens, then once outside their homeland progress to refugees as defined by the UNHCR, but once they arrive in South Korea their UNHCR status as refugees is void. Since North Korea is not a legal state according to the South Korean Constitution, by this definition North Koreans cannot be refugees. Deprived of the protection and assistance that would normally be granted to those with refugee status, North Korean defectors in South Korea found themselves caught between artificial reality (status as South Korean nationals) and actuality (defectors) (see Wolman, 2013 on the dual nationality of North Korean defectors). However, despite the theoretically guaranteed South Korean citizenship bestowed on any North Korean arriving in South Korea, it is hardly a certainty. This is evidenced by a recent case of the South Korean government's decision to send two North Korean fishermen (allegedly defectors) back to North Korea. This decision created a huge controversy, but at the same time it exposed the overly ambiguous laws regarding North Korean defectors that leave too much room for interpretation (*The Financial News*, 2019).

While that case was an exception and North Korean defectors normally obtain South Korean citizenship and the related legality on arrival, they do not immediately join the general populace. Upon admittance, North Korean defectors must attend reformation camps where they are enrolled in various programs promoting adaptation in political, economic, and social spheres. Once they complete the programs, they are given permission to leave the camps at which point they receive financial support mandated by the Law on the North Korean Defectors. South Koreans question the fairness of the financial support and privileges granted to North Korean defectors, which seems to be a source of aggravation. Along with the financial settlement from the government, North Koreans receive housing, job training, employment, and university admissions. All of which are seen as "unfair" advantages especially by a South Korean society that is so highly competitive that North Korean defectors' perceived edge inspires resentment (Chun, 2019, 96–98).

Socially speaking, this resentment leaves North Korean defectors in an ambivalent position that clearly indicates the gap between reality and principle. In principle, many South Korean people feel favorably toward North Koreans based on the theory of "the one ethnicity of five thousand years."[2] But should they discover North Korean defectors living in their neighborhood, the reality is very different. While South Koreans embrace the abstract notion of North Koreans as people of the same ethnicity, they hesitate to extend this acceptance in everyday life simply because they see these privileges as giving North Koreans an "unfair" advantage (Yoon and Song, 2013). According to the Unification Perception Survey published by the Institute for Peace and Unification Studies at Seoul National University, South Koreans consider North Korean defectors to be closer relations than either Ethnic Korean Chinese or South Asians. However, when it comes to interacting as co-workers or choosing future spouses, South Koreans express their intention to maintain a certain social distance from North Korean defectors (Jung et al., 2019).

ALMOST LIKE US, BUT NOT QUITE: MEDIA REPRESENTATION OF NORTH KOREAN DEFECTORS

As members of the same Korean ethnicity, *Han minjok*, North Koreans are considered "blood" relations, but as citizens of a country South Korea is technically still at war with, they are also viewed as the enemy (see Lankov, 2006). In other words, North Koreans are sometimes treated as long-lost brothers, and at other times as an evil twin depending on the circumstances. This ambivalence has become more pronounced as North Korean defectors living in South Korea has become a reality. Providing that the North Koreans as next-door neighbors is an abstract notion of an undefined future, attitudes toward them are generous and even welcoming. Once North Korean defectors are a physical presence in the community, however, their differences become evident, which both disturbs and discomfits.

Most South Koreans, however, never meet a "real" North Korean defector and whatever impression they have of North Koreans is formed by television programs on entertainment or current affairs. News-based programs covering current affairs invite North Korean defectors to appear as witnesses to the deplorable state of the secluded society, discussing serious issues such as politics, human rights, and the dire economic situation there. Entertainment shows invite young and attractive North Korean defectors, usually women, to give gender-skewed perspectives on the lifestyle, customs, and popular culture of North Korea. In these shows, North Korean life is depicted as strange and outdated especially when compared to life in South Korea. When North Korean defectors mention values, traditions, or habits that for them are normal but in South Korea seem strange, the more media attention they get (Kang et al., 2017). Since portrayals of a lifestyle similar to South Korea's is unlikely to draw media attention, more dramatic and extreme cases are discussed instead to create media hype (Oh, 2016). When female North Korea defectors exaggerate aspects of North Korean culture and society to attract media attention, Lee (2014) has argued that they are consumed not just as political defectors but also second-class citizens in South Korea. Ultimately, it is the exotic beauty of young and attractive North Korean women that is the focus of this type of media representation.

Media representation of North Korean defectors reflects the same ambivalence South Koreans have: they are the same but not the same. Although ethnic commonality is accepted, explaining the differences between North Korean defectors and South Koreans in terms of lifestyle and customs and the political and social needs still need to be addressed. To solve this cul-de-sac, one strategy is to approach that the North Korean lifestyle as simply being behind South Korea's by a couple of decades. In other words, even though contemporary North Korean culture appears strange to present-day South Koreans, it is not unlike the lifestyle and old-fashioned habits of their grand-parents or great-grandparents. This narrative assumes some level of similar-ity, but in different time frames (Chun, 2015, 288–289).

Placing the object of representation within a historically different time than our own time is a very efficient strategy of "*othering*" the object. Instead of rejecting difference, this method finds a safe way to make it understandable and acceptable. Johannes Fabian's concept of "denial of coevalness" is a quite usefulness approach in this context (Fabian, 1983). Fabian originally coined this term to describe the context of anthropologists and fieldwork. Once the fieldwork is completed, anthropologists often write about their subject people in ways that place them in a temporal frame other than the anthropologist's. This manner of distancing which Fabian called "denial of coevalness" has the effect of blurring the political context and negating the historical importance of the anthropologist's experience. South Korean media representation of North Korean defectors resonates with Fabian's critique in that it also por-trays the power relations of people with different political, social, and cultural assets in a way that creates boundaries and blocks critical awareness. In the following section, I examine how the image of North Korean defectors is perpetuated by three keywords that most often describe them.

DEFINING NORTH KOREAN DEFECTORS IN SOCIAL DISCOURSES: BUILT-IN BORDER FENCE

There is a consistency in the way North Korean defectors are represented in South Korean society. Media representations of North Korean defectors in South Korean society are guilty of defining individuals from various back-grounds with a variety of experiences as a homogenous collection of people by using three keywords with regularity. The word "displaced" highlights North Korean defectors' uprootedness; "community" stresses the social nature of North Korean defectors; "nationality" defines the level of integra-tion of North Korean defectors to South Korean society.

Displaced

The title of defector is understood as someone who "defected" from the place where they were born and raised. By this definition, adding the word defec-tor after North Korean merely sounds factual and in no way no problematic. However, always adding defector after North Korean focuses on "defecting" and accentuates their state of "being displaced." Regardless of whether North Korean defectors have settled successfully in South Korea or defected from

South Korea to North America and Europe, being labelled as defectors has firmly entrenched North Koreans in a state of being "displaced."

A focus on displacement can attach negative behaviors to North Korean defectors. For instance, since they are displaced, they will be unfamiliar with new situations that some might confuse as incapability and inadaptability. Their experiences in defecting and residual fear from discovery might have them acting in ways that can be misconstrued as mental instability. To help understand North Koreans, having information about life in their home country could be useful, but essentializing a particular group based on their place of origin comes with its own problems. For instance, focusing too much on home and factors that forced North Koreans to defect to understand their displacement tends to cast them as victims of socio-politico-economic circumstances. This unfairly detracts attention from their motivation, intention, planning, calculation, and sentiments before, during, and after the defection.

Community

North Korean defectors' communities can be divided into two categories: ones before defection and ones after defection. The first category includes hometowns, places of employment, and regions with ancestral associations in North Korea. The second category includes brokers and religious groups that helped them defect, North Korean defector-based communities, and reform camp alumni communities. Media representations tend to depict communities before defection in a negative light to emphasize the distressing conditions in North Korea and in doing so laud South Korea. Conversely, the communities after defection are portrayed in a relatively positive way but particularly for their usefulness in accelerating the adaptation process.

The communities before and after defection share one important trait: they are considered as existing outside the North Korean defectors and wield formidable power over them. Normally, it is the intentions and acts of members of a community bring that about changes and modifications. However, in the media most representations of North Korean communities appear to be fixed and unchanging, and the communities act as either positive or negative influences on North Korean defectors. Rigidly dividing communities as either good or bad negates their complexity but also discourages North Koreans from confessing involvement in communities that might be deemed unsavory, which hampers understanding defectors' motivation for joining and the benefits. Adaptation is a long and complex journey. Impartial attention to defectors' relationships with and within their communities will open a window to better understanding the issue of agency on the part of North Korean defectors.

Nationality

Modern discourses and policies on the phenomenon of refugees seem incapable of separating the issues from the concept of nation. Discourses on refugees' long and painful journeys follow a predictable series of events—born and raised in a country where they are persecuted or oppressed, defection to another country where they are segregated or accepted but often as second-class citizens. Seeing refugees unmoored inspires a paradoxical desire to at least conceptually assign membership to a particular country.

Surveys of North Korean defectors often ask whether they identify as North or South Korean. Sometimes the question takes a euphemistic approach such as asking which team they would cheer for in North–South Korea sports matches. Although these questions are designed to encourage North Korean defectors to self-identification, it narrows identity to one nation, enforcing the assumption that single-country belongingness at a given time is the norm. Those who criticize the *talnam* North Korean defectors are often affronted by their decision to leave South Korea after experiencing life there. There is a prevalent belief that if you dislike North Korea enough to leave for South Korea, then you should do whatever it takes to be a good citizen of South Korea. The idea that widespread patriotic sentiment and commitment to a single country should be the norm raises ethical concerns.

To better understand how this idea affects North Korean defectors, we asked, How do North Korean defectors understand the single-nation identity? Is it "normal" to only have a sense of attachment to a nation that provides one with a legal and institutional safe net? Is it legitimate to criticize the ethics of those who are not exclusively devoted to a single nation? Is it legitimate to criticize how one defines one's own nation?

Erving Goffman (1959) developed the theory of Impression Management using the theatre as a metaphor for life. According to Goffman, just like actors on a stage, individuals make conscious and unconscious decisions in their everyday interactions to reveal the traits that will create acceptable images of themselves to others. At the same time, they conceal information that might conflict with the personality they want to project. With his signature dramaturgical approaches, Goffman employed theatrical concepts as front stage and back stage to illuminate individuals' strategic choices and behaviors depending on the circumstances and audiences. This theory is crucial in that it acknowledges the roles of both agency and structured play in everyday life.

Impression Management Theory is also relevant for the purposes of this chapter, especially when addressing the discrepancy between media representation and self-presentation of North Korean defectors as well as where they intersect. Interviews with North Korean defectors gave us first-hand information and insight into their ideas and intentions which are clearly different from the prevailing media representations. What we noticed was that the interviewees intentionally inserted positive images—in contrast to the widespread and negative representation of North Korean defectors—into their narratives for their audience, in this case the interviewer.

Interviewees with North Korean Defectors

As a pilot study, a total of four North Korean defectors were interviewed for this chapter which is admittedly not representative of North Korean defectors in South Korea. What's more, the North Koreans we interviewed do not fit the standard norms in terms of educational background, occupation, and social status. However, the fact that some aspects that have been neglected or excluded in the prevalent image of North Korean defectors are being considered here is positive. All four interviews were conducted as open-ended interviews.

There are two considerable obstacles to recruiting interviewees among North Korean defectors for scholarly work. First, North Korean defectors genuinely fear that disclosure of their identity and personal information to strangers could threaten their own safety as well as the safety of their family and relatives left behind in North Korea. Second, the fact that personal information of refugees is strictly controlled and kept confidential by the South Korean government and related governmental agencies reinforces their concerns. Hence the author of this chapter had to rely on personal networks of friends and colleagues for a recommendation so that possible participants would consent to interviews.

SELF-PRESENTATION OF NORTH KOREAN DEFECTORS: FINDINGS AND ANALYSIS

Out of respect for our interviewees' privacy, we have not included any identifying traits such as their ages or backgrounds in the following section. Only their gender is revealed since all of them are female. In addition, we have not included direct quotations in compliance with requests made by our interviewees. The interviewer made every effort to faithfully paraphrase their stories.

These interviews revealed that North Korean defectors' foci in presenting who they are and what they value greatly differ from their representation in the media or policy discourses. Throughout, the interviewees focused on four factors in their discussion of self-identification: desire to be acknowledged as fellow South Koreans, inclination to distance themselves from other North

Korean defectors, willingness to take charge of their own lives, and everlasting longing for a family reunion.

Identity as North Koreans

When it comes to the theory of identity, this chapter takes a postmodern approach. Unlike the essentialist discourse on identity that argues that the core qualities of an individual are unchanging and everlasting, the postmodern approach to identity is based on the constructionist view (Cerulo, 1997, 391–393; Schachter, 2005, 140–141). The postmodern tradition in identity theory has several branches determined by their emphasis on roles, performances, and power of knowledge. Regardless of their emphasis, all branches agree that an individual may have multiple identities which may be changed, contested, negotiated, appropriated, and manipulated depending on the circumstances and motivations.

When the interviewees were asked to estimate the percentage of their identities they would classify as North Korean, all responded in the lowest range of 5–10 percent. According to the annual survey of North Korean defectors conducted by the Institute for Peace and Unification Studies at Seoul National University, approximately 80 percent of the total respondents identified as South Koreans rather than North Koreans (Jung et al., 2019). The IPUS survey takes a categorical approach that gives the interviewees one choice between identifying as either North Korean or South Korean. Our research instead offered percentage ranges, recognizing that North Korean defectors have multi-layered identities and it is not as simple as being one nationality or the other.

It is important to note that the stigma of being a North Korean defector seems to be a constant in the life of that individual. For example, even if a North Korea defector has lived in South Korea for twenty years as a contributing member of society, they are forever North Korean defectors, distinguished from native South Koreans. Barely rating themselves as North Korean, the self-presentation of our four interviewees, including one who has been in South Korea for only about one year, is in sharp contrast to the South Koreans' perspective of them. When asked to elaborate on the reason for almost disavowing their North Korean origins, they explained that they did not have luxury of time to consider anything beyond adapting to South Korean society.

It is natural that a chasm should exist between self-presentation and media representation, but the discrepancy between the two often causes confusion and distress for North Korean defectors. One of the interviewees told me that even though she does not consider herself to be North Korean anymore, once people around her learn that she is from North Korea, their attitudes towards her seem to change. Instead of being accepted as Korean, she is labelled the North Korean defector, a label that to her mind no longer represents who she is since she herself has embraced being South Korean. Both the subtle and overt responses of South Koreans to a nationality she has disowned leave her feeling discriminated against and isolated.

Community and Social Network

It is true that in some cases in the conscious creation of self-presentation or self-identification what individuals say may not always be consistent with what they do. For instance, when we asked our interviewees how involved they were with other North Korean defectors and if they accepted support from North Korean networks, they all claimed to have little to no contact. However, after compiling and reviewing the entirety of the interview sessions, it was obvious from casual mentions of interactions with other defectors that they had quite extensive dealings with other North Koreans and their networks.

Then why did they purposely minimize the extent of their interactions in their self-presentation? It seems that they are very aware of how it might be perceived by the interviewer (or other people) if they admit to interacting closely with other North Korean defectors. And when they rated their identity as North Korean defectors at 5 to 10 percent, the interviewees were again distancing themselves from other North Korean defectors to emphasize their self-presentation as South Koreans. In answering what community or group has offered them the most assistance and support, the interviewees named South Korean occupational or professional groups, omitting any mention of North Korean networks. Their answers to direct questions show some consistency in their attempts to measure and manage a social distance from other North Korean defectors and thus manage the possible impressions that may arise therefrom.

From an anthropological perspective, assessing the factuality of the response is not of primary interest here. Rather, examining how the interviewees intend to present themselves to others is more significant. For example, when one interviewee was asked for the source of a certain piece of information, it turned out fellow North Korean defectors had provided it. This contradicted the interviewee's declaration of having very limited contact with other North Korean defectors just a few minutes earlier in the interview. The interviewee went on to clarify that the friends who had shared the information just happened to be North Korean defectors, and that she had not deliberately set out to build a relationship with North Korean defectors. All four interviewees' attempts to distance themselves from other defectors and instead align themselves with South Koreans in a conscious self-presentation reflects their aspiration to control their own images. This is very different from the images of victims perpetuated by the media representation of North Korean defectors.

Agency in Making Selections and Decisions

Another subject that media representation and self-presentation diverge on is North Korean defectors' agency. One of the key words that configures media representation of North Korean defectors is "passiveness." By continually depicting them as victims of political oppression, social control, and economic deprivation in North Korea, this creates an image of powerlessness. The primary focus of the media on the insurmountable hardships and North Korean defectors' desperation to escape does not give them credit for their bravery and determination to leave. When the narrative does shift to their new lives in South Korea, it focuses on the policy support and aid they receive as refugees. As stories emerge of North Koreans struggling to adapt to South Korean society, the media focuses on the flaws in the system of support, without considering what the North Korean defectors themselves might think. In both cases, the external influences are at the center of attention, relegating North Korean defectors to the roles of either victims or receivers without agency.

From what our interviewees indicated, however, we learned that the process of defection required a considerable amount of planning, determination, decision making, and comprises. Contrary to popular beliefs, defection is not a spontaneous action but a deliberate process based on a complicated exchange of information among multiple players and brokers. Since defections is illegal, they cannot easily verify the information they receive, leaving North Korean defectors at risk of being discovered or betrayed. Despite depending on others for help and information, our interviewees stressed that the act of defection was the result of their decisions and choices. They were very eager to own the situation, regardless of whether it was positive or negative (see also Yoon, 2012).

The subject of North Korean defectors' agency is relevant not only before, during and after their defection but also as the ultimate reason for their defection. All four interviewees gave variants of the same story: they left North Korea not because they were starving and poor but because they expected a better future with greater opportunities in South Korea. One of the interviewees admitted that had she stayed in North Korea she would most likely have lived quite comfortably. She added that she did not regret her decision to leave because she still believed that life in South Korea would be better.

Another interviewee confessed that she had enjoyed quite an affluent lifestyle in North Korea, but she decided to come to South Korea nonetheless since she craved freedom. Without the freedom to make her own choices, life was not worth living, she said. She added that her decision to leave North Korea was not motivated by political oppression or economic difficulties but the need to be independent. This contradicts the media representation and dominant discourse that depict the North Korean defectors as victims and passive receivers. Without exception, our interviewees believed themselves to be active agents in control of their own lives, eager to take charge of the situation and their narrative.

Family and Diaspora

The one element that weaves through the past, the present, and the future of the North Korean defectors is family. When asked to describe emotional attachments to or the psychological effects of being removed from North Korea, their future plans in South Korea, and the possibility of one day visiting/returning to North Korea, one keyword repeats: "family." The sense of attachment to North Korea might in some part be attributed to fond childhood memories, but more likely than that is the fact that their loved ones are still there. The most difficult challenge to life in South Korea is the absence of family and not knowing if those family members remaining in North Korea are safe. Reuniting with family is the primary reason they give for the hope they might one day visit North Korea.

Half of our interviewees were part of a "chained defection," a term that describes defection to South Korea through with the assistance of family members already settled there. These family members helped the interviewees come to South Korea by providing information on brokers and money through remittances. All our interviewees expressed their intention to bring other family members to South Korea in the future, extending the "chained defection." Three of four interviewees said they were sending money to their families in North Korea and were in contact with them on a regular basis via phone calls. The one who is not currently sending money to North Korea said she planned to start once she found a better paying job.

Considering the images South Korean education and media depict of North Korean society and family dynamics, one might think the North Korean family relationship is purely utilitarian. From what the outside world can see, North Korea is a highly controlled society where the political party displaces the traditional family relationship. Individuals are even encouraged to monitor their own family members to maintain the socialist order. The interviews, however, show that the emotional importance placed on family is quite similar between the two Koreas. Furthermore, the North Korean defectors identified with those families (*Isangajok*) that were separated by the division of the Korean peninsula. Like those families, North Korean defectors, too, are casualties of the hostile political circumstances between the two Koreas.

CONCLUSION: IDENTITY, SELF-PRESENTATION, AND SOCIETY

Only 34,000 North Korean defectors live in South Korea. As a tiny fraction of the entire population, chances that South Koreans interact with the North Korean defectors in their real life are rare. Nevertheless, people have formed an image of North Korean defectors based on media representations. News-based televisions programs that invite North Korean defectors to give testimony on the poverty, starvation, and oppression perpetuate negative images of North Korea. Circulating incorrect or exaggerated information on North Korean society interferes with the North-South Korean relationship and Unification. Although problematic, few people seem concerned that these broadcasts are misrepresenting North Korean defectors. Frequent but superficial news reports on the activities of North Korean defectors who align themselves with extreme right-wing politics also disproportionately influence the general public's perception of North Korean defectors in South Korea (see Song, 2017; Sung, 2019).

Media representation of North Korean defectors has reduced them to caricatures of themselves. They are victims of political oppression and economic poverty under a dehumanizing regime. They are alien to South Koreans due to different lifestyles and value systems. They seek fame by demonizing their place of origin with embellished, exaggerated, or even made-up stories. While these unflattering images are reproduced and perpetuated, South Koreans learn more about the existence of North Koreans from tragic news stories of suicide usually due to heavy financial losses or difficulties adapting to South Korea (Jung et al., 2018).

The truth of the 34,000 North Korean defectors can be found somewhere between these dramatized images and extreme tragedies. The unsensational reality is that they live everyday lives while struggling with different systems, values, and expressions to reconcile the familiar with the new. What this chapter attempts to show is that their self-presentation is often far different from what the media has been conveying to most South Koreans. North Korean defectors are more complex and multi-layered than the victims and receivers they are portrayed to be. That is not to say that North Korean defectors' self-presentation is closer to the reality per se. As Goffman's analysis of everyday presentation of self stipulates, self-identification and related conversation and behavior are products of strategic choices which are fashioned by individual intention as well social structure. Hence, the purpose of this pilot study is to highlight the need for more nuanced and multifaceted approaches in addressing the lives of North Korean defectors in South Korea.

As mentioned in the beginning, this is a pilot study and not a cross-sectional study of North Korean defectors. The intention has been to reveal different aspects of North Korean defectors other than the hitherto circulated images by paying attention to their self-images and voices, keeping in mind that those self-presentations are also social constructs. The purpose of this chapter is admittedly limited in scope and scale, but it does not necessarily have to remain so. As a pilot study on the identity and image of North Korean defectors, it is a first step to more active and productive discussions on the topic in the near future.

NOTES

1. This chapter is a revised version of the previously published article "Representation and Self-presentation of North Korean Defectors in South Korea: Image, Discourse, and Voices," *Asian Journal of Peacebuilding* 8(1): 93-112, 2021.

2. Some scholars argue that the popular belief in "one nation of Korean people" is not so much about fictive blood as a long history and culture of Korean people. See Han, 2007, 19–22.

REFERENCES

Aldrich, Russell. 2011. "An Examination of China's Treatment of North Korean Asylum Seekers." *North Korean Review* 7(1): 36–48.

Baek, Dae Seung and An Tae Jun. 2016. "The Influence of Adolescents' National Identity on Their Unification Consciousness." *Open Education Studies* 24(1): 39–58.

Bhabha, Homi K. 2004. *The Location of Culture,* London & New York: Routledge.

Cerulo, Karen A. 1997. "Identity Construction: New Issues, New Directions." *Annual Review of Sociology* 23: 385–409.

Choi, Won-O. 2012. "Multicultural Society and North Korean Defectors: Understanding through a Perspective of Diaspora." *Unification Humanities Research* 54: 257–283.

Cho, Choon Bum and Han Ki Ju. 2017. "Differences in Social Adjustment of North Korean Refugees According to Demographic and Social Characteristics and Social Adaptation in South Korea." *Multiculture & Peace* 11(1): 271–292.

Cho, Young Ju. 2015. "Narrative Strategies and Discursive-Performative in North Korean Refugee Women's Oral History: Focusing on Mothering." *North Korean Studies Review* 19(1): 309–338.

Choo, Hae Yeon. 2006. "Gendered Modernity and Ethnicized Citizenship: North Korean Settlers in Contemporary South Korea." *Gender and Society* 20(5): 576–604.

Chun, Kyung Hyo. 2015. "Perspectives on North Korea between Same-nation-ness and Multiculturalism: Otherization in South Korea." *Social Science Studies* 23(1): 274–300.

Chun, Kyung Hyo. 2019. "To Be (Together) or Not to Be (Together): Toward Active Peaceful Coexistence." *Unification and Peace* 11(2): 75–106.

Chung, Byung-Ho. 2008. "Between Defector and Migrant: Identities and Strategies of North Koreans in South Korea." *Korean Studies* 32: 1–27.

Fabian, Johannes. 1983. *Time and the Other: How Anthropology Makes its Object.* New York: Columbia University Press.

Goffman, Erving. 1959. *The Presentation of Self in Everyday Life.* New York: Anchor Books.

Han, Kyung-Koo. 2007. "The Archaeology of the Ethnically Homogeneous Nation-State and Multiculturalism in Korea." *Korea Journal* Winter: 8–31.

Han, Mi Ra. 2015. "Transnational Mother Experience of North Korean Women Defectors." *Multiculture & Peace* 9(2): 160–178.

Jun, Myung Hee. 2012. "North Koreans' Lives in the United States." *Korean Academy of Social Welfare* 64(4): 89–111.

Jung et al. 2018. *North Korean Unification Perception Survey 2017.* Seoul: Institute for Peace and Unification Studies.

Jung et al. 2019a. *Unification Perception Survey 2018.* Seoul: Institute for Peace and Unification Studies.

Jung et al. 2019b. *North Korean Unification Perception Survey 2018.* Seoul: Institute for Peace and Unification Studies.

Jung, HyangJin. 2005. "North Korean Refugees' Emotionality and Its Social Implications: A Perspective from Cultural Psychology." *Comparative Cultural Studies* 11(1): 81–111.

Kang, Chae Yeon. 2018. "A Study on the 'Migration of Identity' Paradigm of North Korean Defectors." *The Journal of Multicultural Society* 11(2): 5–36.

Kang, Jun Woong. 2011 "Becoming South Korean: South Korea's Disciplinary Governance and North Korean Settlers' Identity Formation." *Korean Sociology* 45(1): 191–227.

Kang, Min-Kyung Kang, Baek Seon-Gi, and Nam Siho. 2017. "Min-Kyung Kang, Seon-Gi Baek, Siho Nam." *Journal of the Korea Contents Association* 17(1): 567–584.

Kim, Joo Sam. 2016. "The Adjustment of Korean Chinese and North Korean Refugees into Korean Society and Their Role in the Process of National Unification." *Journal of Diaspora Studies* 10(2): 291–319.

Kim, You-Yeon, Son Myung-Ah and Kim Seok-Ho. 2018. "Effects of Family and Social Relations on Happiness of North Korean Adolescent Refugees in South Korea." *Korean Journal of Population Studies* 41(2): 179–205.

Kim, Yoo Jung. 2014. "Parentification Experience of North Korean Women Refugees." *Journal of Social Science* 40(2): 77–108.

Kwon, Soo Hyun. 2011. "Individual Attitudes toward North Korean Immigrants." *Journal of Korean Politics* 20(2): 129–153.

Kwon, Sookdo. 2018. "Suggestion of Improvement Plan of Settlement Support System for North Korean Defectors for Social Integration." *Unification Studies* 22(1): 71–108.

Lankov, Andrei. 2006. "Bitter Tastes of Paradise: North Korean Refugees in South Korea." *Journal of East Asian Studies* 6(1): 105–137.

Lee, Byung Soo. 2014. "A Duality in North Korean Defectors Value Orientations and Differentiation of Identity." *Unification Humanities* 59: 121–150.

Lee, In Hee and Choi Hee Jung. 2017. "Factors Influencing Social Adaptation of North Korean Defectors." *Journal of Korean Public Health Nursing* 31(2): 341–351.

Lee, Soo Jung and Lee Woo Young. 2014. "Social Relations and Attitudes between South Korean Migrants and North Korean Refugees in the Korea Town, New Malden, U.K." *North Korean Studies* 18(1): 137–174.

Lee, Sun-Min. 2014. "How Can North Korean Women Defectors Speak?: A Critical Analysis of Television Talk Show, *Now, Going To Meet* (Channel A)." *Media, Gender, & Culture* 29(2): 75–115.

Moon, Seungho. 2010. "Multicultural and Global Citizenship in the Transnational Age: The Case of South Korea." *International Journal of Multicultural Education* 12(1): 1–15.

Oh, Won Hwan. 2016. "The Politics of Identity of North Korean Refugees." *Korean Journal of Broadcasting and Telecommunication Studies* 30(3): 5–41.

Park, Myung-Kyu et al. 2011. *North Korean Diaspora*. Seoul: Institute for Peace and Unification Studies.

Schachter, Elli P. 2005. "Erikson Meets the Postmodern: Can Classic Identity Theory Rise to the Challenge?" *Identity* 5(2): 137–160.

Seo, Yu Kyung. 2013. "Two Fundamental Problems of the Current Support Policy on North Korean Defectors and Solution for Multiculturalist Social Integration." *Korean Political Review* 21(2): 301–327.

Seol, Jin Bae and Song Eun Hee. 2017. "Risk or Opportunity?: Ambivalence and Social Integration among North Korean Refugees." *Crisisonomy* 13(4): 19–43.

Shin, HaeRan. 2019. "Extra-territorial Nation-building in Flows and Relations: North Korea in the Global Networks and an Ethnic Enclave." *Political Geography* 74:1–9.

Sohn, Ae-Lee and Nae-Young Lee. 2012. "Study on the Attitude of South Koreans Toward North Korean Defectors: Focusing on National Identity and Multi-Cultural Acceptability." *Journal of Asia-Pacific Studies* 19(3): 5–34.

Song, Jiyoung. 2017. "Co-evolution of Networks and Discourses: A Case from North Korean Defector-Activists." *Australian Journal of International Affairs*, 71(3): 284–299.

Sung, Minkyu. 2019. "Balloon Warriors for North Korean Human Rights Activism: A Critique of North Korean Defector-Activists' Post-Humanitarianism." *Critical Asian Studies*, 51(3): 355–367.

Song, Jay Jiyoung and Markus Bell. 2019. "North Korean Secondary Asylum in the UK." *Migration Studies* 7(2): 160–179.

The Financial News. 2019. "North Korea Residents Are Also South Korean Nationals." November 26. https://www.fnnews.com/news/201911261747101240 (Accessed January 10, 2020).

Wolman, Andres. 2013. "North Korean Asylum Seekers and Dual Nationality." *International Journal of Refugee Law* 24(4): 793–814.

Yang and Lee. 2017. "Study on Life History of an Elderly Female North Korean Defector." *Journal of the Korean Contents Association* 17(10): 120–139.

Yoon, Bo Young. 2015. "A Study on a New Methodological Approach for Understanding North Korean Defectors: Focusing on Marginal Man Theory." *The Journal of Social Sciences* 22(3): 187–216.

Yoon Gyun-Soo & Park Amie Meeae. 2016. "Acculturation as a Frustration Negotiation Cycle: North Korean Women Defectors in South Korea." *Asian Journal of Women's Studies* 22(4): 462–476.

Yoon, In Jin. 2012. "North Korean Defectors' Appropriation of Culture and Social Adaptation." *Korean Studies Research* 41: 37–61.

Yoon, In Jin and Song Yung Ho. 2013. "South Korean Nationalist Perception on North Korean Defectors and Multicultural Perception." *Overseas Korean Studies* 30: 7–40.

Chapter 8

North Korean Nation-Building Outside North Korea

HaeRan Shin

This chapter examines transnational defectors' daily discourses[1] and activities to understand how they contribute to a new version of the nation outside the bounds of the geographical location of the nation state. "Nation" here represents a community of people who share language, culture, and a sense of common history and destiny, while "state" refers to an assembly of institutions ruling over a discrete territory (Agnew, 2003). Social science has committed time and resources to the study of the state as a physical and symbolic territory, and the North Korean state has attracted considerable notice in studies on the Korean peninsula. In those studies when the topic of the nation as a social and cultural entity is raised, it is often as a side note to the state's political governing at the center of the nation (Agnew, 2003; Hsu, 2017). Even migrants' extra-territorial practices (Cauvet, 2011; Collyer and King, 2015) tend to focus on the state and the political apparatus that governs people, resources, and security. Recent attempts by the social sciences to address "extra-territorial nation-building" as it refers to the transnational agents' social and cultural practices of building a nation outside the physical territory have yet to venture beyond the theoretical level. As a result, the daily practices of establishing and developing a national community outside the physical territory have remained primarily the domain of migrant studies with a focus on migrants' identities.

Attempting to introduce some balance to the existing scholarship, Hsu (2017: 166) suggested bringing "the nation" as it represents the community back into the conversation to mitigate its marginal representation. This research builds on Hsu's argument on "bringing the nation back" (2017) by documenting the everyday social and cultural practices and observing discourses that constitute bottom-up nation-building outside the national territory.

The case of North Korean defectors discussed here demonstrates the extra-territorial nation-building practices of defectors and the networks that develop from encounters with other migrants through flows and relations. First, "nation-building in flows" refers to the establishment of global networks that connect North Korean defectors around the world. Migrants and defectors have been increasingly able to maintain their belongingness and continue to be engaged in matters concerning the origin society thanks to information technology development and increased mobilities (Robertson et al., 2016; Vertovec, 2004). The plans and policies that these politically like-minded members of this diaspora[2] conceive of to be implemented in their homeland one day envisage a future North Korea that though still in their minds might well be achieved. Second, "nation-building in relations" refers to the efforts to reinforce North Koreanness to guard against the erosion of their identity that daily interactions with South Koreans and British citizens may cause. Their conceptions of and discussions on their nation, often debating changes they would like to see in their home society, constitute a version of the nation as an imagined community (Anderson, 2006).

Based on ethnographic fieldwork, this chapter chronicles the evolution of a people's North Korean nation both imagined and reimagined. The subjects of this research lived in South Korea for a few months to a few years before relocating to the United Kingdom (UK), to the Koreatown in London's suburb of New Malden. This case study offers a flow-based and relational approach to reveal the key aspects of North Korean defectors' nation-building endeavors. First, it examines their nation-building in flows to study how they initiated and then operationalized global and regional networks to advance their campaign for a new North Korea. North Korean defectors in New Malden not only took the initiative to establish global networks but also founded local organizations that would eventually give rise to an opposition party and exile government meant to challenge the North Korean regime.

Second, it investigates how relations with South Korean migrants in North Korean language schools, churches, and associations in New Malden facilitated nation-building in the community. Recognizing that they needed to adjust to their new environments but were reluctant to adopt a South Korean identity, new versions of North Koreanness developed augmented by character traits from South Korea and Europe.

This chapter contributes to the knowledge of post-territorial and relational approaches to the concept of the nation and national identities is organized as follows. The next section critically reviews previous literature on the state and outlines the importance of nation-building from the agents' perspectives while addressing flow-based and relational approaches. The two following sections introduce the research methods and the circumstances of the case, respectively. The first finding section discusses the case of North Korean defectors' global and European networks and nation-building in flows that focuses on discourses deliberating on an alternative sovereignty. The last section illustrates nation-building in relations that is the basis for the transnational identity and North Koreanness that has emerged since interactions with South Korean migrants has increased. To finish, the conclusion explores the theoretical and policy implications of this research.

THEORETICAL FRAMEWORK: EXTRA-TERRITORIAL NATION-BUILDING IN FLOWS AND RELATIONS

"Extra-territorial nation-building" refers to the symbolic and material place-making of the defectors' particular desire to re-imagine their origin societies in practice. This study uses nation-building rather than state-building, because though there are territorial similarities between nation and state and they can and often are used interchangeably (Agnew, 2003), the two terms do have distinguishing qualities. While the term nation can refer to either the territory or the people and their national identity constituted by their social activities, discourses, and cultural practices, the term state is exclusively associated with state sovereignty (Hsu, 2017).The discussion on the nation-state and its territory-building process (Carling, 2008; Collyer and King, 2015) has received much attention, but the notion of nation as it refers to community has been neglected (see Agnew, 1994; Carling, 2008; Collins, 2012; Collyer and King, 2015; Novak, 2011; Yamazaki, 2002, for example).

Discussions on extra-territorial state-building (Perkins and Neumayer, 2008; Sen, 2016, Shin, 2019, 2021) have focused on voting, security control, and sovereignty of the state outside the state territory in the migrants' destination society. Nation-building is not simply a matter of mapping, building, and inhabiting, but also one of crossing, circulating, and moving (Vásquez, 2014; Dyck, 2005; Wu, 2000; McCann, 2002; Pierce et al., 2011). To expand on the discussion of nation-building (see Jirón et al., 2016, for example) and nation-construction on a large scale, this chapter studies transnational agents and the part that diaspora plays in the nation-building process and shaping the identities of nations (Cauvet, 2011). Previous discussions on migrants' identity that have been developed predominantly in terms of transnationalism (Katila and Wahlbeck, 2012) and adaptation to the receiving society (Erdal, 2013) have overlooked the concept of a national identity. A national identity is not only a popular sentiment but also a program for political action that distinguishes the self from the other (Agnew, 2008). In this case study, North Korean defectors' formation of a national identity develops into nation-building, a process in which people reimagine the country of their origin outside the national physical territory.

Recognizing that the political changes necessary to allow them to return home are not currently feasible, many turned their efforts to a re-creation of their homeland in the host country. Defectors' particular geopolitical circumstance creates a seemingly contradictory situation that sees them embrace their national identity while rejecting the North Korean state but more so the politics. In the early days after their escape, North Korean defectors defined North Korea by the push factors that forced their defections, such as deprivation, political persecution, and starvation. At first, North Koreans were mainly asked about their lives and experiences under the Kim regime. As those stories lost their novelty, they began to discuss and consider the kind of roles they could play to undermine the current regime and would play when the time came to rebuild their nation.

North Korean defectors inspired by the success of other exiles established networks, especially Chinese defectors, to support rebuilding North Korea and an exile government to challenge the current administration and possibly lead the country in future. Previous studies discussed those exiles from China (Le Bail and Shen, 2008; Ma, 1993), Russia (Kolstø, 1999; Korobkov and Zaionchkovskaia, 2004), and East Germany (Dietz, 2000) whose networks had been cited in studies as instrumental in assisting their home country through political and financial transitions. There were also studies on Tibetan (McConnell, 2016) and Polish (Engel, 1993) governments-in-exile whose social and cultural organizational activities that include ethnic associations and religious activities (Sheringham, 2010; Vásquez and Knott, 2014) that studies showed involved political mobilization of national identities (Penrose and Mole, 2008).

The associations that are the basis for the flows, relations, and territories and the development of mobile and flow-based ways of place-making (Wigley, 2016) have now attracted geographers' notice (see Collins, 2012, for example). As people's mobilities span multiple countries (Bashi, 2007; Lee, 2011; Olwig, 2007; Sperling, 2014), contemporary migration creates complex experiences of adaptation, betweenness, transnationalism, and translocalism (Halilovich, 2011). Extra-territorial nation-building in flows due to increased global mobilities and the impact of technology on global networks, flows, and mobilities is more viable now than ever before. As the use of communication technologies increased (Hannam et al., 2006; Larsen & Urry, 2016; Sheller, 2007), the dynamics of post-state phenomena driven by globalization has been growing (for example, see Cauvet, 2011; Collyer and King, 2015; Brenner, 1999a).

Extra-territorial nation-building in relations takes place within ethnic enclaves (Varady, 2005). From a native speaking population's view, migrant neighborhoods with a high concentration of ethnic minorities are distinguished, if not isolated, from the host society (Cutler et al., 2008; Murdie and Ghosh, 2010; Smith, 2001). Those neighborhoods with a unique multicultural atmosphere (Pang and Rath, 2007) and are a social and cultural field (Levitt and Schiller, 2004) formed through transnational practice, contacts, and materials (Müller and Wehrhahn, 2013; Dahinden, 2009; Carling, 2008; Levitt and Schiller, 2004; Levitt, 2001) can on occasion attract curiosity and come to be viewed as tourist sites by locals. Some studies revealed that locals' forays into the enclave might bring about integration and adaptation but also stratification and conflict (Liu et al., 2012; Yoon, 2013; Wang et al., 2015). As result in the case of this research, the North Korean defectors' national identity has developed through interactions with South Korean migrants living in New Malden, local British people, and the organizations within their ethnic enclave.

RESEARCH METHODS

The fieldwork for this study was conducted in New Malden from August to December 2017. Mixed ethnographic research methods were used, including participant observation, in-depth interviews, and archival analysis. I have obtained the required ethics approvals from my institution. To provide a comprehensive perspective on the European North Korean network and global network, I conducted in-depth interviews with network members in London and Brussels as well. Interviewee observations and the analysis of results were in part derived from a previous but still recent case study (Shin, 2018, 2021). The interviewees included key actors in a South Korean ethnic association, North Korean ethnic association, the South Korean elderly association, North Korean dance group, the National Unification Advisory Council, and a European network of North Korean defectors. The interviews were semi-structured with a flexibility that allowed the interview subjects to share stories that did not necessarily pertain to the questions being asked. The interviews were conducted in Korean and each session lasted one to three hours and was tape-recorded with the subject's permission.

I also conducted participant observation in a Korean language school for North Korean children from September to December 2017. The author's position as participant and observer was made clear from the beginning, and the North Koreans being aware of the researcher's dual role sometimes asked me to keep something that they shared off-the-record. The school held classes on Saturdays in a hall rented from a local church in New Malden. Since my ten-year-old son attended the school,[3] I could participate in class preparation and clean-up. While setting up tables and chairs, laying out snacks for the children, and cleaning up afterward, I had the opportunity to observe the dynamics of other parents. Once the classes were in session from 1:30 to 5:00 pm, I joined the other parents in coffee shops or a parent's home for the duration of the class. During this time and with the parents' understanding and consent, I could monitor ordinary daily discussions about their children or issues within the North Korean community. Further participant observation was conducted during several events organized either by South Korean groups or by North Korean groups but would generally include members from both groups. I cross-checked the interview data with the information that I acquired through participant observations and archives.

Analyzing the information that I gained from my previous research, I was able to provide background knowledge of the organizational activities and daily discourses on defectors' home country. I amalgamated this information with the analysis of the data on the discourses and activities that led to the nation-building process in flows and relations from my current fieldwork to provide evidence of progression.

CASE INTRODUCTION

Since 1953, ten to thirty thousand North Koreans have defected from North Korea, the majority escaping to Russia and China. As of 2004, an increasing number of North Koreans have defected to the UK, usually traveling through China to find temporary asylum in South Korea first. Though twenty-three countries have granted North Koreans the status of refugee, the Chinese government has continued to return defectors caught in China to North Korea to maintain diplomatic relations. China's refusal to offer refuge rendered North Korean defectors as undocumented migrants evading discovery and subsequent repatriation to North Korea. Of the twenty-three countries to accept North Koreans, South Korea has accepted the most with 31,338 defectors registered with the Unification Ministry as of 2017. Since Kim Jong-un came to power in 2011, however, defection rates have been declining.[4,5]

According to research by the European Alliance for Human Rights in North Korea, there are approximately 1,400 North Koreans defectors in all of Europe.[6] Outside of South Korea, the UK harbors the largest number of refugees at 630 and provides welfare benefits exceeding what is offered by many other countries.[7] One Eurostat report calculated that nearly 90 percent of North Koreans of the estimated 820 to arrive in European Union countries from 2007 to 2016 settled in Germany and Britain.[8] In fact, many North Korean exiles had already determined that the UK was their destination of choice based solely on the information circulating among the defectors that the welfare provided there was superior to most.

Of the North Korean defectors residing in the UK, most live and work in the New Malden suburb of London. New Malden as the original location for the South Korean embassy attracted Koreans to the area as early as the 1970s, and the late 1990s saw an influx of Joseonjok—Korean Chinese—to the area. As of 2015, however, New Malden has become renowned as the largest North Korean community in Europe and has been labeled the "North Korean village." New Malden is unique in that nowhere else is there such a high concentration of North Koreans living side by side with South Koreans in what could be considered as a test site for a reunified Korea.

During their stay in South Korea, North Koreans' attitudes towards their home country became further complicated by the conflicting agendas of right-wing conservatives and left-wing liberals. Right-wing conservatives in South Korea have argued for the type of reunification that would see North Korea being absorbed by South Korea. To support their bid to bring North Korea under South Korean rule, they mobilized defectors to denounce the ruling party's human rights violations and plead for South Korean intervention. The left-wing liberals, however, have focused on the Sunshine Policy initiated by the Kim Dae Jung regime that stressed cooperation and not subjugation of North Korea. Since neither party asked North Koreans what they wanted, the assumption was that North Koreans fall in line with the political agendas set by South Korean politicians.

As a result, North Korean defectors' organizations and activities developed into two different groups with quite different agendas as outlined in Table 8.1. To identify the groups according to the motivation for their activities, they have been labeled as 'global network' group and 'local settlement' group. The labels describe the focus of each group in the discursive rebuilding of North Korea.

The global network group has aligned itself with the right-wing conservatives in South Korea as well as Korean Christians, the church being one of the key supporter of this political group. This group favors integration with South Korea, values the European socio-economic system, and has publicly denounced North Korea thereby denying North Koreanness. As the group most interested in creating global networks of North Korean defectors, it is primarily a proponent of nation-building in flows. According to one interviewee, the election of the liberal Moon Jae In was perceived as a threat to their cause, aware that the progressive government would not support efforts for reunification.

The local settlement group's views on how North Korea should be approached align with South Korean liberals and the current Moon government. This group has focused on resettlement in the UK first and discussions on reforms for their home country after. The local settlement group was responsible for the school and organizational activities that have created a

Table 8.1: Two groups of North Korean defectors in New Malden

Group	Nation-building	Connection with South Korean political group	Focus	Main organization	Transnational identity	Religious affiliation
Global network group	Nation-building in flows	Right-wing conservative, anti-Moon regime	Criticizing North Korean human right issues	Global network of North Korean defectors	Assimilating to South Korea, Europe pride	Christian orientation
Local settlement group	Nation-building in relations	Liberal, pro-Moon regime	Settling down in New Malden	Children's Korean language school	Maintaining North Korean identity, Europe pride	None specified

positive environment for North Korean defectors. They criticized the global network group's propensity to reiterate outdated information and exaggerated accounts regarding human rights issues to the media and in lectures. They argued that those defectors had not experienced the stories of hardship themselves and repeated rumors that they had heard without verification. Members of the local settlement group have been less inclined to seek attention by railing against the North Korean regime and more concerned with settling down in New Malden with a dedication to nation-building in relations.

Each group believing that their way was the right way, they struggled for dominance of the North Korean ethnic association, and for a time there existed two associations. In 2016, they re-united, and the elected chair was a member of the local settlement group.

NATION-BUILDING IN FLOWS: A GLOBAL NETWORK AND AN ALTERNATIVE SOVEREIGNTY

The global network group sought out fellow North Korean defectors that agreed with their cause in countries around the world to form a united association. "The North Korean defectors' global network" was inaugurated in 2013 and held its first official meeting in London that year. A European network was also formed with headquarters in London and Brussels. The global and European networks' activities and discourses constitute the extra-territorial nation in flows whose nation-building is not contingent on or tied to one specific place. Instead their activities and discourses result in extra-territorial nation-building that transplace a vision of a future North Korea.

To gain support for their cause they appealed to the media to broadcast their message and objectives. One actor who worked with Radio Free Asia and Voice of America explained that in order to inform Europeans about the need to push North Korea toward democracy media coverage was vital. He complained, though, that media outlets such as EU Today were reluctant to broadcast the exile government's agenda since it opposed the South Korean government's Sunshine Policy for North Korea. They discussed the establishment of an exile government, believing that an open challenge to the North Korean regime would attract significant international media attention. They also would start a political party, stating that it would be more efficient and inspire a greater loyalty in its members than an ethnic association.

When a key member of the global network group was asked if he believed the exile government could replace the North Korean government, he responded:

> I know that what I am saying, establishing an exile government, sounds like non-sense. It would not replace the North Korean government. Yet the presence of an exile government itself would be meaningful since many people in North Korea neither like nor trust the South Korean government.

This interview subject argued that though the exile government would likely never rule it had symbolical and political significance nonetheless. He explained that in the event North Korea severed all communication, the exile government could represent the interests of North Koreans at home and abroad. He went on to compare a North Korean exile government and the South Korean government to relations between Taiwan and China in that though there are disagreements an uneasy truce can exist nonetheless.

It is not the exile government and/or political party themselves that are the focus of this research, however, but the fact of these activities to establish alternative narratives of a sovereign government. The discourses of North Korean defectors' global network in effect constitute an extra-territorial sovereignty outside the nation-state that conjure another version of North Korea as social and discursive entity. Preparations to establish an exile government required those North Koreans in the network to consider how they could share ideas to initiate the changes for a future North Korea as they thought it should be.

Although ideologically global network group aligns with South Korean right-wing conservatives and some members of this group do favor assimilating with South Korea, the model for their exile government was not South Korean. The global network group was impressed by the European socio-economic system and wished to emulate it, believing a government based on this system would be the best option to lead a new North Korea into the future. One interview subject stated that if his safety were guaranteed he would return to North Korea without hesitation to help rebuild the country and improve the social system. He said,

> South Koreans wouldn't be able to govern a new North Korea because they do not understand North Korea at all. North Koreans in North Korea wouldn't be able to govern it either because they know only about North Korean ways. We've lived in North Korea, South Korea, and Europe. We would be the best alternative.

This interview subject deemed South Koreans' inability to understand North Koreans as one of the main obstacles to the success of their style of government in North Korea. He explained that misunderstandings would arise from South Koreans' mistaken belief that North Koreans would welcome their intervention when in fact North Koreans are more likely to reject South Korean rule. He argued that the leadership of a reincarnated North Korea based on a global experience such as North Korean defectors' experience of outside societies was in the best interests of both South Korea and North Korea.

Their preference for the European system was in some part a reaction to and rejection of the pressure South Korean society put on North Koreans to assimilate. Though some right-wing thinkers embrace a wholly unified Korea, this interviewee believed that this may seem fine in theory but not reality, and that even a federation would be perceived as a threat by North Koreans. A number of those defectors explained that the pressure to conform to South Korean society and the aggressive campaign by South Korean churches to join a congregation, pledging themselves to God and publicly confessing their perceived sins, dismayed them. It was too reminiscent of the coercion and expectation of obedience in North Korea that they were trying to escape. If this was South Korea's approach to individual North Korean defectors, the sense was that it would be much the same but on a larger scale if South Korea was ever in charge of the country of North Korea.

South Korean support was necessary for the exile government, an interview subject stated, arguing that the exile government would depend on the South Koreans' approval in important matters such as meditations with the North Korean government. Should lines of communication open and if North Korea were changed enough to accept an exile government, he felt positive changes would ensue. He offered the example of China's powerhouse economy that resulted from eased restrictions and an invitation to Chinese defectors to invest in the country to illustrate the positive changes he envisioned for North Korea.

The obstacles confronting North Korean defectors aspirations to be mediators in dealings with North Korea were that neither the left wing nor the right wing in South Korea was interested in involving them. Left-wing politicians were pursuing change through negotiation and were concerned that the North Korean government might view the involvement of defectors as a reproach. To avoid unnecessarily provoking the North Korean regime, left-wing politicians excluded defectors from their negotiations. Unlike the left wing, the right wing did not seek to open lines of communication with North Korea and therefore did not require mediators, defectors or not. Right-wing politicians did, however, offer North Korean defectors a role in their campaign to bring down the North Korean government and that was to stridently denounce the human rights violations repeatedly.

Although North Korean defectors have not been included as they would wish to be, that has not stopped them from envisioning their homeland once liberated. A new political system would need to be implemented, and defectors weighed the liberal democracy of South Korea against the social democracy in North Europe. One key actor believed that, should the North Korean political system collapse or be overthrown, the country should emulate European democracy and not South Korean. To exemplify his preference, he compared the essential projects to benefit the public that European politicians proposed to the often-wasteful growth-oriented construction projects that South Korean politicians promised just to win votes. Interestingly, all interviewees from the global and European networks were critical of the exile government that had been established in the US in general and the sources of financial and political support in particular. While some support comes from churches, it is the involvement of the Parent Coalition, which is a union of Korean right-wing extremists, that has other networks refusing to collaborate with them.

When right-wing president Park Geun Hye was impeached and Moon Jae In's liberal party was elected in 2017, the global network group lost an important ally. With the inauguration of Moon, North Korean defectors and their networks affiliated with the right-wing politicians in South Korea adopted the South Korean concept of *Jongbuk Jwapa Palgaengi* (pro–North Korea Left Red)[9] to criticize left-wing liberals. One interviewee, who prepared for a North Korean exile government in the UK, even argued that the liberal regime put North Korean defectors' security in jeopardy and that the Minjoo liberal political party would end in disaster for all concerned.

Now is a difficult time. They [North Koreans who live in South Korea] feel insecure. They thought that they could rely on the conservative right-wing party, but it collapsed. Now left-wing liberals took power.

Although North Korean defectors' fear that their security was threatened was groundless, apprehension and uneasiness motivated many to unite against a perceived crisis. The same interviewee on a visit to South Korea marshaled support for an exile government, drawing on connections he had made during the eleven years he had lived in South Korea to recruit other defector leaders. He was genuinely invested in bringing about the democratization of his homeland and did what he could to achieve that aim from outside North Korea.

According to the news from home conveyed through the Han Chinese brokers to one interviewee, people have begun to refer to Kim Jong Un, the leader of North Korea, by his first name. This is considered to be highly disrespectful and would have been unimaginable before. He explained that though this may be a small act of defiance it was nonetheless a sign of change. He expressed concern that the outside world had either not noticed or simply not acknowledged these gradual changes and therefore not adjusted their estimation of North Korea to reflect the country's evolution.

NATION-BUILDING IN RELATIONS: TRANSNATIONAL NORTH KOREANNESS

Nation-building in flow relies on global networks, but nation-building in relations is derived from daily interactions and encounters such as those between North Korean defectors and South Korean migrants in the UK. In North and South Korea, fraternization with the enemy population is illegal, but in New Malden, encounters between North Koreans and South Koreans are a daily occurrence. North Korean defectors might interact with local British, but they must interrelate with South Koreans, as they are the majority within the New Malden community. North Koreans' collaborations with South Korean migrants expose them to continual prejudice against North Koreans and North Korea. As they formulated a two-prong approach to disengage or at least distance themselves from South Koreans and form their own community, they created a distinct identity as North Koreans.

Establishing a school for their children was the first proactive step in setting themselves apart from South Koreans and preserving their identity as North Koreans. Most of the interviewees who had chosen to migrate from South Korea to the UK were motivated by the need to provide their children a more comfortable and less discriminatory environment. The parents who had children during the time they lived in South Korea complained that the government did not consider that the educational needs of North Korean children might differ from South Korean children's need. In the almost twenty years since North Korean defectors started arriving in South Korea, the government had done little to retain or reeducate so North Koreans could raise their human capital and become contributing members of South Korean society.

One interviewee worried that left to the South Korean or UK education systems, their children would lose their heritage. He explained that older children, such as his son who had arrived in South Korea at the age of fifteen, already spoke Korean and understood that when the time came they would help rebuild North Korea. His concern centered on those younger children whose formative years were spent in South Korean and the UK and needed to be reminded to speak Korean and taught that the democratization of North Korea would be a shared effort. They decided that to ensure their children learned Korean and about their heritage, they would have to educate them themselves.

After their migration to the UK, children's education remained a key issue for North Korean parents especially as their concerns grew over their children speaking English only. Wishing to preserve their language and prepare their children for a possible return to a new North Korea, parents organized a North Korean children's language school for the second generation of defectors in 2016. The parent of a child who devoted himself to establishing the North Korean school said,

> I was afraid our North Koreanness would disappear if our children completely assimilated to South Korea in the South Korean language school.

North Koreanness started to coalesce and take form as parents and children congregated in a school uniquely their own where they could honor their country without prejudice. While the school was not political in itself, through its support for and development of a North Korean identity it contributed to nation-building in relations. Some North Korean parents admitted that they feared that their children would be influence by South Korean attitudes and start to lose or even reject those traits that differentiate them if they attended the South Korean language school.

Another parent who worked devotedly to keep the school open said,

> I thought we need at least one thing that is our own.

This simple statement explained the North Korean language school's organizers' rejection of the South Korean government's attempt to integrate their school with the registered South Korean language school. Involved South Koreans and the global network group criticized the North Korean school for stubbornly defying amalgamation. Members of the North Korean school were unmoved by this criticism. They viewed their school as a repository for their language and identity, a place where their children could learn without discrimination. Their active resistance to assimilation by South Koreans and the ensuing emergence of North Koreanness are pivotal to their nation-making.

There were certain practices from North Korea that they employed in the management of their school. For example, the group was proud to offer children's education free of charge as it is in North Korea. They found the tendency of South Korean schools to charge parents exorbitant fees for their children's education inappropriate. Neither did they did not want to pressure their children to learn the way children were pressured in South Korean schools, in some part due to the costs. The founding committee paid for the North Korean school's rental space in a local church and teachers' salaries with donations from the community. Parents were only asked to pay 5 to 7 British Pounds per month for the children's snacks that would be distributed during the Saturday afternoon break. To avoid hiring help and limit expenses, parents organized a rotating roster that assigned snack and cleanup duties through an online community chat.

As the school became established, it not only offered education and stood as a cultural symbol of North Korea, it became the center of the North Korean community and provided a foundation for new networks to build upon. The school's central role in the community was in part due to a weakened North Korean ethnic association plagued by internal conflict among members and lack of a unified objective. The church, once the center of the North Korean community, was torn apart by the conflict among members North Korean Association and was consequently disbanded, leaving a void in the North Korean community. Using education and non-political activities to attract people without creating conflict, the school filled the void left by the church and made up the deficit in leadership left by a disorganized ethnic association. Later, the North Korean ethnic association invited the school to join together, and one of the mothers was elected to preside over the association.

The North Korean school was important to the community as a cultural hub, but it contributed to outside discourses that captured media attention as well. A number of documentary filmmakers and Korean television companies (KBS, YTN) produced documentaries about New Malden and the North Korean school. They explored the organic integration of North and South Koreans and in ethnic enclaves outside Korea as well as the evolution of Korean education. The North Korean school was neither wholly North nor South Korean but hybrid and integrated. The founder was from South Korea, and the foundation committee included a mix of North and South Koreans, as well as three teachers from North Korea and three from South Korea. They taught Korean as a second language since the majority of the children attending were born and raised in the UK and chose textbooks and references books without political overtones.

The second step in North Korean defectors' nation-building in relations and creation of a North Korean identity that defines them as other than South Koreans was achieved through social activities. Usually, these activities were hosted by organizations such as the South Korean or North Korean ethnic association, the North Korean children's Korean language school, the South Korean elderly association, the National Unification Advisory Council (NUAC), and cultural groups. Initially, South Koreans organized and controlled everything, but over time collaboration on events, joint sponsorship and committee memberships for North Koreans has increased. For example, the South Korean elderly association and the NUAC has applied to their headquarters in South Korea for permission to admit North Korean members. The South Korean ethnic association has taken it one step further and invited two North Koreans to become committee members.

As participation in organized activities in New Malden inevitably increased interactions, North Koreans were reminded of their experiences in South Korean where the North Korean national identity was considered dangerous and undesirable. One interviewee told me that on the first day in the adjustment support program for North Korean defectors (Hanawon) they were told that they should assimilate to South Korea and convert to Korean Christianity. The implications that North Koreans should abandon their national identity combined with the pressure to embrace a South Korean identity inspired resistance rather than compliance. One interviewee explained,

> I escaped from North Korea because I did not like the North Korean regime. It doesn't mean that I did not like North Korea, my country. Why should I be anti-North Korea?

This statement was made during a friendly gathering of liberals at the home of a fellow North Korean. When asked if they felt relief now that they had escaped the dictatorship in North Korea, they instead discussed the pressure to adopt South Korean ideals and their resentment of it. Another defector at the same gathering stated that he loves his home country and asked why it should be wrong to display the North Korean flag at their events. He added that South Koreans parade their national flag at every opportunity and event and North Koreans should too. Yet another admitted that after she and her children had hung up the national flag she teased them that they might be bombed since North Korea is viewed as a global threat.

Another North Korean defector revealed that just the sight of the North Korean flag can bring tears to her eyes and feel homesick for country she loves. Even though she risked her life to escape the terrible conditions in North Korea and faced imprisonment or execution if caught defecting, she is proud to be North Korean, she said. They explained that though they abhor the current regime they love their country, and while changes in governing are necessary, they value and would keep certain policies such as free education. Many North Koreans were disillusioned by the value system in South Korea and cite the differences as one of the many reasons they are against Korean reunification.

Their primary aversion to reintegration arose from the fear that South Koreans would dictate the changes in North Korea in a manner similar to their treatment of North Korean defectors in South Korea and New Malden. Identifying the flaws in both the North Korean and South Korean systems of governing, most defectors envision a future North Korea as a hybrid of North and South Korea, like the North Korean language school. Ironically, the local settlement group's nation-building was promoted and clarified during the interactions with South Korean migrants. Their building of a different version of North Korea in relations with others was a project that negotiated a boundary between selves and others and create a new version for the selves.

The friction between North Koreans and South Koreans is evident in a setting even as innocuous as the school, where awkward encounters denote a continuing uneasiness with each other. That the transnational community is stratified by the origin societies and economic development in a geopolitical hierarchy that places South Koreans at the top and North Koreans firmly at the bottom reinforced divisions. New Malden is a microcosm of the greater geopolitical macroeconomics of South Korea, North Korea, and the UK that play out in New Malden and shape relations there. The geopolitical relationship between the UK and South Korea and that of the UK and North Korea has to an extent informed the interactions between South Koreans and North Koreans in New Malden.

CONCLUSION

Based on the agents' political and social activities in this study, North Korean defectors' extra-territorial nation-building was a social and cultural process. First, the global network of North Korean defectors' ideas, discourses, and activities to establish an exile government imagined a version of the nation of North Korea in an example of extra-territorial nation-building in flows. Second, North Korean defectors' community-based activities to uphold a North Korean identity and distinguish them from South Korean and Korean-Chinese migrants created a version of North Korea in the UK through nation-building in relations.

This chapter extends the geographical imagination of the nation by defining nations not as territorial spaces but the sense of community that comes from human agents' transnational practices, networks, and discourses. This does not discount the value of the originating territories and nations rather the idea being that agents take the essence of nation with them to re-imagine and re-create it in a new territory or country. In this sense, the study of transnational migrants provides an avenue to further developing the field of geopolitics. The implications of this paper in East Asian contexts are articulated in the example of territories defined by migrants' daily lives and activities, their migrations, geopolitical economic positions, and national identity.

This chapter also provides a significant practical application. Since the completion of this fieldwork in April 2018, the leaders of South Korea and North Korea have met in the region of *Panmunjeon*, the Joint Security Area. The consequence of these two leaders' willingness to meet face-to-face led to expectations of re-established flows, improved relations and eased hostilities between the two countries, and the re-building of both countries. Extra-territorial nation-building through flows and relations in diverse and innumerable ways, therefore, is anticipated although the two countries' relations have been inconsistent and on occasion suffered setbacks. As this case study has demonstrated, the members of the North Korean diaspora already have agendas of their own for nation-rebuilding. North Koreans themselves have demonstrated through nation-building beyond the national territory that they have found a way to straddle North and South Korean influences and embrace European influences as well. Should they ever have an opportunity to utilize their knowledge and experiences, they could very well heal the rift between these two countries.

NOTES

1. In this study, discourses refer to spoken or written communication in daily life. Discourses not only represent what people think but also influence each other's ideas and discourses.

2. *Diaspora* means a group of people who are scattered from their original country to other countries, or the act of spreading to separate geographic locale.

3. Just like any language school, the North Korean language school was open to every child regardless of their nationality. The author's child was not the first South Korean to attend the school, but he was the only non-North Korean in the school during the period.

4. https://www.nrc.no/news/2018/february/ten-things-you-should-know-about-refugees-from-north-korea/

5. http://www.unikorea.go.kr/eng_unikorea/relations/statistics/defectors/

6. https://www.eahrnk.org/articles/policy-and-research/a-case-for-clarification-european-asylum-policy-and-north-korean-refugees

7. https://theconversation.com/why-does-the-uk-deport-north-korean-asylum-seekers-92129

8. http://english.yonhapnews.co.kr/news/2018/04/10/0200000000AEN201804100 03200315.html?sns=tw

9. This term has been often used to criticize left-wing liberals even when they had nothing to do with North Korea. As the national security law has defined those *Jongbuk Jwapa Palgaengi* as the enemy of the state, the labeling has been effective.

REFERENCES

Agnew, John. "The territorial trap: the geographical assumptions of international relations theory." *Review of international political economy* 1, no. 1 (1994): 53–80.

Agnew, John. "Borders on the mind: re-framing border thinking." *Ethics & Global Politics*, 1, no.4 (2008): 175–191.

Agnew, John. 2003. *Geopolitics: re-visioning world politics*. London: Routledge.

Anderson, Benedict. 2006. *Imagined communities: Reflections on the origin and spread of nationalism*. Verso Books.

Bashi, V., ed. 2007. *Survival of the knitted: Immigrant social networks in a stratified world*. Redwood City: Stanford University Press.

Brenner, Neil. "Globalisation as reterritorialisation: the re-scaling of urban governance in the European Union." *Urban studies* 36, no. 3 (1999a): 431–451.

Brenner, Neil. "Beyond state-centrism? Space, territoriality, and geographical scale in globalization studies." *Theory and society* 28, no. 1 (1999b): 39–78.

Carling, Jørgen. "The human dynamics of migrant transnationalism." *Ethnic and racial studies* 31, no. 8 (2008): 1452–1477.

Cauvet, Philippe. "Deterritorialisation, reterritorialisation, nations and states: Irish nationalist discourses on nation and territory before and after the Good Friday Agreement." *GeoJournal* 76, no. 1 (2011): 77–91.

Collins, Francis Leo. "Transnational mobilities and urban spatialities: Notes from the Asia-Pacific." *Progress in Human Geography* 36, no. 3 (2012): 316–335.

Collyer, Michael, and Russell King. "Producing transnational space: International migration and the extra-territorial reach of state power." *Progress in Human Geography* 39, no. 2(2015): 185–204.

Cutler, David M., Edward L. Glaeser, and Jacob L. Vigdor, "When are ghettos bad? Lessons from immigrant segregation in the United States." *Journal of Urban Economics* 63, no. 3 (2008): 759–774.

Dahinden, Janine. "Are we all transnationals now? Network transnationalism and transnational subjectivity: the differing impacts of globalization on the inhabitants of a small Swiss city." *Ethnic and Racial Studies* 32, no. 8 (2009): 1365–1386.

Deleuze, Gilles, and Félix Guattari. 1972. *Anti-Oedipus*. Trans. Hurley, Robert, Mark Seem, and Helen R. Lane. 1983. Minneapolis: Minnesota University Press.

Dietz, Barbara. "German and Jewish migration from the former Soviet Union to Germany: Background, trends and implications." *Journal of Ethnic and Migration Studies* 26, no. 4 (2000): 635–652.

Dyck, Isabel. "Feminist geography, the 'everyday,' and local–global relations: hidden spaces of place☐making." *Canadian Geographer/Le Géographe canadien* 49, no. 3 (2005): 233–243.

Engel, David. 1993. *Facing a holocaust: the Polish government-in-exile and the Jews, 1943–1945*. UNC Press Books.

Erdal, Marta Bivand. "Migrant transnationalism and multi-layered integration: Norwegian-Pakistani migrants' own reflections." *Journal of Ethnic and Migration Studies* 39, no. 6 (2013): 983–999.

Halilovich, Hariz. 2011. "(Per)forming 'trans-local' homes: Bosnian diaspora in Australia." In *The Bosnian diaspora: Integration in transnational communities,* edited by Marko Valenta and Sabrina Ramet, 63–81. Surrey: Ashgate Publishing Limited.

Hannam, Kevin, Mimi Sheller, and John Urry. "Mobilities, immobilities and moorings." *Mobilities* 1, no. 1 (2006): 1–22.

Hsu, Jinn-Yuh. "State transformation and the evolution of economic nationalism in the East Asian developmental state: the Taiwanese semiconductor industry as case study." *Transactions of the Institute of British Geographers* 42, no. 2 (2017): 166–178.

Jirón, Paola A., Walter Alejandro Imilan, and Luis Iturra. "Relearning to travel in Santiago: The importance of mobile place-making and travelling know-how." *Cultural Geographies* 23, no. 4 (2016): 599–614.

Katila, Saija, and Östen Wahlbeck. "The role of (transnational) social capital in the start-up processes of immigrant businesses: The case of Chinese and Turkish restaurant businesses in Finland." *International Small Business Journal* 30, no. 3 (2012): 294–309.

Kolstø, Pål. "Territorialising diasporas: The case of Russians in the former Soviet Republics." *Millennium* 28, no. 3 (1999): 607–631.

Korobkov, Andrei V., and Zhanna A. Zaionchkovskaia. "The changes in the migration patterns in the post-Soviet states: the first decade." *Communist and Post-Communist Studies* 37, no. 4 (2004): 481–508.

Larsen, Jonas, and John Urry. 2016. *Mobilities, networks, geographies*. New York: Routledge.

Le Bail, Hélène, and Wei Shen. "The return of the 'brains' to China: What are the social, economic, and political impacts." *Asie Visions* 11 (2008): 1–31.

Lee, Helen. "Rethinking transnationalism through the second generation." *The Australian Journal of Anthropology* 22, no. 3 (2011): 295–313.

Levitt, Peggy, and Nina Glick Schiller. "Conceptualizing simultaneity: A transnational social field perspective on society." *International Migration Review* 38, no. 3 (2004): 1002–39.

Levitt, Peggy, ed. 2001. *The transnational villagers.* Berkeley: University of California Press.

Levitt, Peggy. "'You know, Abraham was really the first immigrant': Religion and transnational migration." *International Migration Review* 37, no. 3 (2003): 847–873.

Li, Wei. "Anatomy of a new ethnic settlement: The Chinese ethnoburb in Los Angeles." *Urban Studies* 35, no. 3 (1998): 479–501.

Liu, Ye, Zhigang Li, and Werner Breitung. "The social networks of new-generation migrants in China's urbanized villages: A case study of Guangzhou." *Habitat International* 36, no. 1 (2012): 192–200.

Ma, Shu-Yun. "The exit, voice, and struggle to return of Chinese political exiles." *Pacific Affairs* (1993): 368–385.

McCann, Eugene J. "The cultural politics of local economic development: meaning-making, place-making, and the urban policy process." *Geoforum* 33, no. 3 (2002): 385–398.

McConnell, Fiona. 2016. *Rehearsing the state: The political practices of the Tibetan government-in-exile*. John Wiley & Sons.

Müller, Angelo, and Rainer Wehrhahn. "Transnational business networks of African intermediaries in China: Practices of networking and the role of experiential knowledge." *DIE ERDE–Journal of the Geographical Society of Berlin* 144, no. 1 (2013): 82–97.

Murdie, Robert, and Sutama Ghosh. "Does spatial concentration always mean a lack of integration? Exploring ethnic concentration and integration in Toronto." *Journal of Ethnic and Migration Studies* 36, no. 2 (2010): 293–311.

Novak, Paolo. "The flexible territoriality of borders." *Geopolitics* 16, no. 4 (2011): 741–767.

Olwig, Karen Fog. ed. 2007. *Caribbean journeys: An ethnography of migration and home in three family networks*. Durham: Duke University Press.

Pang, Ching Lin, and Jan Rath. 2007. "The force of regulation in the land of the free: The persistence of Chinatown, Washington DC as a symbolic ethnic enclave." In *The sociology of entrepreneurship*, edited by Martin Ruef and Michael Lounsbury, 191–216. Bingley, UK: Emerald Group Publishing.

Penrose, Jan, and Richard C. M. Mole. "Nation-states and national identity." *The SAGE handbook of political geography* (2008): 271–284.

Perkins, Richard, and Neumayer, Eric. "Extra-territorial interventions in conflict spaces: Explaining the geographies of post-Cold War peacekeeping." *Political Geography* 27, no. 8 (2008): 895–914.

Pierce, Joesph, Deborah G. Martin, and James T. Murphy, "Relational place□making: the networked politics of place." *Transactions of the Institute of British Geographers* 36, no. 1 (2011): 54–70.

Robertson, Zoe, Raelene Wilding, and Sandra Gifford. "Mediating the family imaginary: Young people negotiating absence in transnational refugee families." *Global Networks* 16, no. 2 (2016): 219–236.

Sen, Sudipta. 2016. *A distant sovereignty: National imperialism and the origins of British India*. Routledge.

Sheller, Mimi. "Bodies, cybercars and the mundane incorporation of automated mobilities." *Social & Cultural Geography* 8, no. 2 (2007): 175–197.

Sheringham, Olivia. "Creating 'alternative geographies': Religion, transnationalism and everyday life." *Geography Compass* 4, no. 11 (2010): 1678–1694.

Shin, HaeRan. "The Geopolitical Ethnic Networks for De-bordering: North Korean Defectors in Los Angeles and London." *Asian Journal of Peacebuilding* 9, no. 2 (2021): 209–232.

Shin, HaeRan. "Extra-territorial nation-building in flows and relations: North Korea in the global networks and an ethnic enclave." *Political Geography* 74 (2019): 102048.

Shin, HaeRan. "The territoriality of ethnic enclaves: Dynamics of transnational practices and geopolitical relations within and beyond a Korean transnational enclave in New Malden, London." *Annals of the American Association of Geographers* 108, no. 3 (2018): 756–772.

Smith, Michael Peter. 2001. *Transnational Urbanism: Locating Globalization.* Malden, MA: Blackwell.

Sperling, Jessica. "Conceptualising 'inter-destination transnationalism': The presence and implication of coethnic ties between destination societies." *Journal of Ethnic and Migration Studies* 40, no. 7 (2014): 1097–1115.

Varady, David P., ed. 2005. *Desegregating the city: ghettos, enclaves, and inequality.* Albany: SUNY Press.

Vásquez, Manuel A., and Kim Knott. "Three dimensions of religious place making in diaspora." *Global Networks* 14, no. 3 (2014): 326–347.

Vertovec, Steven. "Cheap calls: the social glue of migrant transnationalism." *Global networks* 4, no. 2 (2004): 219–224.

Wang, Zheng, Fangzhu Zhang, and Fulong Wu. "Intergroup neighbouring in urban China: Implications for the social integration of migrants." *Urban Studies* 53, no. 4 (2016): 651–668.

Wigley, Edward. 2016. "Every day mobilities, place and spirituality: Constructing subjective spiritual geographies in contemporary Bristol, UK." Doctoral dissertation, University of the West of England.

Wu, Fulong. "The global and local dimensions of place-making: remaking Shanghai as a world city." *Urban Studies* 37, no. 8 (2000): 1359–1377.

Yamazaki, Takashi. "Is Japan Leaking? Globalisation, reterritorialisation and identity in the Asia-Pacific context." *Geopolitics* 7, no. 1 (2002): 165–192.

Yoon, Sharon J. "Mobilizing ethnic resources in the transnational enclave: Ethnic solidarity as a mechanism for mobility in the Korean church in Beijing." *International Journal of Sociology* 43, no. 3 (2013): 29–54.

Conclusion

Looking to the Future

HaeRan Shin and Kyung Hyo Chun

In this edited volume, we examined how North Korean defectors' mobilities, settlement, and identities have evolved over time. Since they left their country of origin, their mobilities have primarily developed around their hopes and plans for their families and North Korea. Until they can affect change in North Korea, their strategies for their survival and growth revolve around living in a country that offers better welfare and education for their children. As they have settled and re-settled in various countries, they have muddled through encounters with South Koreans in all major aspects of their lives: careers, children's lives, and community activities. North Korean defectors' daily life is made up of geopolitical tension, different countries' policies, and interactions with South Koreans and the host destination's populace. Their mobilities, settlement, and identities have responded to and been shaped by external factors in the destination countries such as the politics and welfare policies, as well as population's attitudes towards them.

These defectors had their own opinions on their actions. Some admitted that they felt in defecting they had betrayed their country, but they felt that South Korean migrants had also betrayed their country by leaving. They defected knowing that their actions could jeopardize the safety of the family members they left behind, which caused feelings of guilt. However, North Korean defectors refute the notion that their escape would result in their families being imprisoned or threatened with death, stating that this is not the case. Some of them confessed that they miss North Korea, and that they had not abandoned their country so much as escaped from the oppressive Kim regime. They grappled with feelings of disloyal, guilt, and homesickness as they attempted to settle adjust to other countries.

This book's processual approach to North Korean defectors' continuous evolution leads one to wonder what other changes the future may bring.

Naturally, speculation about the future would involve discussions on the state of the two Koreas. Interviews with North Korean defectors have already revealed that some would embrace reunification, but many are ambivalent about a reunited North and South Korea. Though they might wish to see an end to North Korea's dictatorship, they are not sure what system should replace it. Many North Koreans have stated that they would not like to see a South Korean system or the government in Seoul ruling over North Korea. Many hopes instead for changes to the North Korean system that allows the two Koreas to remain separate with the border open to trade but more importantly unrestricted contact between their peoples. How would relations between North Korea and South Korea and their citizens change in the event of a reunified Korea or at least two countries at peace?

That would depend on pertinent geopolitical factors inside and outside the Korean peninsula. It might be that the future remains the same including the current military tension with occasional negotiations and so nothing would change. It could be a case of there being just enough changes that the two different governments could exist without political tension. Or, the two countries could be reunited as one country ruled under a capitalist, socialist or as of yet undetermined system. It would be beyond the scope of this book to predict the political changes for the Koreas in an unknowable future. Nonetheless, this edited volume has introduced discussions that provide interesting implications regarding the potential mobilities of people, capital, firms, and culture and how they may instigate future changes in the two Koreas.

In this conclusion, we extend the discussions on the main themes and consider the implications of our research for academic debates, practices, and policies. We have employed processual, relational, and interpretative approaches to arrive at the findings of this research. The processual approach has helped understand how precarious situations related to the geopolitics have influenced the dynamics of mobilities, resettlement, and identities that are so significant to defectors' lives. Relational approaches examined how the contexts and the dynamics of post-defection life have influenced North Korean defectors' interactions with other population groups. An interpretative approach to North Korean defectors' case studies provided insights to and implications for their meaning-making in a new destination and how that had implications for their home country.

Previous studies chronicled how defectors' and migrants' networks and activities played a role in the changing political climate and financial well-being of their home countries. For example, when China adopted an open-door policy to attract foreign investment, Chinese defectors readily participated in the financial rebuilding of their homeland (Le Bail and Shen, 2008; Ma, 1993). Another example is of ethnic Germans and Jews returning to Germany following the break-up of the Soviet Union (Dietz, 2000) and migration in the post-Soviet states (Korobkov and Zaionchkovskaia, 2004). In the case of North and South Korea, one significant change would be to allow the freedom to move between the two countries. If the border dividing the Korean peninsula could at the very least allow passage so people could interact, exchange ideas, collaborate, and migrate, how would defectors living either inside or outside South Korea react? It is likely the evolving aspects of their identities will become even more complicated than described in this volume as a consequence of their repeated migrations followed by a return to Korea. Let us explore the possible scenarios and discuss their implications. Using the framework of this book, we can think of those responses in terms of mobilities, settlement, and identities to extend our discussions.

EXPANDED AND COMPLICATED MOBILITIES

Following the reunification of German in 1990, the population's mobilities from East to West and the various issues that caused are what we would expect in a reunified Korean peninsula. Even with strict border controls, the mobilities of people, information, and remittances have increased over time. The physical and symbolic borders are not as impervious as they might seem, and North Korean defectors have played an important role in proving their fallibility. They have achieved this not only by sending money and information into North Korea but bringing information out of North Korea through disclosures to governmental research institutes, in YouTube videos and on TV.

Since these activities continue while the border is so stringently controlled, it would not be difficult to imagine the mobilities of capital, people, and things would increase significantly should controls be relaxed. It is also quite likely that defectors' roles as players or mediators will increase as well. Should this situation arise, would those defectors be willing to return to North Korea? Would the North Korean regime be willing to allow those defectors to return? If relations between North and South Korea improved, some of the North Korean defectors interviewed who live in the UK stated that they would move back to the Korean peninsula. They cited a desire to contribute to the modernization of the economy and politics in North Korea as their reasons for returning.

In the event that North Korea defectors return to assist in rebuilding their country, it would be an interesting case to study in terms of the migration–development nexus. While some stated that they would fear arrest and punishment upon their return, a North Korean government genuinely seeking to economically develop the country would welcome defectors and their knowledge of capitalist societies. China, in permitting previous defectors to return as development agents, has demonstrated that their roles in the country's growth have been significant.

Another possibility is that some defectors may assist development by investing in North Korea but living in South Korea or another country. They might have adjusted to their new home or hesitate to live in North Korea again for other reasons and prefer to visit North Korea rather than permanently relocate there. This type of entrepreneurship based on transnational ethnic networks has been growing especially among migrants whose home country is undergoing rapid economic development. For example, Vietnamese marriage migrant women who live in South Korea began by sending remittances home but eventually established businesses and invested in real estate in Vietnam, capitalizing on the country's sudden development. Unfortunately, women who had surrendered their Vietnamese citizenship to become South Korean citizens had to invest through family members due to the Vietnam's restriction on foreign investment that was in place until 2015. However, women who became citizens after the South Korean government's policy was changed to allow marriage migrants to hold both citizenships could invest in Vietnam directly.

Remaining in the destination country would be preferable for many North Koreans defectors since it offers the best of both worlds. They can keep the life they have become accustomed to and test financial ventures in their home country without too much risk. If they live in South Korea, they could easily go for short- or long-term stays in North Korea to oversee their investments. These financial endeavors would not be the responsibility of the defectors alone as many would involve their families and friends as well. Those global ethnic networks of personal and community contacts that North Korean defectors had already established would be of vital support to their investment and businesses in various locations. Family members involved in these ventures would either oversee the business in the home country or they too would engage in repeated mobilities between South Korea and North Korea.

Some North Koreans defectors, however, have stated that they would not return to North Korea even if they could. They would rather stay where they are or move to any other country if that would benefit them but not North Korea under any circumstance. In that case, as discussed in this volume, they can either assimilate to the destination society or absorb some of the host society's traits and retain parts of their North Korean identity (Shin, 2019). As representatives of North Korea, their revelations about their country to the outside world and diminishes the mystery. Then, instead of being defectors from one of the last completely closed societies in the word, they would be like the many other migrants seeking economic success and social recognition in the destination society.

For many North Korean defectors, their repeated mobilities have become a survival strategy for their post-defection lives. Our fieldwork revealed that repeated mobilities witnessed among migrants and refugees, as well as other precarious groups, have for some become an addiction. The mobilities as a strategy of Korean Chinese migrants—*Joseonjok* or *Chosŏnjok* migrants—is an example of this addiction. Those migrants who had always intended to return to China after earning money in a foreign country found they could not stay settled and had grown to prefer circular mobilities. Through repeated mobilities, they come to develop an in-betweenness that often eases the strain of circular or repeated mobility but over time becomes part of their identity.

As *Chosŏnjok* and Vietnamese migrants developed circular mobilities for personal or professional reasons, many also developed businesses that would sell South Korean products in their origin societies. Their business networks often were made up of family members in both the origin country and in South Korea. While it can be an advantage of in-betweenness, it was also true that the mediators, who play the role of linking two sides, often have lost out as the direct networks developed.

In discussions regarding the future, some of our North Korean interviewees expressed an interest in establishing businesses in North Korea like those of *Chosŏnjok* and Vietnamese migrants. Others were less concerned about business and more concerned about where their children, the second-generation, would like to live. Since the second-generation was born in South Korea or another country like the UK, they did not have firsthand knowledge of North Korea, their parents' home country. Yet those raised in a North Korean community were often aware of the situation in North Korea and the tension with South Korea. The children of the defectors tended to be decidedly attached to the destination society, while their parents' appreciation for the host country was complicated by a longing for their home country. Some children of defectors claimed to be from South Korea because their classmates and other children considered K-Pop to be cool. In discussions on the future of Korea, many of those defectors said that they expected their children to play an important role should the opportunity arise.

RE-SETTLEMENTS AND ENCOUNTERS

If North Korea and South Korea are reunited in the future, population mobility and re-settlement would be one of the most pressing issues. After Germany reunified, there was an influx of Germans from the former East looking for better jobs in former West Germany. This created a hierarchy with wealthy Western Germans at the top and poor Eastern Germans at the bottom. The case studies on the London and Los Angeles Koreatowns in this book exhibit a similar hierarchy between North Korean defectors hired by South Korean migrants. This disparity in the job market has caused conflicts between the two groups.

Until there is reunification, it would be difficult to predict with any certainty, but based on the example in Germany, it is likely that North Koreans would migrant to South Korea for jobs. Predicated on examples in London and Los Angeles, a hierarchy would result not only in the workplace but also in everyday life such as in schools, communities, and organizational activities.

Though this is a highly probable scenario, over time different dynamics are just as likely to emerge. In the UK where encounters between North Koreans and South Koreans were well-observed, there has been evidence of a hierarchy, discrimination, and pressure on North Koreans to assimilate to South Koreans' ideals. Over time, however, some North Korean defectors have established their own businesses, and North Korean defectors' organizational activities have proved to be more active than South Koreans'. After the initial transition period of a reunified Korea, their differences would eventually become less pronounced as North Koreans take leadership roles (Shin, 2018, 2021).

If North and South Koreans were looking for an exemplar for a reunified Korea, they could look to those experiences of Korean Chinese migrants who are ethnically Korean but were born and raised in China. When they migrated to South Korea, they were initially welcomed as returning ethnic Koreans. However, as time went on, public perception changed once it became evident that Korean Chinese do not consider themselves to be purely Korean. After that Korean Chinese were viewed with prejudice and resentment, many believing that they were taking available jobs from native Koreans. Based on these experiences, we can anticipate that the general public's perception of North Koreans could evolve along similar lines. It would require further investigations to determine whether migrants deprive South Koreans of jobs or create a labor force for those jobs most South Koreans refused to do. However, even if North Koreans do not take the jobs South Koreans want, the perception that they are can create a negative impression that may adversely affect their professional and personal relations.

While the number of non-Koreans in South Korea has increased over recent years, serious racial or ethnic conflicts have not arisen. The prejudicial attitudes towards Korean Chinese migrants would be the most serious ethnic conflict to date, which manifests in a coldness toward them. It is possible that in a united Korea tension around issues of culture would emerge, though, as many North Korean defectors have expressed a dislike of South Korea's society and attitude of superiority.

North Korean defectors who live in South Korea now have empowered themselves by establishing enclaves where they as North Koreans can thrive in a community all their own. It is a classic migrant coping strategy to create an enclave where they can speak freely and unselfconsciously, shop for familiar items especially food, work for other migrants, and create a community. Places of worship, restaurants, community centers, and associations within these enclaves provide opportunities to reaffirm their identities. Enclaves are an example of migrants' place-making in an effort to secure a space for themselves despite the fact that those spaces are constantly renegotiated among migrants' multiple belongingness.

If the political tension between South Korea and North Korea remains unchanged, North Koreans defectors in South Korea will continue to adapt to survive and hopefully thrive in a society that is foreign to them. They might assimilate or they might just embrace those South Korean characteristics they do admire while preserving their North Korean identities. Their children and grandchildren will face different challenges from the ones that they have. It will be quite interesting to how the second and third generations' identities will evolve further both in the short and the long term.

CULTURAL DIFFERENCES BETWEEN NORTH KOREAN DEFECTORS AND SOUTH KOREAN RESIDENTS

After 70 years of separation, it would be safe to assume that there are now noticeable differences between the citizens of two Koreas. One of the most often asked questions regarding North Korea and South Korea is just how much they differ in terms of language, lifestyle, and culture. North Korean defectors' "cultural difference" is often cited as one of the most crucial factors hampering their successful adaptation to South Korea. While North Koreans are accepted as ethnically the same, their value system, ways of life, speech and communication style create a "cultural difference" that marks them as unlike South Koreans.

Though the differences are undeniable, it is difficult to measure how significant they are to the citizens of North and South Korea. Dominant discourses on North Korean defectors, however, use the concept of cultural difference to explain issues with assimilation without considering how North Korean defectors themselves understand and conceptualize cultural difference. It needs to be understood that South Koreans' perceptions of cultural difference might not align with those of North Korean defectors.

Cultural difference is based on people's assumptions and expectations and therefore subjective. For example, the North Korean accent is considered to be one of the most notable indications of cultural difference. But does the mere fact that having a different accent constitute genuine cultural difference rather than a distinctive pronunciation or intonation? Or, is the act of speaking with a different accent being interpreted as cultural difference based on the assumption that if "someone talks differently from us, then they must have a different lifestyle and culture"? Variations in accents do not necessary indicate that there are meaningful differences in culture since they neither prevent communication, nor are they a sign of different value systems. Nevertheless, the North Korean accent is often given as an example of the cultural difference between defectors and South Koreans. In fact, it is cited as a cultural difference so consistently that North Koreans feel that it is at the root of the discrimination they face. Truthfully, it is not the North Korean accent itself that causes problems rather the negative stereotypes South Koreans associate with the accent that become the basis for prejudice (Chun, 2022).

The cultural differences of minority groups are often associated with negative social aspects of their origin country, although there is no direct relationship between them. In those cases, perceived cultural differences can stigmatize minority groups. Negative images that are first associated with a particular minority in people's minds via media representation and vulgar journalism then becomes engrained through repetition. For example, the *Daerim* area in Seoul is known as a Korean Chinese ethnic enclave but also for its high crime rate, which has been shamelessly stereotyped in films and TV shows. Portrayed as a dark and crime-ridden place on the fringes of society, the focus on violence and illegal activities such as smuggling and human trafficking ignores that ordinary people live there too. These sensationalized criminal elements have combined with a lowly social standing in South Korean society to give ethnic Korean Chinese a mostly undeserved reputation for being disreputable. This reputation is then attached to ethnic Korean Chinese people who through their distinct accent, vocabulary and way of speaking reveal their origin. This is how accents come to be considered a cultural difference.

As mentioned, North Korean defectors also have a distinctive accent and way of pronouncing certain vowels that almost immediately identifies them as not South Korean just like ethnic Korean Chinese. Where South Koreans' negative perspective of ethnic Korean Chinese is quite definite, their distrust of North Korean defectors can vary. Though very few South Koreans have ever had significant interactions with North Korean defectors or even met one, this lack of first-hand experience has not stopped them from forming opinions on them. The media-generated stereotypical images of North Korean defectors, in turn, have stressed cultural differences to create a foundation for discrimination and prejudice (Chun, 2020).

Reducing every distinction so that it falls under the category of cultural difference is not an efficient way to understand another's life or acknowledge that their circumstances are more complex. The true difference between North Korean defectors and South Koreans lies in their contrasting educational, social networking, interpersonal communication, and professional experiences. Some might point to the capitalist system and socialist regime as the causes of these differences. In that case, any divergence should be understood as emerging from social differences rather than cultural differences. Attributing cultural difference or more accurately social difference to a politico-social system runs the risk of reintroducing an unproductive discussion on collective personality, for example, socialist personality, national personality. The issue with applying collective personality here is that it attempts to employ a group's customary conduct in a certain setting to explain an individual's experiences in a different setting. If one assumes conversely that individuals represent the group in a simplified and overgeneralized form and the group represents an individual, this reasoning can become circular. Each individual has experiences unique to themselves, and those experiences are all the more distinct for those individuals who have crossed borders into different countries. Hence, rather than a simplified approach that deals in generalities what is required is a nuanced approach that considers specifics and a particular setting to address the difference between North Korean defectors and South Koreans. A nuanced approach will also reveal not only people's past experiences and present circumstances but offers future projections as well.

It is past time that discussions on cultural identity go beyond methodological nationalism that acknowledges only the nation-state's definition of national identity. Is there really one cultural identity that is both inclusive and distinctive enough to define all the people residing within a nation as one collectivity? Not to mention those discourses on ethnic homogeneity that ceased to be relevant as globalization and transnational migration connected the world in a way that has defied national borders. Considering that people from different backgrounds can amicably coexist in the same space, this contradicts the assumption that cultural identity/similarity (as opposed to cultural difference) is necessary within a nation's boundaries. Though official discourses on North Korean defectors use the term cultural difference to explain their varying degrees of social integration, that it is used in this way at all effectually gives the term validity. Rather than blaming North Korean defectors' maladaptation on cultural differences, it would be better to address the issues they face than attempt to simply explain them away.

In a unified Korea, neither a homogenous ethnic Korean identity nor the discrete cultural identities of North and South Koreans could adequately represent the complex whole of people's various experiences and aspirations. What this edited volume suggests as necessary for a re-envisioned Korean identity is a diverse and multi-layered approach to interpreting the experiences of the self and of others. North Korean defectors' worldviews, values, hopes, and despairs, as well as the different paths they have taken that we have observed will contribute to the formation of a new Korean identity. South Koreans will also need to re-evaluate their previous thoughts on identity and cultural difference, as they face changing social circumstances where previous boundaries are reconfigured and stereotypes are torn down.

A discussion on identity raises speculation about the type of cultural symbols that different social actors of a unified Korea will adopt. Any projections on cultural symbols that might be mobilized in the future would be derived from theories formed from a study of the perceptual process, which is a sequence of psychological steps of using perception to select objects, organizing the perception of objects, and interpreting. Cultural symbols, then, are not merely the product of different cultural backgrounds but rather individuals' strategic choices shaped by their social, economic, and political conditions. What we have assumed as pure cultural difference is in fact choices and preferences that have been influenced by a person's socioeconomic status. North Korean defectors living in the US, UK, Japan, South Korea, and other parts of the world have absorbed diverse cultural symbols in an expression of their identity that transcends cultural differences.

The implications of the empirical studies in this book for defectors is that a connection has been made from their previous experiences and identities in North Korea to their present and future relations and identities. This is significant in that it explains that the motivation for their mobilities and coping strategies for their post-settlement lives originates in their home society. Not only their motivations and strategies but their lifestyles and their daily culture endure after their defection through their ethnic networks and associations as they re-created North Korea abroad. Many defectors left North Korea not out of a desire for a new identity in a new destination but to escape the oppressive regime. Most North Korean defectors were not only proud of their identity but were willing to maintain it. So were even those North Koreans defectors who tried to hide or deny their nationality.

This book offers another implication for North Korans defectors in regards to the parts they might play in a unified Korea or a peninsula at peace. In the event that North Korea follows China's example and implements an open-door policy, those defectors might be invited to contribute to the new economy. There are several possible ways North Korean defectors could assist as North Korea navigates economic and political changes. The migration-development nexus that could see North Korean defectors return with the knowledge and ideas to support the new economy that would be an immense aid in rebuilding the country. The financial and social remittances that have quietly contributed to the country's illicit black market could be expanded to legitimate investment in official developments. In addition to rebuilding the economy, North Korean defectors have much to offer to the cultural land-scape of either a unified Korea or a reformed North Korea. This would be particularly true of North Korean defectors living overseas since their experiences of multicultural communications and interactions would be beneficial in creating a more open and accommodating culture for all Koreans.

REFERENCES

Chun, Kyung Hyo. "Representation and Self-presentation of North Korean Defectors in South Korea: Image, Discourses, and Voices." *Asian Journal of Peacebuilding* 8, no.1 (2020): 93–112.

Chun, Kyung Hyo. "North Korean Defectors as Cultural Other in South Korea: Perception and Construction of Cultural Differences." *Asian Journal of Peacebuilding* 10, no. 1 (2022, forthcoming).

Dietz, Barbara. "German and Jewish migration from the former Soviet Union to Germany: Background, trends and implications." *Journal of Ethnic and Migration Studies* 26, no. 4 (2000): 635–652.

Kolstø, Pål. "Territorialising diasporas: The case of Russians in the former Soviet Republics." *Millennium* 28, no. 3 (1999): 607–631.

Korobkov, Andrei V., and Zhanna A. Zaionchkovskaia. "The changes in the migration patterns in the post-Soviet states: the first decade." *Communist and Post-Communist Studies* 37, no. 4 (2004): 481–508.

Le Bail, Hélène, and Wei Shen. "The return of the 'brains' to China: What are the social, economic, and political impacts." *Asie Visions* 11 (2008): 1–31.

Ma, Shu-Yun. "The exit, voice, and struggle to return of Chinese political exiles." *Pacific Affairs* (1993): 368–385.

Shin, HaeRan. "The Geopolitical Ethnic Networks for De-bordering: North Korean Defectors in Los Angeles and London." *Asian Journal of Peacebuilding* 9, no. 2 (2021): 209–232.

Shin, HaeRan. "Extra-territorial nation-building in flows and relations: North Korea in the global networks and an ethnic enclave." *Political Geography*, 74 (2019): 102047.

Shin, HaeRan. "The territoriality of ethnic enclaves: dynamics of transnational practices and geopolitical relations within and beyond a Korean transnational enclave in New Malden, London." *The Annals of the American Association of Geographers*. 108, no. 3 (2018): 756–772.

Index

About the Editor and the Contributors

ABOUT THE EDITOR

HaeRan Shin has taught at University College, London, and is now a professor in the Department of Geography at Seoul National University. Her research is focused on political geography and migrant studies. She has examined the politics of urban development cases and the issues of transnational migrants and refugees, the dynamics of mobilities, and the territoriality of migrants' networks and their ethnic enclaves. For her research on urban politics and migrant studies, she has used qualitative research methods, including in-depth interviews, participant observations, focus groups, discourse analyses, and archival analyses. In recent years, she has focused on the transnational ethnic networks of North Korean defectors who live outside the Korean peninsula. She has published two monographs, *The Cultural Politics of Urban Development in South Korea: Art, Memory and Urban Boosterism in Gwangjua* (Routledge, 2020) and *We Are All Joseonjok* (Imagine, 2016), and a number of articles in international academic journals including *The Annals of the American Association of Geographers, Political Geography,* and *Urban Studies*. Email: haeranshin@snu.ac.kr.

ABOUT THE CONTRIBUTORS

Kyung Hyo Chun earned her doctorate in anthropology from the University of British Columbia, Canada, and she is currently an assistant professor in the Department of Korean Studies at Ewha Womans University. Before joining Ewha Womans University, she was a senior research fellow at the Institute for Peace and Unification Studies at Seoul National University, conducting research projects on North Korean defectors and social integration between

North-South Koreas. Her areas of research interest include post-coloniality, nationalist discourse, North Korean refugees, commemorations, museum representations, material culture, cultural properties, multiculturalism, and media politics. She coauthored *Many Faces of Peace* (2010), *History and Politics of Socialist Vietnam* (2019), *Variations of Tradition and Solidarity: Life and Culture of Divided Koreans* (2016), and has published articles on politics of memory, cultural representation at museums, and North Korean defector issues. Email: kchun@ewha.ac.kr.

Hyunuk Lee is a researcher with the Korean Hydrography and Research Association in Korea. Before joining KHRA, she was a research professor at Ewha Womans University. She received a bachelor's degree from Ewha Womans University and a master's degree and a doctorate in human geography from the University of Tokyo. Her research focuses on domestic and global migration, but recently, she has been particularly interested in the migration of young people, especially in Korea. She is the author of *Life and Hope of Jumma Refugees: From the Chittagong Mountains to Gimpo in Korea* (2017) and *People Living in Unfamiliar Places* (2016), as well as numerous published articles on migrants in Korea. Email: leehyunuk2019@gmail.com

Heuijeong Kim is a visiting professor in Inha University and a lecturer in Seoul National University. Before joining Inha University, she worked for the Unification Education Division of the Korea Educational Development Institute and lectured in the Settlement Support Center for North Korean Refugees. She received her bachelor's degree in clothing and textiles at Yonsei University and a master's degree and a doctorate in early childhood education at Seoul National University. Her research is focused on the lives of North Korean defector children and their families, education of North Korea, and the unification education. She is the author of *"Parent" Image and Attachment in North Korea* (2019) and *A Study on the Classification of Unification Emotion Structure* (2020), as well as a number of articles on North Korea and North Korean defectors. Email: mokren@snu.ac.kr.

Seok-hyang Kim is a professor in the Department of North Korean Studies at Ewha Womans University. Before joining Ewha, she worked for the Ministry of Unification. She received her bachelor's degree and master's in sociology at Ewha Womans University. She then completed a second master's degree as well as a doctorate in sociology at the University of Georgia in the United States. Her research is focused on people's everyday lives and stories of North Korean defectors. Recently, she has turned her attention to minority issues in North Korea and North Koreans' defection stories. She is the author of *My Hometown Stories in North Korea: Those North Korean Defectors' Memories*

(2018), *North Korean Women Vent Their Desires for Beauty in Jangmadang!* (2019), *Chosenjin, Jaepo, and North Korean Defectors: Three Types of Devooted Lives of Ex-Zainichi People* (2021), and numerous articles related to North Korean people and those defectors. Email: feelfree@ewha.ac.kr

www.ingramcontent.com/pod-product-compliance

Lightning Source LLC
Chambersburg PA
CBHW050639280326

4l932CB00015B/2714